TWAYNE'S WORLD AUTHORS SERIES
A Survey of the World's Literature

YIDDISH

Edward Alexander, University of Washington

EDITOR

Yankev Glatshteyn

TWAS 566

Photograph by Alexander Archer

Yankev Glatshteyn

YANKEV GLATSHTEYN

By JANET R. HADDA

University of California

TWAYNE PUBLISHERS

A DIVISION OF G. K. HALL & CO., BOSTON

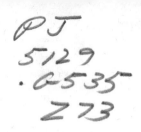

Library of Congress Cataloging in Publication Data

Hadda, Janet.
Yankev Glatshteyn

(Twayne's world authors series ; TWAS 566 : Yiddish)
Bibliography: p. 191–94
Includes index.
1. Glatstein, Jacob, 1896–1971—Poetic works.
PJ5129.G535Z73   839'.09'13   79-21660
ISBN 0-8057-6408-9

For Allan

Contents

About the Author

Preface

Chronology

1. Biographical Sketch 11

2. The Literary Background of Yankev Glatshteyn 19

3. In zikh and Beyond 28

4. Take a Book of Records 62

5. A Shadow on the Snow 102

6. The Silver Crown of Yiddishkeyt 132

7. Songs of Reconciliation 164

8. Conclusion 179

   Notes and References 181

   Selected Bibliography 191

   Index 195

About the Author

Janet R. Hadda currently teaches at UCLA where she has developed a Yiddish Minor Program and instituted Yiddish as a foreign language fulfillment of the M.A. reading requirement. In addition, she is the author of numerous articles focusing on the Yiddish language and its literature.

Dr. Hadda majored in German and minored in English at the University of Vermont, where she received a B.S. Ed. in 1966. After a year of study at Hebrew University, Jerusalem, she earned a master's degree in Germanic languages from Cornell University, and a Ph.D. from Columbia University, where her dissertation subject was the early poetry of Yankev Glatshteyn.

Preface

The conceptualization of this book brought with it a difficult conflict. Yankev Glatshteyn, one of Yiddish literature's brightest artistic luminaries, was also impressively prolific and versatile, his oeuvre comprising ten volumes of poetry, three novels, eight volumes of collected essays, and over one hundred short stories, most of them written under pseudonyms. Clearly, within the confines of a modest-length study, a compromise of scope or depth had to be made.

Glatshteyn himself once remarked in an interview that he considered himself first of all a poet, that his other writings were important to him only insofar as they, too, contained the spark of poetry. I share Glatshteyn's self-appraisal, for while his prose work constitutes a valuable contribution to Yiddish belles-lettres and criticism, his greatness is revealed in the poetry that spans his fifty-year career. Thus, after giving the matter considerable thought, I have decided to forfeit some breadth in order to concentrate on Glatshteyn's poetry here.

Except where the specific date of the original publication is relevant, I have discussed the poems in the context of the volumes in which they first appeared.

In quoting from Glatshteyn's poetry, I have for the most part cited both the original—using the transcriptional system favored by the Institute for Jewish Research (YIVO)—and a translation. Unless otherwise indicated, the latter are my own; I have attempted to provide as literal a rendering of the Yiddish as is possible within the confines of intelligibility.

A number of people have aided me in my work on this study. I would like to thank Rabbi Chaim Seidler-Feller of UCLA Hillel for giving so generously of his time and learning in helping me with the biblical and ceremonial references in Glatshteyn's poetry. I am indebted to Mrs. Fanny Mazel Glatshteyn for filling me in on details of her husband's life, and to Mary Kay Norseng for her friendship and support over the time in which I was working on this project.

My profound gratitude goes to Harold Meyerson for sharing with me the fruits of his brilliant and orderly mind; for the discussions, the many suggestions, the significant criticisms, for the patience and warm encouragement that accompanied me throughout the preparation of this manuscript.

JANET R. HADDA

University of California, Los Angeles

Chronology

1896 August 20, born in Lublin, Poland; son of Yitskhok and Ite Rokhl (Yungman).

1914 Immigrated to the United States.

1919 The poems *1919*, *In roykh* and *Tirtl-toybn* published in the journal *Poezye*.

1920 The *In zikh* manifesto (with A. Glants-Leyeles and N. B. Minkov) published in the poetry anthology *In zikh*.

1921 *Yankev glatshteyn*, poems.

1925 Began his career as a newspaper writer, an occupation he continued until his death; wrote columns, e.g., in the *Morgn-zhurnal*, the *Tog*, and the *Yidisher kemfer;* also edited the periodical *Folk un velt*, the organ of the World Jewish Congress.

1926 *Fraye ferzn*, poems.

1929 *Kredos*, poems.

1934 Traveled to Lublin.

1937 *Yidishtaytshn*, poems.

1938 *Ven yash iz geforn*, a novel.

1940 *Ven yash iz gekumen*, a novel; *Emil un Karl*, a novel for children.

1943 *Gedenklider*, poems.

1944 *Yosl loksh fun khelm*, a long poem (with music by Henoch Kon; illustrations by Isaac Lichtenstein. Previously published in *Yidishtaytshn*).

1946 *Shtralndike yidn*, poems.

1947 *In tokh genumen*, essays.

1953 *Dem tatns shotn*, poems.

1956 *Fun mayn gantser mi*, selected poems; *In tokh genumen*, essays.

1960 *In tokh genumen*, essays (2 vols.).

1961 *Di freyd fun yidishn vort*, poems.

1963 *Mit mayne fartogbikher*, essays.

1966 *A yid fun lublin*, poems.

1967 *Af greyte temes,* essays; *Kh'tu dermonen,* collected Holocaust poems.
1971 November 19, died in New York; *Gezangen fun rekhts tsu links,* poems.
1972 *In der velt mit yidish,* essays.
1978 *Prost un poshet,* essays.

CHAPTER 1

Yankev Glatshteyn: Biographical Sketch

YANKEV Glatshteyn was an American-Yiddish writer in the fullest and deepest sense. In his work, the influences of two diverse cultures are blended to form a new unity, the individual elements of which can be observed but not separated. Thus, although Glatshteyn lived in the United States for fifty-seven of his seventy-five years, the language of his poetry and prose was always Yiddish; although he spent virtually all of his adult years living in New York City and reacting to his immediate environment, his birthplace, Lublin, Poland, always remained a powerful, if intermittent, imaginative stimulus. It was in Lublin that he received his early education and absorbed a system of values that underlay many of his later artistic impressions. It was there, too, that he began to amass the enormous storehouse of images and associations to which he returned again and again, both in family memories and in direct evocations of the city itself.

Yankev, son of Yitskhok and Ite-Rokhl (née Yungman) Glatshteyn, was born on August 20, 1896.[1] On his mother's side, he stemmed from rabbinic stock, and from his father's family he was endowed with a combined heritage of orthodox enlightenment and music—his uncle, Moyshele Glatshteyn, was the city cantor in Lublin, and Moyshele's two sons were choirboys who went on to become composers and music teachers. Much later, Glatshteyn made explicit reference to the significance of music in his own life. During an interview with Avrom Tabatshnik, Glatshteyn observed:

. . . I must go to concerts; I must hear music. There is a connection between this music that I must hear, that I regard as quite as much a nourishment for my spirit as reading, and the music of my word. How poets who have

11

no love for music can nevertheless create musical pieces is a wonder to
me. (p. 49)

Glatshteyn's father was determined to provide his son with the
best education possible. Consequently, one-half of what he earned
each week as a clothing salesman was set aside for Yankev's school-
ing. Until the age of sixteen, the boy received a solid religious and
traditional training. Nonetheless, Yankev was permitted certain lib-
erties. Rather than perform a customary biblical exegesis at the time
of his *bar-mitsve*, for instance, he composed his own sermon, which
was published by the Jewish community. Nor was he compelled to
recite the daily prayers of the strictly observant Jewish male (Whit-
man, pp. 13–14).

More than this, however, Yitskhok wished to expose Yankev to
secular learning and engaged private tutors to instruct him. Since
the father reserved a special place in his heart for Yiddish literature,
he introduced his son to the work of such classical masters as Perets,
Sholem-Aleykhem, and Reyzen, delighting in the boy's keenly in-
terested response. In later life, Glatshteyn stressed the crucial im-
pact of this early education. He claimed, in fact—both in poetry
and in an interview—that his father had sanctified him to a life of
writing Yiddish.

Regardless of what the unconscious or subconscious incentives
may have been, Glatshteyn's attempts at a creative literary career
began early. By the age of thirteen, he had amassed enough material
to warrant a pilgrimage to Warsaw, where, like many other aspiring
writers, he sought the validation of Y. L. Perets and members of
his salon. When he was just seventeen, one of his stories was ac-
cepted by Baal Makhshoves for inclusion in the periodical *Fraynd*,
which was at that time published in Warsaw. This work never ap-
peared as planned, however: growing impatient, its youthful author
reclaimed his manuscript before it could be brought out.

The Lublin of Glatshteyn's youth was situated in Russian Poland
and had been an important commercial community in the nine-
teenth century. Jews had participated in the city's economic ex-
pansion, engaging in both business and industry. In addition, the
city had achieved prominence as a Hasidic center and as a Jewish
council meeting place. At the turn of the century its population
included over 23,000 Jews. In the years immediately preceding
World War I, however, the position of Jews in Lublin deteriorated

sharply: they were publicly abused and suffered, in addition, from a boycott of their businesses. The youngest of Yitskhok Glatshteyn's brothers lived in New York, and it was decided that the seventeen-year-old Yankev could evade persecution by going to the United States. Thus, in June 1914, he arrived in the city that would hence-forth be his home. In that same year, he published a short story, *Di geferlekhe froy* ["The Dangerous Woman"], in the New York publication *Fraye arbeter shtime.*

A difficult period of adjustment to his strange new environment followed for Glatshteyn. Like many immigrants, he attempted to support himself through sweatshop jobs. But no matter what he did (and by his own estimate, he worked in over fifty shops), he found himself unsuited to manual labor. At the same time, he had ceased to write. Glatshteyn later advanced one theory for this hiatus in literary productivity: it was a necessary concomitant of acclimati-zation, one important aspect of which was achieving proficiency in English. Consequently, his writing suffered. Later he explained to Yankev Pat that at the time he had felt "as if I had left my literary heritage on the other side of the ocean" (p. 84). Ruth Whitman postulates another, although related, cause for Glatshteyn's creative silence: after the praise and support he had received at home, he was overwhelmed by the vicissitudes of existence in New York, particularly when the outbreak of World War I disrupted his con-tacts with Poland and isolated him from all he had counted on as familiar (p. 15).

The turning point in Glatshteyn's artistic development can be traced to an unexpected source—his decision, in 1918, to enter New York University Law School. It so happened that one of his classmates was Nokhem Borekh Minkov, who would later be a theoretical leader, along with Arn Glants-Leyeles and Glatshteyn himself, of the new poetic group that called itself *In zikh* ("Inside the Self"). Minkov opened Glatshteyn's eyes to the exciting pres-ence of a Yiddish belletristic milieu in the United States, an envi-ronment in which writers such as Mani Leyb, Yoysef Opatoshu, and Zisha Landoy flourished. These were artists who had dedicated themselves to the task of broadening, deepening, emancipating, and beautifying the language and themes of Yiddish literature. In this atmosphere, Glatshteyn began to write again.

His revived efforts were not, however, met with uniform enthu-siasm. A favorite anecdote told of Glatshteyn concerns his reaction to the advice of Sh. Yanovsky, editor of the *Fraye arbeter shtime*, who counseled him to abandon his literary aspirations and concentrate instead on his career in law. Undaunted by the realization that Yanovsky would refuse to print his poetry, Glatshteyn adopted a pseudonym: Klara Blum. In this felicitous disguise, Glatshteyn managed to publish fifteen poems in the *Fraye arbeter shtime*,[2] even receiving editorial praise before the truth emerged and Klara Blum's career came to an end.

Fortunately, Glatshteyn's reception among his poetic colleagues was more cordial. Leyeles, who was slightly older, became a mentor of sorts for the young writer, and both Moyshe Leyb Halpern and H. Leyvik encouraged him to persevere. Reminiscing years later with Pat, Glatshteyn recalled his first visit to Leyvik, an account that indicates how the standard-bearers of Yiddish literature, for all their fire and verve, simultaneously endured considerable hardship:

[I] recited poems in order to get his opinion. At that time, H. Leyvik made a living by bringing home work from L. Miller's epaulet workshop. H. Leyvik stood by the table affixing epaulets, and I recited my poems. I was ordained by him. (p. 85)

Glatshteyn's energy could no longer be channeled into the study of jurisprudence. Years later, in an amusing retrospective essay,[3] Glatshteyn recollected that he and Minkov would from time to time recruit "deputies" to attend classes for them while they went for walks along Fifth Avenue. Moreover, they typically allowed their work to be neglected until exams were imminent, whereupon they appealed for aid to another immigrant student, Eleas Liberman, who—unlike them—was destined for a brilliant legal future.

Ultimately, however, the ministrations of their friend were not enough to save the two. Minkov transferred to a school in Brooklyn where standards were less stringent than those of New York University. There he completed his studies, although, as Glatshteyn wryly commented, his diploma never launched him on a career as a lawyer, but rather furnished him with the academic qualifications necessary for a position at the New School as lecturer in Yiddish literature. Glatshteyn himself never even obtained a degree, having failed several exams at the end of his final year in school; instead, he admitted jokingly at the conclusion of his reminiscence: "What became of me—is an open book."

In 1919, Glatshteyn made his poetic debut in the pages of the journal *Poezye,* whose contributors included such well-known writers as Halpern, Mani Leyb, and Yehoash. The appearance of three poems, *1919, In roykh* ["In Smoke"], and *Tirtl-toybn* ["Turtledoves"], revealed Glatshteyn unquestionably as the creator of an experimental style whose hallmark was a brilliant wordplay with which he was to be identified by the Yiddish-reading public during the first half of his career. The publication in 1920 of an *In zikh* anthology containing a reprint of the *Poezye* selections as well as ten additional poems and a manifesto coauthored with Minkov and Leyeles served to reinforce the impression that an artist of substance had joined the ranks of American Yiddish literature.

Glatshteyn's new concentration on poetry did not signify that his original interest in prose had disappeared. He had married in 1919 and when his wife, Nettie, became pregnant in 1923 Glatshteyn determined to earn a living by teaching. This venture proved unsuccessful, however, and he turned to newspaper work—an occupation he had previously eschewed as unseemly for a poet. As one way of moderating his ongoing conflict over his new calling, Glatshteyn hid behind a variety of pseudonyms. So disguised, he embarked upon a long and respected career as a columnist, first in *Di naye varhayt,* where he was a member of the editorial board and in which he published weekend feuilletons, and later, beginning in 1926, in the *Morgn-zhurnal.* At the same time, he continued to write short stories, about one hundred of which—bearing the pseudonym Y. Yungman, his mother's maiden name—appeared in the *Morgn-zhurnal* alone.

Until the mid-1930's Glatshteyn's creative life followed the basic pattern that had emerged a decade earlier. He maintained his poetic career, publishing prodigiously and involving himself in editorial work as well. In 1926, together with Mikhl Likht, he edited the monthly literary journal *Loglen;* from 1928 to 1929 he was the editor of *In zikh,* and between 1934 and 1938 he served on its editorial board. Simultaneously, he continued to write his column, *Prost un poshet* ["Plain and Simple"], for the *Morgn-zhurnal.*

Nevertheless, absorbed as he was with his career as a Yiddish writer in America during this period, Glatshteyn closely followed events in Europe and their impact on Jewish life. In 1934 he returned to Poland and visited his family in Lublin, a journey he later transformed into two autobiographical novels: *Ven yash iz geforn* and *Ven yash iz gekumen* (which appeared in translation as *Homeward Bound* and *Homecoming at Twilight*). This trip to his homeland evidently helped catalyze in Glatshteyn a heightened awareness of looming catastrophe and Jewish vulnerability. Years before the actual destruction of Eastern European Jewry, he felt compelled to voice his concern. As he later asserted to Avrom Tabatshnik:

I wrote "Wagons" here, after I returned from Poland and I began to feel—beginning in 1934 when they began the gruesome experiments on the bodies of German Jews—I began to see tragedy on the march. That's when I wrote "Wagons." It's a symbolic poem, a good one in my opinion; first, because it expresses the unvoiced fear of a generation, and second, because the fear is not direct and concrete, but an aura hovers over the poem like a shadow of the yet-to-come. (pp. 49–50)

Superficially, Glatshteyn's situation did not alter substantially during and after World War II. He kept up his career as a journalist, supplementing his work for the *Morgn-zhurnal* with a weekly column in the New York newspaper *Yidisher kemfer*. Between 1945 and 1957, Glatshteyn published approximately six hundred articles under the heading *In tokh genumen, arum bikher, mentshn, un zakhn* ["In Essence—About Books, People, and Things"], essays devoted to book reviews and literary analyses, as well as discussions of general and Jewish cultural problems. Glatshteyn was also a coeditor of *Yidisher kemfer* between 1954 and 1955. In addition, he became editor of the World Jewish Congress monthly, *Folk un velt.*

Over the years Glatshteyn's early evaluation of journalism had changed; he was no longer ashamed to be writing for a newspaper. In fact—he confided to Yankev Pat—he had been pleased when, in 1938, the editor of the *Morgn-zhurnal* insisted that he drop the pseudonym Itskus and assume his real name. Indeed, Glatshteyn came to believe,

The writer does not have two pockets for his work—one for writing on current public affairs and the other for poetry. There must be one pocket. The writer, even if he is a poet, must be connected with reality, with battles in society, with ideologies. (p. 89)

Glatshteyn's postwar poetry was similarly marked by his acceptance of a new responsibility. The tragedy envisioned by Glatshteyn in the 1930's had come to pass more hideously than he could possibly have foreseen. If, as he himself suggested, the poem "Wagons" expressed "collective fear, the terror of a generation" (Tabatshnik, p. 49), then his work after the Holocaust documents not only the annihilation in Eastern Europe of his family and its entire culture, but also the sufferings of those who, like Glatshteyn, had somehow survived to bear the burden of witness. Particularly in his volumes *Gedenklider—Memorial Poems, Shtralndike yidn—Radiant Jews,* and *Dem tatns shotn—My Father's Shadow,* Glatshteyn vented his anger, despair, and loneliness at the fate of both living and dead. In this way he charged himself with the awesome task of recording no longer collective terror, but its aftermath, collective grief.

Glatshteyn continued to view his poetic efforts within an experimental framework; however, his later output was certainly not marked by the same sort of formal daring that had characterized his earliest work. To some extent, this was merely a function of age and changing sensibility. As Glatshteyn said during his interview with Tabatshnik:

I have a great longing for free verse. I think my free verse has deteriorated a little, and I say this quite frankly. . . . The free verse of the first Inzikhists, the pioneer Inzikhists, sought a new musicality, the discipline of human speech, the rise and fall of human speech, the distilled music of human conversation. Seeking this discipline, and simultaneously seeking the ideal short poem, I gradually turned to rhyme, and I did not notice that in turning to rhyme I was gradually losing the music of free verse. (p. 48)

But there was perhaps another reason for the different structure of Glatshteyn's poetry, one that his colleague Leyeles described poetically: *Ven keyn grenets iz nishto far di yesurim,/Veytik-oys a sig fun shtreng-getsoymtn furem.* ("When there is no boundary for agony,/Ache out a fence of strictly tamed form.").[4] Glatshteyn himself delineated the postwar artistic problem as the paradoxical necessity of responding to events so appalling that they defy portrayal. This, then, was the new experimental challenge. Or, as he put it to Tabatshnik:

Language is entirely bankrupt in relation to what happened. An ordinary chronicle of the destruction is a thousand times more "modern" than the language of poetry with its limited poetic vocabulary. . . . The Yiddish poet must become the aesthetic chronicler of what happened, and he must fix it for all time. In comparison with what we have hitherto regarded as poetry, the responsibility of a Yiddish poet today, it seems to me, is a fearsome responsibility. (pp. 40–41)

Glatshteyn never gave up attempting to be an aesthetic chronicler. The passage of time somewhat assuaged his anguish over the Holocaust, but his social concern never subsided. Sensing that the time had come for tying up loose ends, he attempted a kind of summing up in his final volume of poetry, *Gezangen fun rekhts tsu links—Songs from Right to Left*. Even there, however, the need to confront and to inquire could not be hidden.

The year 1971 was an important one not only for Glatshteyn but for the Yiddish-speaking world as well, for it was the seventy-fifth anniversary of his birth. That autumn was a time of celebration in New York, Glatshteyn's adopted city. On November 19, in the midst of these commemorations, Glatshteyn died suddenly of a heart attack. He was survived by his three children, his second wife and longtime companion, the artist Fanny Mazel, and sorrowing lovers of Yiddish the world over.

CHAPTER 2

The Literary Background of Yankev Glatshteyn

IN 1920, the American Yiddish literary scene was jolted by the emergence of a new school: *In zikh*—the Introspectivists. Under the leadership of Yankev Glatshteyn, Arn Glants-Leyeles, and Nokhem Borekh Minkov, eight young poets issued an anthology entitled simply *In zikh—Inside the Self*.[1] The volume opened with a manifesto (pp. 5–27) in which its authors joined together against their literary forebears and called for major changes within Yiddish poetry. Their goal, as they summarized it, was: "Individuality in everything and introspection in everything."

The *Inzikhistn* themselves reflected the uneasy merger of two cultures. Nourished by traditional Eastern European Jewish education, they had also enjoyed a taste of university life in the United States; onto a foundation rooted in the history and development of Yiddish poetry, they grafted a growing awareness of the contemporary English and American poetry exemplified by Pound, Eliot, and the Imagists. Armed with this arsenal of innovation and legacy, *In zikh* sought to topple the hegemonic literary establishment of their day and introduce what in hindsight may be termed Yiddish modernist poetry in America.

In zikh's predecessors, *Di yunge* "The Young Ones,"[2] had themselves rebelled against the public orientation of writers like Moris Rozenfeld, Dovid Edelshtat, and others who, in their turn-of-the-century descriptive and exhortatory writings, had agonized and agitated for a better world. In contrast, *Di yunge*—although themselves poor laborers—rejected the constraints of a journalistically dominated literature. Refusing to yield to what they saw as a demand for political and national commitment, these artists fled instead to a search for beauty and a celebration of their "decadence."

19

In following their impulse to raise the aesthetic standard of Yiddish literature, *Di yunge* began to revamp it internally, concentrating on the inherent musicality of Yiddish, which they had only to tap, and infusing it with a new, cosmopolitan vocabulary. Seeking, moreover, to assure Yiddish literature a more international stature and to grant it self-sufficiency, they combined their own writing with translation—necessarily indirect at times—from such diverse sources as Japanese, Arabic, and American Indian poetry as well as from less exotic European and American originals. More interested in mood evocation than in communicating a message, they applauded art for art's sake and sneered at their forerunners for writing poetry that they regarded as merely the means to some political or social end.

The *In zikh* manifesto was more a thematic and linguistic declaration of independence than a literary coup, although its authors were somewhat disingenuous when they professed appreciation of their precursors. In fact, their unacknowledged target was *Di yunge*. The chief goal of *In zikh*, its founders asserted, was poetic truth, the union of life and art. This objective could only be attained through introspection, through absorption in a kaleidoscopic flow of egocentric associations and suggestions that, when viewed from the outside, might appear contradictory, unclear, sometimes even unconnected to the subject matter under discussion. The work of *Di yunge*, which had attempted to transmit mood in a rounded, concentrated fashion, was thus exposed by *In zikh* as a lie, for it denied the awesome labyrinth of the human psyche and refused to accept the host of feelings that inevitably resulted from experience. The introspective method, furthermore, defied the notion—implicit in *Di yunge*'s quest for beauty—that certain topics were inappropriate for poetry: according to the *Inzikhistn*, any stimulus that catalyzed the train of association and suggestion, thereby revealing the ultimate and unique operation of an individual soul, was potential material for poetic scrutiny. Only by plumbing the confusing depths of the self, the *Inzikhistn* insisted, could the complicated essence of modern life be properly and honestly expressed.

As self-conscious Yiddish poets, the *Inzikhistn* used their general concepts of individuality and introspection to probe as well the specific question of their Jewishness. Like *Di yunge*, they disavowed any *a priori* national or religious responsibilities, but their concern was different. "Whatever a Jewish poet writes in Yiddish is *ipso facto* Jewish, by dint of that alone," they declared. "Special 'Jewish themes' are unnecessary." And, just as they accepted the fullness of their Jewish identity, they also proclaimed the self-sufficiency of Yiddish, their belief that in their language, the highest possible poetic achievements could occur.

Indeed, the major contribution of the *In zikh* group must be seen in language rather than thematics. Their attainment, however, did not stem from innovations in language *per se*. Rather, it was accomplished in the realm of poetic structure and in the creation of new uses for Yiddish as it already existed. Here the *Inzikhistn* made their most substantial break with the past, thrusting Yiddish poetry into the maelstrom of modernist theory and practice. Their manifesto announced, and their anthology illustrated, the systematic inauguration of free verse in American Yiddish poetry. Citing as their goal a separate form for each poetic theme, they stressed melody rather than the constraints of meter and rhyme.

Every poem must have an *individual rhythm*. . . .the rhythm of a poem must be completely suited to that poem. One poem cannot have the same rhythm as another poem. Every poem is, in reality . . . an *unikum*. . . . We introspectivists believe that free verse is most suitable for rhythmic individuality. . . . The melodic quality of a poem—an undoubtedly important thing—is not dependent on rhyme. Rhyme is merely *one* element of melody—and the most meager. . . . The combination of sounds, the *individual* sound combination is truly necessary . . . unusually important.

The *Inzikhistn* concluded their manifesto by turning away from most of their predecessors and embracing instead their Modernist colleagues in other literatures. Like their contemporaries, the *Inzikhistn* hoped to realize the full potential of their own language, to purify Yiddish by stripping it of superfluous and hackneyed elements. Accordingly, their formal statement of purpose contained a summary of practical as well as theoretical aims: (1) The language of *In zikh* would parallel the introspectivist ideal of individually reflected life by seeking to approximate the structure and cadence of speech. Specifically, the *Inzikhistn* would not allow restraints of rhythm or rhyme to disturb the natural flow of spoken Yiddish in their poetry. (2) Banal figurative expressions were cliches and therefore lies to be avoided. (3) Unnecessary adjectives—which were useless and cumbersome—also had to be eschewed. (4) The *Inzikhistn* disdained the quest for intrinsic beauty and supported

instead the use of appropriate language, without regard to its sup-
posed aesthetic value: a word used properly was always beautiful.

The *In zikh* group, as defined in its own manifesto, banded to-
gether in order to facilitate the development of its separate mem-
bers. Of all the eight participants in the original anthology, none
has aroused as much discussion and investigation as Yankev Glat-
shteyn, one of *In zikh's* principal theorists. From the beginning of
his career through the mid-1930's, Glatshteyn was known chiefly
for his brilliant and extravagantly creative—if controversial—ma-
nipulation of Yiddish language and poetic structure. By the end of
his life, however, he had achieved recognition, both within the
Yiddish-speaking world and beyond, as a major literary spokesman
for Jewish nationalism. This apparent split in poetic focus and tone
inspired a critical disagreement around Glatshteyn that pivoted on
the legitimacy of dividing his work into two distinct stages.

Critics such as Y. Rapoport and Shmuel Lapin,[3] for instance,
argued that Glatshteyn had undergone a metamorphosis generated
by the Holocaust and its reverberations. Having entered the ranks
of Yiddish poetry as a rambunctious and irresponsible artist, they
contended, Glatshteyn had been forced to recognize his true ob-
ligations and had met the challenge with unexpected sensitivity and
depth. Others, including Glatshteyn's *In zikh* colleagues B. Alkvit
and Arn Glants-Leyeles,[4] rejected this notion of transformation. For
them, Glatshteyn had always been an artist of major stature; but
in a critical world which made literary judgments on the basis of
extraliterary criteria, his earlier work had gone unappreciated. Now,
it was his sense of Jewish responsibility that won him acclaim.

Both sides in this dispute are partially correct, since although
Glatshteyn's poetry did indeed change with the Holocaust, an over-
all framework of issues and attitudes unifies his oeuvre. Yet neither
argument does justice to his complex unfolding. For whereas two
well-defined periods in Glatshteyn's poetic life may be clearly dis-
tinguished, they are in fact the same pattern of development ex-
perienced twice, once when he was starting out as an *Inzikhist,* and
again around the time of the Holocaust. On each occasion, the poetic
cycle began with expressions of rebellion and fury, coupled with a
defensive, threatened stance. In both instances, this agitated and
unhappy frame of mind yielded with time to a mood of reconcili-
ation, greater openness, and satisfaction.

Despite the basic constancy of the pattern, there is some deviation between its initial emergence in 1919 and its repetition some twenty years later. The major difference is Glatshteyn's perception of the threats he faced, even though, throughout his career, he was to see his problems as cosmic in scope. In the earlier period, he considered himself isolated within and persecuted by a hostile universe. Historical circumstances and his contemporary surroundings affected him only insofar as they generally provoked in Modernist artists a response to the anxieties and confusions of post-World War I existence. By the late 1930's, in contrast, the danger of total annihilation was engulfing not only the lone individual, but Glatshteyn's entire people. He recognized this destruction, moreover, as an historical anomaly with vast ramifications that could be neither avoided nor dismissed.

Even in this later period, however, Glatshteyn could not ignore the jeopardy in which he in particular was placed, especially in his capacity as a Yiddish poet. Thus, at the very same moment that he manifested the growing community awareness that was to solidify his position with previously unsympathetic critics, some of his finest poetry remained personal and private; and some of his most interesting and powerful work concerned the ambivalence with which he regarded his new role. Similarly, Glatshteyn's move toward resolution, although on both occasions concerned with adjustment to a larger framework, was broader the second time than the first. In the 1920's and early 1930's, it signified principally an easing of his egocentric position; towards the end of his life, it meant not only reconciling himself personally and in the present, but entailed coming to terms with a world that had been almost completely obliterated.

This cyclical continuity in Glatshteyn's emotive development—which implies sameness as well as change—also applies to his choice of subject matter. Here, Glatshteyn himself provided an important clue: in his last volume of poetry, *Gezangen fun rekhts tsu links—Songs from Right to Left* (New York, 1971)—he reprinted from the year 1919 the first poems he had published in America under his own name: *1919, In roykh* ["In smoke"] and *Tirtl-toybn* ["Turtle-doves"][5]. Read in the context of his entire poetic output, these works clearly constitute the first stage of Glatshteyn's involvement with issues that were to engage him throughout his entire career: social and political concerns, problems of love and sexuality, the state of Yiddish literature and language. Furthermore, his identity as a committed Jewish artist, while muted at various junctures during his long and prolific existence as a poet, is already evident at this initial point. These three very early works, which were obviously still important to Glatshteyn at the end of his life, can thus serve a two-fold purpose. In juxtaposition with later poems, they provide a basis for charting the changes that unquestionably occurred in his writing. At the same time, they highlight the degree to which Glatshteyn remained faithful to his own intellectual and emotional imperatives, if not to the theories and ideals of the *Inzikhistn*.

The narrator of *1919* is a consciousness in crisis. He has lost all trace of his former identity as *yankl bereb yitskhok* ("Yankel, son of Yitskhok"); he remains no more than *a kleyntshik pintele a kaylekhdiks* ("a tiny little round dot"), rolling along in confusion, evidently powerless to find or change direction. Though literally wrapped up in himself, he cannot avoid the assaults of modern city life. Newspaper extras fall from on high, squashing his already waterlogged head with the world's catastrophes; his glasses have been permanently stained red by some creature with a long tongue. Unable to bear the pressure, the narrator imagines that something in his head will snap and short-circuit, leaving behind no more than *a kupke shmutsiklekhn ash* ("a little heap of dirty ashes").

The narrator's entrapment assumes cosmic dimensions. Having lost or given up his Jewish identity and taken on a more universal, literally "well-rounded" personality, he nonetheless finds himself beholden to an *oyber-har* ("sovereign") who has used heaven to seal mankind into earth: *Der oyber-har hot mit dem himl-bloy/Di gantse erd arumgeringlt/Un nito keyn retung*. ("The sovereign has with the celestial blue/Encircled the entire earth/And no salvation."). The real horror for the narrator, however, is not so much the physicality of his imprisonment as its permanence: as the little dot, he will spin *in eter af eybikeytn/Mit royte vualn arumgehilt*. ("in ether for eternities/Wrapped in red veils."). The collapse of his inner self thus will not liberate the narrator but force him instead into an overwhelming awareness of violence and alienation from which he has absolutely no hope of escape.

Unlike the disintegrating consciousness of *1919*, the narrator of *In roykh* does not internalize his sense of impotence and isolation; rather, he seeks to strengthen himself by subjugating a woman. This poem begins as a *kinder-shpil*, a "game for children," and the interaction that follows is indeed revealed as an immature power struggle. The narrator's ostensible adulthood is symbolized by the cigar on which he puffs, daring the female—according to the narrator, a tiny little girl in a large chair—to tolerate the smoke. Childishly defiant, she sticks out her red tongue, and the narrator responds by threatening to envelop her in smoke. This time, hundreds of tongues stretch out at him, making him feel like a *groysn nar/Mit di halb-farzhmurete oygn.* ("big fool/With the half-squinting eyes."). At the end of the poem, the little girl suddenly becomes a tiny dot that proceeds to disappear, leaving the narrator, still a big fool, with his vision completely distorted.

These game players are not children, however, and at issue in their struggle, no matter how immature, is sexual power. Seeking to prevail, the narrator warns the woman (for she is more than a little girl) that, although she may laugh and stick out her tongue at him, he will dazzle her: *Bald vet di shtub shvarts vern fun roykh/Un mir veln zikh lozn valtsirn in roykh/Un flien mit im.* ("Soon the room will become black with smoke/And we will begin to waltz in the smoke/And fly with it."). However, the narrator's scheme to enfold the object of his desire in romantic ecstasy results in failure. Just before she disappears, after sticking out her tongue and forcing the narrator to squint in order to avoid the insult, the woman issues a bold sexual challenge: *Fun vaysn heldzl/Tsit zikh arop dayn rozeve kleyd.—/A yam mit blendende vayskeyt.* ("From your little white neck/Your pink dress strips itself off.—/A sea of blinding whiteness."). In the end, it is the man who, far from reducing the female to unthreatening proportions, is himself forced to capitulate and face desertion.

Like *In roykh*, Glatshteyn's poem *Tirtl-toybn* depends on associations with childhood, but its purpose and style are very different. In this, the most sanguine of Glatshteyn's first three poems, the narrator uses free association to transport himself through time. Stimulated by a flash of light on a knife blade, he returns to the earliest *kheyder* (traditional religious school) years of his childhood,[6] focusing on one word, *tirtl-toybn* ("turtle doves"). Essentially, the poem is an examination of that word seen through the eyes of a small child, for whom it assumes tangibility. The word pursues him *Mit dem veykhn kneytsh fun tirtl,/Mit dem lashtshndikn kneytsh.* ("With the soft wrinkle of turtle,/With the cuddly wrinkle."). The narrator-as-child repeats the word until it momentarily disintegrates, thereby emphasizing the fragile and sophisticated connection of sound and meaning in language: *O tirtl-toybn/Tirtl-toybn/Tirtl-tirtl/Tirtl-toybn.* ("O turtle-doves/Turtle-doves/Turtle-turtle/Turtle-doves.").

Although the narrator of *Tirtl-toybn* is able to lose himself in childhood through most of the poem, the adult mind behind the child never completely disappears from view. Summing up his specific experience, the narrator simultaneously considers the process of recollection in general: *Un es zingt./Un farfolgt./Un farvigt./Un dermont:/Tirtl-toybn/Tirtl-tirtl,/Tirtl-toybn.* ("And it sings./And persecutes./And rocks./And reminds:/Turtle-doves/Turtle-turtle,/Turtle-doves."). The lines themselves are as short and uncomplicated as those of a child; yet, despite their simplicity they reveal subtle distinctions in perspective. *Zingt,* "sings" and *farvigt,* "rocks" both describe plausible reactions of a child, although they are equally suited to an adult's reminiscence of the past; *farfolgt,* "persecutes" is more complicated than the other two, since it is a sophisticated concept indicating abstract evaluative perception rather than active physical response. *Dermont,* "reminds," however, clearly involves the adult narrator's state of mind, his detached reflection on his own flashback.

Regarded as a unit, Glatshteyn's debut poems form a spectrum of focus: at one end there is the narrow and particular perspective of *Tirtl-toybn* and, at the other end, the cosmic vision of *1919.* Somewhere between the two lies the social interaction in *In roykh.* In terms of structure, these three works possess a number of characteristics in common. Each avoids any attempt to achieve the sensitive, "poetic" beauty so prized by *Di yunge.* Instead, they are punctuated by terms that are recklessly "unpoetic" in both sound and meaning: *umgelumpert* ("clumsy"), *krakh* ("crash"), *blyask* ("glare"), *farzhmuret* ("squinty"), *morisshtul* ("Morris chair"), *tsigarnroykh* ("cigar-smoke"). Moreover, in each case, Glatshteyn has entirely disregarded the concepts of stanza, rhyme, and scannable meter to produce one continuous strophe with lines of uneven length. In this sense, the poems are closer to spoken Yiddish than are those of *Di yunge.* However, a preponderance of short lines, especially in *Tirtl-toybn* and *In roykh,* yields an impact that is not conversational. On the contrary, *1919* and *In roykh* seem anxious and exclamatory, whereas the echo of *Tirtl-toybn* suggests a lullaby. Form has been tailored to content.

Though *1919*, *In roykh*, and *Tirtl-toybn* encompass the diversity of Glatshteyn's interests, all three are distinguished by the egocentricity celebrated in the *In zikh* manifesto. The narrators of these poems experience the world wholly as it occurs in and through them. The narrator of *1919* perceives himself as the center of a cosmos that is contracting around his consciousness; the narrator of *Tirtl-toybn* retreats into the private realm of his past, where present time and space are irrelevant; the narrator of *In roykh* is aware of his adversary only insofar as she affects him directly.

In each of these early works, finally, the narrator feels threatened and embattled: the little dot of *1919* interprets all evidence of political foment as an attack upon himself—news stories squash his head, his glasses are smeared with red—everything seems designed to destroy him. The narrator of *In roykh* unwisely engages in a power struggle with a woman who first humiliates and then abandons him. *Tirtl-toybn*, which is more positive in tone than either *1919* or *In roykh*, nonetheless contains a hint of threat in the term *farfolgt*, "persecutes"; even in a memory, then, Glatshteyn's earliest narrators cannot avoid a sense of seige.

Glatshteyn was soon to go beyond the tenets of *In zikh* to diverge widely from the egocentric, threatened world view that marks his earliest work. In a curious way, however, his career flows according to one *In zikh* notion about poetic viewpoint: that it be kaleidoscopic, that it mirror the untidy multiplicity of responses possible in any single situation. Glatshteyn's oeuvre is a kaleidoscopic vision over time. His perceptions of socio-political, romantic, and literary matters would alter during the course of his career, yet at the conclusion of his final volume, he would return to the same configurations he had originally observed.

CHAPTER 3

In zikh and Beyond

THE major change that took place in Glatshteyn's poetry between the time of his emergence as a member of *In zikh* and the time immediately preceding the Holocaust—a period of approximately sixteen years—involved attitude more than subject matter. His interests remained similar; his reactions did not. At first, Glatshteyn's work reveals a pervasive sense of isolation and helplessness. The narrators of these early poems are self-centered, frightened, and isolated; they are threatened by, and in furious opposition to, both society in general and specific individuals. By the end of this period, however, a new poetic personality had emerged, reflecting the mind of an involved, self-confident, and responsible individual. Keenly aware of realistic dangers and conflicts, Glatshteyn had nonetheless reached a point of reconciliation with the surrounding world that freed him for a full response to it even before the catastrophe of World War II and the Holocaust.

In his first two volumes, *Yankev glatshteyn—Yankev Glatshteyn* (New York, 1921) and *Fraye ferzn—Free Verse* (New York, 1926), Glatshteyn was engaged in the attempt to assert himself, to which the title of his first book bears striking testimony. The predominant impression yielded by these works is that of an overwhelmed individual fighting to establish himself socially, romantically, and professionally. The preoccupation with self described in *1919* with particularly graphic clarity continued to be a major influence in his earliest complete volumes.

I *The Threatened Self*

The narrators of Glatshteyn's poems in this period are too caught up with the difficulties of surviving as immigrants in a modern metropolis, and too concerned with the perils in their lives, to concentrate on anything else. Instead, they probe the effects on themselves of their new milieu. The city, with its speed, venality, and anonymity, inspired within Glatshteyn feelings of alienation, dismay, and disgust. In the three short poems entitled *Shtot* ["City"],[1] the narrator describes a loss of self so strong that it causes in him not only fragmentation, but dissolution into the environment. There is an emotional, as well as a physical, level to the narrator's condition. Similarly, objective and subjective reality are confused in the narrator's view of the city. In fact, New York is often no more than a reflection of his inner state.

The key word in these three poems is *khaleshn,* which means both "to faint" and, colloquially, "to be very hungry." The first poem describes the narrator's fainting spell without, however, referring to it directly. Already in the opening line, the narrator speaks of detachment from himself: *Hot zikh mayn bleykhkeyt geleygt af di gasn,* ("My paleness lay down in the streets,"). He declares that his fainting had occurred around, rather than within, himself: *Durkh di farlofene oygn mayne/Hot di shtot gekhalesht.* ("Through my filmy eyes/The city fainted.").

Not until the second poem does the narrator acknowledge that he too had fainted. As he is awakened, the screaming around him begins anew; but the narrator remains disintegrated: *Tsvey groyse oyern zaynen nor/Af dr'erd gelegn* ("Only two big ears/Lay on the ground"). The ears take in the scream of the city: *Hu, hu. hu, ha. hu, hu. hu, ha.* This play on the Yiddish term *hu-ha,* "hullaballoo, to-do, bustle," served to concretize the frantic big city atmosphere.

In the last of the *Shtot* poems, the narrator focuses on the genesis of his malady: his own participation in the city's madness. This way of life had started for him when, unable to overcome the impetus of an initial push from the outside, he had begun whirling like a top, an urban actualization of the helpless cosmic spinning so feared by the narrator of *1919.* But the narrator of *Shtot* had found himself enjoying this motion and the hysterical excitement of pursuing his own spinning. Only when he paused for a moment to catch his breath did everything faint before his eyes, the city's *hu-ha* hanging dead in the air. The conclusion of *Shtot* thus forms a circular link with its start, since the third poem ends just at the point where the first one begins: as the city faints before the narrator's eyes. In this way, the work as a whole structurally imitates the rotation of its narrator.

The image of spinning, in *1919* as well as in *Shtot*, represents the ordeal of existence in a hostile modern world within which the individual has no control. When applied to New York City in particular, this twirling milieu stands for commercial culture that threatens dignity, integrity, and even survival. In Glatshteyn's early poetry, the influence of a money oriented society causes the subversion of ideals or the thoughtless annihilation of those who do not conform. The immigrant's position in this strange new environment is especially problematic. In *Iyev in nyu york* ["Job in New York"],[2] the biblical hero has succumbed to the values of the money culture. Job is blind and reduced to begging for a living; he is unremarkable amidst the noise of New York City, quietly saving up enough money to buy himself a street organ. But Job lives his beggarly life slyly, pocketing most of the coins he receives and leaving only a few to lament piteously from his beggar's tray. He has lost his biblical morality and anger; everything is subservient to money, for this is all that really counts in the rush of New York. The last lines of the poem emphasize Job's new outlook: *Elipaz, du fun teymon, un bildad, du shukhi,/Treyst mikh mit ayer kuperner treyst.* ("Elipaz, you from Yemen, and Bildad, you Shuhite,/Comfort me with your copper comfort.").

In *Park evenyu* ["Park Avenue"],[3] even God must accede to the demands of established money. As a Carnegie Hall violinist, He plays before Caesar, who sits comfortably in a plush loge; and *got hot zikh farneygt far tsezarn.* ("God bowed before Caesar."). The narrator seems at first to accept this situation, describing without complaint how the heavy coaches of Park Avenue go by, leaving him covered with the dust of their momentum-filled lives. Casually, he comments that from under the weight of the coaches' wheels, *Kliglen zikh aroys di verimlekh mit fligelekh tsu der zun,/Mit fligelekh tsum lebn.* ("The little worms puzzle their way out, with little wins towards the sun,/With little wings towards life.").

By the end of the poem, however, it is clear that the narrator is concerned and angry about this kind of abuse. His attention turns to two Italian immigrants, both of whom are street-organ players and one of whom is blind. Unlike Job, however, these two immigrants are unable to collect enough "comfort" to hide some of it away, since they are rewarded with only one penny between them for serenading the "rich windows" of Park Avenue. Also unlike Job, they are intent upon achieving some higher goal: the narrator reveals that it is they who are the little worms with wings stretched towards the sun: *Un tsvishn rod un shteyn raysn zey zikh tsum lebn.* ("And between wheel and stone they aspire to life."). Despite their aims, however, or perhaps because of them, they constantly risk being crushed by heavy coaches that represent the power and invulnerability of established wealth.

The attempt to evade the city's influence provides no solution either, for there is no escaping this culture. The narrator of *Eygns* ["Property"][4] begins by comparing his world to the paltry, materialistic one inhabited by small businessmen. These petty merchants have nothing more to care for and protect than *reshtlekh eygns* ("remnants of property"). Yet they bolt the doors of their stores and leave part of themselves—their shadows—behind at all times. The shadows come and rouse them early in the morning so that they can resume their *tog-tants* ("day-dance") over fragmented and remaindered possessions. This description of their habitual motions sounds suspiciously like a *toytn-tants* ("dance of death"), and the implied similarity is an unmistakable comment upon the essence of an existence governed by commerce.

The narrator, in contrast, avoids the frantic nature of business life. He, too, has a guardian shadow, but it protects the nocturnal silver of the moon and, at dawn, presents him with a bit of gold from a fresh sun. The aesthetically oriented narrator presumably holds claim to a fortune far greater than the meager possessions of those merchants whose scurrying activity he rejects. At the same time, however, something in the idyllic picture is awry, for the moon is shining on the tip of Woolworth's, that epitome of an odds and ends business turned into mammoth financial success. The intrusion of this concrete localized image into what is otherwise a generalized and abstract poem has a jarring effect, imbuing the entire work with gentle irony. The point of the poem changes subtly as the narrator's ability to remove himself from the world of materialism is called into question. As he attempts to get away from business and finance, he finds that even nature can provide only scant and ambiguous refuge.

Glatshteyn's New York is not only a place of ready capitulation or immediate defeat; it is also a city that provokes its citizens to open rebellion, individual and shortlived though it may be. *Luter Bodi* ["Luther Boddy"][5] is based on the true story of a young black man from Harlem who killed two detectives in January, 1922. The public was predictably scandalized: Boddy, once caught, was summarily indicted, subsequently convicted and executed.[6] In Glatshteyn's poem, however, Boddy is not a criminal but, quite the contrary, both hero and model for his people. Like Robin Hood, to whom he is compared in the poem, Boddy's morality transcends the constraints of a society that wishes to dominate and humiliate him. In his moment of triumph, he becomes invincible, mocking death as he rides astride the back of night.

Unlike the immigrants of *Park evenyu*, who sought mercy from the rich and highborn, Boddy had refused to become a gracious adornment in wealthy waiting rooms, because, as the narrator explains, *Host dayne oygn shpiglen nit gevolt in undzere opgeglantste shikh.* ("You didn't want your eyes to reflect in our polished shoes."). Nor would Boddy accept the red fool's cap of a servant. But his is not simply rebellion for its own sake; this is the narrator's point. Rather than viewing the killing of two detectives as willful violence, the narrator recognizes a good deed behind the crime: by committing murder, Boddy has helped his exhausted fellow blacks. Technically free but in fact still enslaved, they are for once able to relax: *Af harte gelegers ruen mide negers./Rut dos mide last-ferd fun der vayser velt./Ale hiter toyt, ale hint farsamt./Durkh der vayser velt trogt zikh vi a vikher der shvartser robin hud.* ("On hard beds rest tired negroes./The white world's tired work horse rests./All guards dead, all dogs poisoned./Through the white world black Robin Hood moves like a whirlwind.").

Luter bodi is very specific in its references to blacks; their way of life is described and some of their special problems delineated. The imagery of the poem reinforces this specificity: mothers use Boddy's name to frighten their chocolate children; the streets of night are grey and black with torches of pitch burning on them; the very first word of the poem refers to Luther Boddy as black. Yet, for all its outward particularity, this poem addresses a problem common to all of Glatshteyn's early characters and narrators—how to maintain a dignified and integrated sense of self in the midst of a thoughtless, sometimes brutal environment.

In the poem *HOMO*,[7] Glatshteyn expanded his anger and defiance to cosmic dimensions with messianic undertones. The narrator introduces himself by daring the forces of nature to ravage both the people and the land that surrounds him; he expresses undaunted faith that a savior will emerge to aid them, even if their fields are ruined and the wombs of their women cursed. The nonsupernatural essence of this apocalyptic figure is hinted at by the very title of the poem. Moreover, the title's Latin-character orthography suggests a messiah who is not only human, but secular in identity. The text of *HOMO* confirms the initial impression yielded by its title: *Fun undzer zomen vet er kumen./Er vet kumen./Er vet muzn kumen.* ("From our seed he will come./He will come./He must come."). Speaking in an elevated prophetic tone, the narrator commands the winds of the world to spread a black decree: *Az mit dem letstn bisl koyekh/Veln mir dem shteyn fun undzer erd tseakern* ("That with our last bit of strength/We will plow up the stone from our ground"). Humanity will not be stopped. Should the light of heaven be extinguished, mankind will nonetheless continue its battle blindly. If deprived of language, the narrator declares, *Undzer brumen vet farshtumen dem vizltirs un dem leybs.* ("Our roar will silence that of the bison and the lion."); and *HOMO* concludes with a prediction that despite adversity, and although the sick and the feeble will die before their final goal can be achieved, the foundations of heaven will eventually be smashed.

The message of *HOMO* is that the meek will inherit not only the earth, but heaven as well. However, God does not figure in this universe, even as a force to be overthrown. Rather, power is concentrated in nature itself without any guiding principle or energy behind it. Thus, the messianic fantasy of heaven overthrown by man represents a conflict between power and weakness similar to that discussed by Glatshteyn elsewhere. And, although the narrator appears at first to exude a defiant confidence in the victory of humanity with the aid of a savior, his assertion throughout the poem that: *Er vet kumen./Er vet muzn kumen.*("He will come./He must come."), in the end sounds more like a plaintive wish than a statement of apocalyptic anticipation. The problems faced by humanity, then, are no more soluble in an abstract, cosmic realm than in a concrete, social one.

II *Hostile Relationships*

The same sense of frailty, vulnerability, and awareness of danger that plagued Glatshteyn as he explored the socio-economic context of modern, urban existence gnawed at him as well in his perception of human relationships. The narrator of *Du* ["You"],[8] for example, is weakened and exhausted by the power of a fiery lover who, flaming inwardly like an eternal light, threatens to consume him before she burns herself out: *Zoygst mayn blut mir oys,/Zoygst mayn markh mir oys,/Makhst mir shvartse ringen unter mayne oygn.* ("You suck out my blood,/You suck out my marrow,/You make black rings under my eyes.").

The narrator's reaction to seduction at the hands of this predatory female is a mixture of perceived danger and delight. Interpreting her first move as a *shlangen-krikh* ("snake-crawl"), he is suddenly swept up in a wild dance of sex; now the black rings relate not to his eyes, but to sexual intercourse: *Hop-galop./Hop-galop./Grubn tife./Shvartse ringen.* ("Hop-gallop./Hop-gallop./Deep caves./Black rings."). As the poem ends, the narrator repeats several of his earlier observations about the woman, trailing off inconclusively with the words: *Un vos far a koyekh in dir - - -* ("And what power in you - - -"). This return to previous impressions, as well as the failure to achieve closure, suggest that the narrator will continue to be surprised, seduced, and tired out by the woman, powerless to alter a cycle of behavior based on overwhelming desire.

A reversal of the predator-victim relationship, however, presents problems of its own. In *Finfundraysik* ["Thirty-Five"],[9] the narrator confronts a thirty-five year old woman who has aged prematurely but still desires him, if only, he believes, to warm her old age. Yet the narrator remains unimpressed by the woman's active and exciting past, and concentrates on his loathing for her lascivious thoughts: *Mir iz dervider, ven du haltst mayn hant in dayner/Mit dayn velkn veln.* ("It revolts me when you hold my hand in yours/With your withered wanting."). The implication of this switch in power roles is a sober one: here, the alternative to feeling sexual attraction and thus risking destruction by surfeit of passion is to be, instead, the object of passion but to feel uninvolved, or even disgusted by it.

One specific alternative to the pain and confusion of sexual relationships is the avoidance of commitment to one individual, a possibility Glatshteyn explores in the poem *Ovntbroyt* ["Supper"].[10] In this work, a self-centered man is caught between two women, refusing or unable to see either of them as unique or to accept responsibility for the feelings he arouses in them. Both the overall structure of *Ovntbroyt* and its content are built on tension and ambiguity. On one level, this is simply a poem about three people at a supper party, responding to one another as they eat; on another level, however, *Ovntbroyt* focuses on volatile sexual tensions for which the supper is merely a social disguise. In addition, it probes the personal and interpersonal conflicts that inundate all three. The narrator and two women sit together at sunset; outwardly silent, they are seething beneath the surface: *Di mayler shvaygn, nor di hertser klapn.* ("The mouths are silent, but the hearts pound."). All three are described as guests at this table; they do not feel as relaxed as they would at home. However, their discomfort is rooted in a more complicated matter, for there exists between them an unpleasant ambivalence. The narrator is aware of simultaneous love and deadly hatred for the women. They, for their part, are also in the grip of tangled emotions. One woman concentrates on the danger that dominates the meal: the reactions of the other woman emerge in greater detail: . . . *ir libe tsu undz un ir sine tsu undz/Un ir libe tsu mir un ir sine tsu ir/Zingt aroys durkh der tsepralter tir* (". . . her love for us and her hatred towards us/And her love for me and her hatred towards her/Sings out through the wide-open door").

The two women are obviously competing for the attentions of the narrator. However, he sees them only insofar as they relate to him. At the beginning of the poem, the narrator refers to the three diners as *Ikh un zi un nokh a zi.* ("I and she and another she."). Unlike the narrator, they exist only in terms of their gender. As the poem progresses, the women become less, rather than more, distinct. This process reaches its culmination in the line: *Un in harts fun zi dos mesersharf zingt* ("And in the heart of she the knife-blade sings"). According to Yiddish grammar, the phrase would be *fun a zi* or *fun der zi*, i.e., "of a woman," "of the woman," where *zi* is a noun; or, alternatively, *fun ir* "of her," in which instance the dative case follows the preposition *fun*. In Glatshteyn's formulation, however, the woman's identity and purpose rest completely in the fact that she is female.

Indeed, the entire supper scene is a metaphor for sexual relations, a loaf of bread and a sharp knife functioning as its symbols. The narrator describes the bread, in the first line of *Ovntbroyt*, as fresh and *shvanger mit zetikeyt* ("pregnant with nourishment"). Later, mentioning the knife, he comments that it is *farmatert fun roytn farlang* ("exhausted from red desire"). Just as the narrator is more important in *Ovntbroyt* than the women, so, too, does the knife

take precedence over the bread. And although both women toy
with the knife, it is the narrator who uses it to approach the passive
bread: *Dos meser un ikh haldzn shtayf eyns dem anderns moyre./Ikh
fokh arum broyt mit tsiterdike hent,* ("The knife and I stiffly embrace
one another's fear./I wave around the bread with trembling hands").

There is no resolution to the social and sexual tensions released
in *Ovntbroyt*. Even at the end, the women do not overcome their
positions as foils for the narrator's ambivalence and indecision: *Dos
meser tantst fun mir tsu ir un fun ir tsu ir./Un shvaygndik esn mir
fun libe un has/Dos ovntbroyt.* ("The knife dances from me to her
and from her to her./And silently we eat of love and hate/Supper.").

In Glatshteyn's earliest poetry, there are no satisfactory relation-
ships between men and women. A partial exception to this bleak
outlook is *Harlem: zuntik* ["Harlem: Sunday"].[11] Here, however,
romance must be relegated to the realm of fantasy in order to prevail
even temporarily. Much as in his response to social difficulties in
HOMO, Glatshteyn inflates fantasy to the level of absurdity in *Har-
lem: zuntik*, while never forfeiting the poignancy that underlies the
wish. As in *Luter bodi*, the protagonists of this poem are blacks, a
group whose socio-economic status offered Glatshteyn an objective
basis for his own threatened world view at the time.[12]

A fundamental progression from general to specific and from out-
side to inside operates on several levels in *Harlem: zuntik*. It func-
tions with respect to scenic description, where initial concentration
on building facades yields to particular interest in the occupants of
two rooms; temporally, as well, an emphatic distinction is made
between the workday week and Sundays, the focus of the poem
coming to bear on the latter; most importantly, however, the hon-
ing-in motion is a crucial element in developing the central theme
of *Harlem: zuntik:* the conflict and huge discrepancy between reality
and fantasy, between the outward, public lives of human beings
and their secret, private dreams.

The narrator begins by discussing the architecture of Harlem,
setting up as he does so a sense of the neighborhood's sinister
darkness and establishing as well a tone of chilly confidentiality that
sets the scene for later descriptions of sexual fantasy: *Vos veysn
shvartse vent fun gang fun di teg?/Vos veysn fintstere vent fun vokh
un fun ru?/Zey veysn, zey veysn vi ikh un vi du.* ("What do black
walls know of the course of the days?/What do dark [sinister] walls
know about the week and about rest?/They know, they know as I

and you do."). The metonymic connection of buildings with those who inhabit them is expanded in the next lines of the poem, as the walls of Harlem are reigned in, enslaved and whipped by their daily burdens. If these walls are patient, however, there is a weekly reward—Sunday. The narrator presents the glories of this day in an ironically elevated tone: the sun is a golden crown, morning is announced with the resounding of a horn. The absurdity of the scene becomes clear as two lost birds cheerfully greet a Harlem tree with the words: *Gut zuntik, gut zuntik.* ("Good Sunday, good Sunday."), a play on the Yiddish Sabbath greeting, *gut shabes.*

The truth is that the inhabitants of Harlem lead a sad and empty existence: *Der elnt fedimt a vokh mit a vokh/Un neyt oys un shtept oys a groteskn geney/A mitndervokhikn mantl fun groy/Mit farbike lates fun zuntiks.* ("Misery threads weeks together/And embroiders and quilts a grotesque needle-work/A mid-week coat of grey/With colorful patches of Sundays."). Thus, the pleasures of a day off are not an integral part of life, but rather fragments of enjoyment grafted onto essential drabness. Far from being the lighthearted and free-spirited creatures of then current stereotypes, unmarried men and women weep out the unhappiness of their existence in lonely furnished rooms. In fact, the only productive creatures on the block are female cats and dogs—an ironic twist to the image of black promiscuity prevalent at the time of *Harlem: zuntik.*

Realistic fulfillment denied them, the men and women of Harlem spend their Sundays indulging in fantasy. The narrator relates one of these, that of a man to whom he gives the name Leon. Leon's is an urban fantasy: another man might daydream while contemplating a river, but for Leon the catalyst is a window in the building opposite his own. Whereas in fairy tales, happiness sometimes waits across a golden bridge, Leon's bridge bears a suspicious resemblance to a clothesline linking his building and the next. Barefoot, wearing only underwear, Leon moves back and forth along this bridge; in his imagination, he possesses supernatural powers: *Leon halt oysgeshtrekt a shemevdike hant/Un tsertlt a brust fun kegniberdiker vant.* ("Leon holds out a shy hand/And fondles a breast of the wall opposite."). With this gesture, he enacts a fusion of environment and self similar to the fantastic projections described by the narrator of *Shtot.*

The object of Leon's attentions is Amalye, as the narrator calls her. Leon—so it appears—sees her throw off her nightgown and approach her mirror, where, because she is no longer young and slender: . . . *zitst an alte kishef-makhern*/*Vos kneytsht ir layb, makht veykh ir brust, makht fet ire fis.* (". . . an old sorceress sits/Who pinches her body, softens her breasts, makes her legs fat."). Amalye's thoughts merge with his own in Leon's mind, and she advises herself, or is encouraged by him, to reject the mirror and be reflected instead in his eye. Amalye joins Leon in spanning the space between their two buildings. In keeping with the heightened atmosphere of fantasy, the bridge that unites them has turned to gold.

The narrator admits that, although these characters actually have different names, he has chosen to call them Leon and Amalye in keeping with the style of romantic novels. As he does so, *Harlem: zuntik* itself begins to resemble a Yiddish dime novel, both in its elevated, German-influenced, proselike language, and in its content. Leon arrives at Amalye's home in an elegant chauffeured automobile and knocks at her door with noble hands. He enters, embraces her, calls her *himlishes vezn* ("heavenly creature"). Realizing that she is naked, his head begins to pound—and abruptly, the vision disappears. During Leon's fantasy, time has been passing, and now the Harlem street is transformed into a sleepy forest, a kind of urban Eden after the Fall; Amalye fashions herself a fig leaf belt and Leon covers himself by putting on his trousers. And in both their heads the pulses beat insistently: *Hey-ra-ten!Hey-ra-ten!* ("Mar-ry!Mar-ry!").

The last line of *Harlem: zuntik* returns once more to the neighborhood's buildings, over the walls of which Sunday respite grows like a creeping vine. The image implies both insulation and gradual entrapment, separating Leon and Amalye after their sexual sin as well as punishing them for it. But, of course, it has all been a fantasy; there has been no romance, no interaction.

With this study of lonely Harlem blacks, Glatshteyn draws together a number of strands that run through his poetry of the early and mid-1920's: the hopelessness of attempting to achieve any satisfying relationship with another human being; the general abuse suffered by the individual in society, and, more specifically, the trampling of downtrodden humanity in an urban milieu; finally, the use of fantasy to posit what seems to be impossible in the world of reality.

III *Artistic Battles*

Es tsitert di knoyt fun undzer dor./Ho, mentshn regedike./Lomir, af gikh, oyskritsn in marmor undzere maysim./In bikher farshraybn undzer nomen. ("The wick of our generation is trembling./Ho, transitory people./Let us quickly carve out our deeds in marble./Record our names in books."). With these opening lines of the poem *Undzer dor* ["Our generation"],[13] Glatshteyn inaugurated his first volume of poetry and, in a sense, his career as well. It is a strange pronouncement, judging from the confident and vigorous tone of the *In zikh* manifesto, which had appeared only shortly before *Yankev glatshteyn* and of which Glatshteyn was a primary executor. Considering his early mood of threatened pessimism and his fear of impotence and annihilation, however, this vision is not incongruous, even though it is unusual in that the narrator is not totally isolated in his situation. Moreover, as in other instances where the feeling of doom inspired an aggressive stance, *Undzer dor's* redoubtable predictions have their corollary in an attack aimed at *Di yunge*, who represented to the *Inzikhistn* the American Yiddish literary establishment.

Poetic criticisms are the substance of another early poem, *A farziglter briv* ["A sealed letter"],[14] but they remain shrouded in ambiguity. On a straightforward level, *A farziglter briv* is a vaguely morbid description of a young woman receiving a letter from the realm of death, but careful observation of the poem's structure and between-the-lines reading of its content reveal otherwise. Superficially, the work is a typical *Yunge*-type mood evocation, full of the hackneyed hush that is often associated with poems about death. However, this initial impression is undercut by several elements, the first being precisely *A farziglter briv's* stereotypical subject matter and imagery. A woman's solitude, the coolness of her body, the late hour, wax candles, silence—these are the sort of clichés eschewed by the *In zikh* group. Their abundance in the poem is suspicious. At the same time, jarring notes intrude on the general, dreamily lugubrious nature of this work: it is amusing, rather than suggestive of darkness and mystery, to picture a dead mailman delivering a letter from the dead, which its recipient, rather than reading, files in a *toytn-arkhiv* ("death-archive"), preferring instead to envision the face of her deceased lover.

Similarly, the form of *A farziglter briv* is a peculiar combination of the predictable and the unusual. Compared in general with Glatshteyn's earliest poetry, this work is strikingly rich in rhyme; at the same time, however, the very first rhyme pair: *brivn-treger/geleger* ("mail-man/bed") undermines the potential of rhyme as a unifying element meant to enhance the flow of the poem. A more obvious device used to rupture the smoothness of mood evocation is the remarkably long and clumsy line: *Der yontev kumt alemol shpet tsu ir in hoyz, ober fort nit umzist gevart.* ("The holiday always comes to her home late, but once again she had not waited in vain.").

When these elements are considered together, it is evident that *A farziglter briv* seeks to stress, by ironic example, the disparity between the trappings of mood and the mood itself. In this way, the narrator criticizes the heavyhanded attempts that, in the opinion of the *Inzikhistn*, characterized the work of *Di yunge* at its most anemic and self-derivative.

IV   *The Importance of Language*

Quite unlike this circumspect but negative response to literary rivals and the fear with which he contemplated his future, Glatshteyn approached language itself in a vibrant and positive fashion; it is here, in fact, that the most clearly affirmative attitudes of his earliest writing are expressed. For Glatshteyn, language possessed a life of its own; his belief in its tangibility—a central theme in the poem *Tirtl-toybn*—is apparent in other works as well. Just as if they were human, words not only act autonomously, but also have the power to affect others, emotionally and physically. In *In der fintster* ["In the dark"],[15] for example, the narrator relates the following scene: *Raytn verter in melodiyen-raykh af goldene raytvegn./Nest zikh a vort af mayn kop un glet mayne hor./Shpilt zikh a vort mit a shotn af der vant.* ("Words ride in the melody realm on golden chariots./A word nests on my head and strokes my hair./A word plays with a shadow on the wall."). The notion of language as constantly capable of being created also led to Glatshteyn's early invention of nonce words and neologisms, e.g.: *bam(e)zuzet* ("covered with mezzuzahs"), *verimen* ("to act like a worm"), or *nertomedik* ("eternal light-like").[16] This practice was to become an identifiable characteristic of his work.

The poem *Shlos fun yo* ["Castle of Yes"][17] is Glatshteyn's most graphic song of praise to the vitality of language. In this work words become the goal of a quest, comprising as well the scenery of the narrator's all-consuming journey: *Af raytvegn neyn./Durkh krume vegn oyb./Tog ikh un nakhtik ale mayne yor.* ("On chariots [of] no./Through crooked paths [of] perhaps./I spend the days and nights of all my years."). In the pulsating rhythm of a wild ride, the narrator explains that he is traveling towards the *Shtol un shteynernem shlos fun yo.* ("Steel and stone castle of yes.").

His head, depicted here metaphorically as the tower on his shoulders, shouts that, rather than consisting of steel or stone, the castle is merely an insubstantial dream; reality, far from being "yes," is in fact . . . *neyn. neyn. neyn.* (". . . no. no. no."). The narrator's description of his head as a tower reinforces the main point of *Shlos fun yo:* by refusing to use the term "head" and choosing "tower" instead, he admits the importance of mind but asserts that the development of language should not be locked within the framework of intellectual abstraction. And, to emphasize this issue, he concludes by rejecting what his head tells him, continuing his faith that *Durkh aruf. arop. arum.* ("Through upwards. Downwards. Around."), he will finally reach the steel and stone castle of yes. In this way, the narrator casts his lot with language as an emotionally affirming spirit in his life, overriding constraints and providing him with the prospect of security in the end, despite its precarious and difficult aspects. For the threatened poet, then, language is the only source of comfort and celebration.

V   Glatshteyn's Changing Perspective

Kredos—Credos (New York, 1929) and *Yidishtaytshn—Yiddish Meanings* (Warsaw, 1937) reveal a new period in Glatshteyn's poetry. His fearful attitudes were diminishing and, with them, his self-centered response to what had previously seemed a threatening world. By the late 1930's, Glatshteyn's poems reflect deep involvement with the world into which he casts his individual narrators, and they, in turn, are integral parts of that world. As his vision broadened, Glatshteyn began to concentrate on new aspects of the

situations he discussed, so that, for example, psychological moti-
vation or social and developmental processes became as important
to him as individual and personal reaction. These changes, occurring
in all areas of his work, underlie the concentrated power of Glat-
shteyn's response to the Holocaust, particularly the destruction of
Eastern European Jewry, as well as his subsequent return to issues
of a more general nature.

In these volumes, Glatshteyn's discussion of social and political
matters is marked by two major innovations: a less self-centered
view of events and situations and, at the same time, deepening
interest in his own Jewishness and his notions about Jewish life.
While the first of these innovations is significant, and its results
obvious in such works as *Sako un vanzetis montik* ["Sacco and Van-
zetti's Monday"], *Der firer* ["The leader"], or *Shvartse khoges*
["Black (non-Jewish) holidays"][18] it is through the second change—
Glatshteyn's coming to terms with his Jewishness—that the depth
of his development is fully revealed. In a variety of works written
before his famous *A gute nakht, velt* ["Good night, world"], he
anticipates the defiantly Jewish consciousness of that poem. Now
a specifically Jewish viewpoint informs his examination of subjects
that had interested him all along. These works, whose Jewish per-
spective ranges from central to incidental, testify to Glatshteyn's
decision, whether conscious or not, to confront more completely
this side of his existence.

VI   Society and Self: Continued Conflict

In *Luter bodi*, an historical figure from the world of crime had
served as a catalyst for Glatshteyn's discussion of the outsider in
America. He employs this device again in a later work, the four-
part poem *Shini mayk* ["Sheeny Mike"].[19] However, here the pro-
tagonist is not black but Jewish, and Glatshteyn emphasizes the
importance of Sheeny Mike's family and background as elements
in his development. In the first poem, though, the narrator does
not dwell on Sheeny Mike's connection to Jewishness, but concen-
trates instead on his deviation from heritage. The first line, *Shini
mayk shloft in a bronzenem orn.* ("Sheeny Mike sleeps in a bronze
coffin.") exposes an essential conflict. Sheeny Mike, by his name,
is evidently Jewish, and the Yiddish term *orn* explicitly signifies a

coffin for a Jew, yet this casket is bronze, not the simple wooden box generally used in traditional Jewish burials.

Moreover, the dead hero is not dressed in the burial shroud customarily worn by Jews; rather, he lies foppishly decked out. The remainder of the poem amplifies this initial contradiction. Sheeny Mike had been a gang leader; his men stand around on the corners of his realm—twelve city blocks—smoking and steeling themselves against tears. In contrast to this view of Sheeny Mike is the spectacle of his parents, who, together with his gang, mourn for their son. They are traditional Jews: his father is bearded and his mother wears the wig donned for the sake of modesty by married women. Through synecdoche, this Jewish identity is emphasized still further, indicating that although Sheeny Mike's mother is more lenient than his father in assessing her son, the essence of both is their religious outlook. The mother's wig praises Sheeny Mike: *Az er hot alte tate-mame/Nit gelozt faln mentshn tsu last.* ("That he never let his old parents/Become a burden to people."). For this she believes he should accumulate merit in the divine reckoning. The father's beard, however, is ashamed because everyone within the twelve-block empire knows that Sheeny Mike has died violently, and that he is now resting in a bronze coffin.

The second poem of this series is a flashback to Sheeny Mike's youth that sheds light on early humiliations. In death, his Jewishness is muted, but in the narrative view of his life, the particular burdens of Jewish immigrant existence emerge as the central reality from which he flees. The narrator relates how Sheeny Mike had dreamed of his future kingdom as he observed the dirty city from a tenement roof. Elevated symbolically as well as actually, he had risen above his father, who, sitting in the house below, had with half-blind eyes: *Gelernt mit kinder dem taytsh/Fun shulkhon—a teybl un kisey—a tsher.* ("Studied with children the meaning/Of *shulkhon*—a table and *kisey*—a chair."). His father's position as a *melamed*—a teacher of small children—while never a prestigious job, was even more demeaning in America than in Europe because, as an immigrant, he was forced to translate from Hebrew into a language not native to him.

Sheeny Mike's mother, in apparent contrast to his father, had been aware of her son's ambitions, realizing that he was climbing the ladder, not of success as in the stereotypical American dream, but rather of the world of crime: *Fun keshene ganev tsum same shpits,/Tsum groysn srore, meylekh un bafeler,/Iber di gantse arum un arum tsvelf blok.* ("From pickpocket to the very pinnacle,/To the lord, king and commander,/Of the entire twelve blocks."). The poem concludes with a lament, evidently the mother's, that the ancestors of the family, the pious water-carriers and butchers, had remained in the cemeteries of Europe, unwilling or unable to intercede in heaven as Sheeny Mike's father brought poverty into their house. The connection is clear: because of the passivity and lack of vision exhibited by his father, Sheeny Mike turned to dreams of success which, for him, took the form of power through crime. The pious, working-man's life of his European heritage would not suffice for him in America, paling beside his ambitions. This desire for mastery conceived on a tenement roof in a kind of Pisgah vision— *Do, af dem dakh hot er dokh dem kholem fun zayn kinigraykh derzen.* ("Here, on the roof, indeed he discerned the dream of his kingdom.")—is ultimately unfulfilled; but its partial realization suggests, in Glatshteyn's work, a narrowing of the chasm between fantasy and real-life possibilities.

In the third and fourth poems in this series, Sheeny Mike's empire is described in its full blossom and after its conclusion; Sheeny Mike himself becomes less the Jew and more the gangster. In fact, the final poem does not mention Sheeny Mike's family at all, concentrating instead on his bereaved sweetheart, to whom he had seemed so noble. Another aspect of Sheeny Mike's personality is revealed here: the wild and angry lover, able to enthrall by passion as well as by his own brand of royal power. Completely stripped of his Jewish connections, he functions finally simply as a man of immense verve and charm, transcending his vulgarity, lively even in the silence of his death.

The lines of *Shini mayk* are a strange blend of legend-making and simultaneous subtle undercutting of the legend. In each poem, Sheeny Mike rises nominally to the rank of hero, only to be cast back into his meager context. In the first poem, for example, he is described as *Der shrek un der hiter, der meylekh un gebiter* ("The fear and the protector, the king and commander"). This line, with its regular rhythm and inner rhyme, radiates a clichéd simplicity and predictability that makes it resemble a folk-song; but the expectations it arouses are shattered in the very next line, as Sheeny Mike's empire is revealed, in ironic overstatement, to be "around and around twelve whole blocks." Similarly, in the last poem, two lines describe Sheeny Mike in a throbbing rhythm, first elevating and then degrading him: *Der raytndiker riter,/Der temper yung, der shiker,* ("The riding knight,/The dense youth, the drunkard,"). The contrast is evident in the other poems as well. A dramatic list of Sheeny Mike's achievements is juxtaposed with the revelation that this "king" lived at home with his impoverished Jewish parents. Even his grand vision, revealed through weighty alliteration— *Shvere shlepshifn shnaydn dos koytike vaser,/Shtinkendiker roykh farsazhet di dekher* ("Heavy tugboats cut the dirty water,/Stinking smoke covers the roofs with soot")—leads only to the paltry realm of twelve city blocks and to an early and futile death.

Futility is the final comment on Sheeny Mike's revolt, as romantic and hopeful as it had been. His wished-for dynasty, a new kind of tradition born of Jewish immigrant failure on American soil, is never realized. In the end, Sheeny Mike's attempt to overcome his past and his parents' present is no more successful than Luther Boddy's had been. At this stage, then, the criminal protagonist—inevitably doomed—remained a compelling figure to Glatshteyn as he continued to confront the conflict between society and self.

VII *Love: Commitment and Causality*

By the late 1920's, Glatshteyn's poems concerning personal relationships were moving away from the threatened tone of his earliest period. During this time, he broadened his perspective and began to feel sympathy for women.[20] As his attitude became more positive, Glatshteyn began to write about friendlier, warmer relationships, ones based on empathy, trust, and, eventually, commitment.

This is not to say that resolution of conflict was easy or necessarily permanent. The process could be tortuous and incomplete, as the poem *Unter fremdn dakh* ["Under a strange roof"][21] reveals. This work, like *Ovntbroyt*, concerns a romantic triangle, but here the similarity ends. The triangle consists of two men and one woman, rather than two women and one man; moreover, instead of a situation in which the women serve merely as foils for the man's ambivalent reactions, *Unter fremdn dakh* describes a growing love relationship between the narrator and a married woman, a union that is eventually culminated sexually.

At first the narrator compares himself to a priest listening as the woman confesses her love for her husband. He spends months supressing his own desires to become closer to her, burdensome though this self-control is: *Ir libe far im iz govorn gevoynheyt vi a hoyker/Un efsher iz doz geven der hoyker af mir* ("Her love for him became as familiar as a hunchback/And perhaps the hunchback was on me"). However, although the narrator talks about himself, he concentrates as well on the changing reactions of the woman and on thoughts about her husband, who is a critical figure in the romance despite his physical absence.

The woman claims exaggerated faithfulness to her husband, devotion so slavish that she continually oscillates between his arms and the brink of some danger. She repeats this confession compulsively, as if attempting to convince herself of its validity. The woman's verbosity emerges as a central motif in *Unter fremdn dakh*. The very first verb used to describe her is *gevertert* ("worded"); her words constitute an obstacle, rather than a means of communication, between herself and the narrator. He attempts to bridge the barrier, but his efforts are in vain: *Zibetsn shleyern hob ikh geshlept fun ir kheynevdike reyd/Un zi iz alts geshtanen far mir/Lang un hoykh in ir kimono.* ("I pulled seventeen veils from her charming speech/And she still stood before me/Long and tall in her kimono.").

In the end, however, the woman uses her power of speech in order to seduce the ostensible priest. Exploiting the enslavement by her husband revealed in her confessions, she pleads: *Leyz mikh oys, bafray mikh fun mayn libe tsu im,*—("Deliver me, free me from my love for him,—"). The priest's cross melts, signifying both the end of his sexual avoidance and the warmth of his feelings. He undresses the woman by stripping away her last thin veil of speech. Just as language had previously obstructed communication between the two people, their intimacy begins with its removal.

The narrator desires complete union with his lover—understanding so total that words become unnecessary. He think of her as a cello and awaits the purity of clear music which he hopes will come from her. But the woman, who has exposed herself and finally become vulnerable, is now more trapped than before. It is not enough that she lives with a man: *Vos geveltikt iber di vinkelekh fun hoyz,/Iber dem orimen tish un tsebrokhene shtuln/Un iber ir vi a teyl fun zayn gotgebentshter orimkeyt.* ("Who rules over the corners of the house,/Over the poor table and broken chairs/And over her as a part of his God-blessed poverty."). Now she is subservient to the narrator as well. Kneeling under the yoke of their lovemaking, she closes her eyes with exhaustion; she suffers from dreadful guilt, fashioning her love into strips and beating herself with them. The narrator soon finds that his cello, far from delighting him with beautiful music, breaks her silence only by crying.

The narrator does not fare much better. He, too, experiences feelings of guilt, gradually allowing the contradictions of the affair to enter his consciousness. As he becomes aware of his own conflicts, he is suddenly reminded as well of the woman's longlasting devotion to her husband. He thus avoids facing the fact that her marriage is tantamount to imprisonment, represented by *Di kargshaft fun gehern un farmogn/Un di engshaft fun a bet far tsvey* ("The scantiness of belonging and possessing/And the narrowness of a bed for two").

Under fremdn dakh reveals a narrator capable of strong positive feelings about a woman and able to recognize her individuality: he is clearly different from the narrator of *Ovntbroyt* in his sympathy, thoughtfulness, and willingness to concentrate on the sensitivities of another. Despite this, he abdicates responsibility in the end, allowing himself to believe that his lover is tied to her husband after all. The issue of commitment is one that the narrator ultimately decides not to confront.

The narrator of *Fun undzer yokh* ["About our burden"][22] is very different from the one in *Unter fremdn dakh*. The title of the poem indicates the nature of the relationship he describes: implying readiness to take on a burden, it assumes as well that this burden will be shared.

The involvement of the lovers in *Unter fremdn dakh* faltered precisely as the last obstacle to the union crumbled. The opening lines of *Fun undzer yokh*, on the contrary, reveal a relationship thriving without barriers: *Dos letste ventl tsvishn undz iz gefaln/Un ikh hob gezen, az zi iz nit tsoyberlekh.* ("The last screen between us fell/And I saw that she was not magical."). For the narrator, this realization is a source of pleasure—he has no sense of impending destruction or misery. The excitement of seduction, with its concomitant elements of self-deprecation, guilt, and flight, is no longer important to him; instead, he joins together with a woman who is his friend, to live with her and accept the responsibilities of their common existence: *Far ir hob ikh keyn netsn nit geshpreyt./Vos far a yeger ken ikh, mishteyns gezogt, zayn/Mit dem pak fun oysgekligte yorn./Zi iz aleyn tsu mir gekumen.* ("I spread no nets for her./Alas, what kind of a hunter can I be/With this pack of clevered-out years./She came to me herself.").

The narrator's sense of comfort and resolution is rooted in the fact that, while he does not fear being destroyed by an adversary, neither does he expect ultimate communication with his woman. As he puts it: . . . *vi noent man un vayb zoln nit shlofn/Zaynen zeyere khaloymes farshidn./In shlof zaynen zey elnt/Un shlisn oys eyner dem andern.* (". . . no matter how close man and wife sleep/Their dreams are different./In sleep they are lonely/And shut one another out."). Dreams are now part of an alternate realm, supplementing rather than opposing real-life experience. Moreover, the narrator's acceptance of the essential isolation of all individuals does not preclude desire for closeness with the woman to whom he feels committed; paradoxically, their communication, though limited, achieves the intimacy so desired by the narrator of *Unter fremdn dakh:* understanding that needs no words. Thus, this relationship, far from collapsing when there are no external barriers, flourishes with gentleness and warmth.[23]

A second paradox is the freedom that results from shouldering responsibility. The metaphor for this apparent contradiction is the narrator's shingling the roof of his house in order to protect his woman and himself; elevation and lack of encumbrance stem directly from his pursuit of stability. His position is radically different from that of the narrator in *Unter fremdn dakh* who, while assuming no actual burdens, never attained an equivalent measure of freedom.

Although in Glatshteyn's poems of the late 1920's and 1930's feelings of threat and impotence posed by encounters with the opposite sex were diminishing, these impulses were not forgotten; however, Glatshteyn sought to understand the motivations behind such emotions. In *Nakht, zay shtil tsu mir* ["Night, be quiet to me"],[24] one of a brilliant group of poems in which he attempts to recreate the sensations and ideas of childhood and adolescence, Glatshteyn explores a child's response to perceiving himself abandoned.

The narrator of *Nakht, zay shtil tsu mir* finds himself prey to anger, jealousy and despair when his mother leaves the room to join her husband. The child is frightened of the night, which he experiences as a living force; nonetheless, he invites it to join him under the covers, deriving pleasure from his own fear. The reason for his rashness soon becomes clear: furious at his mother for deserting him, he hopes to gain revenge by allowing himself to be harmed as a result of her neglect. Convinced that, in the dark, a shadow is preparing to kill him, he labels his mother a murderess for her lack of concern: *Zi iz avek, in tatns bet,/Un ir art nisht, vos morgn/Vet men mikh gefinen a dervorgn,* ("She left, to [go to] my father's bed,/And she does not care that tomorrow/They will find me choked,"). The child tries to pretend that he is unperturbed, but his show of courage evaporates, revealing a fear as powerful as the desire for retribution: *Art mikh oykh nisht./Art mikh nisht./Art mikh oykh nisht./Art mikh nisht./Art mikh oykh/Nisht.* ("It doesn't bother me either./It doesn't bother me./It doesn't bother me either./It doesn't bother me./It does/N't bother me either."). Finally, still wanting his revenge, but succumbing to the fear as well, the child asks the night to maintain no more than a distanced contact with him by watching him through the window.

The child's ideas are clearly designed to reveal to the reader more than the narrator himself understands. Unable to articulate the depth of his sense of abandonment, he objectifies his emotions, allowing his misery to be reflected in the perception of murderous intentions lurking within a hostile night. Neither does he recognize that his pretense of strength only exposes its opposite.

The child's attempts to master strong emotions resemble the responses of other narrators in Glatshteyn's work. The projection of an inner situation onto the environment was clear in *Shtot;* repetition in order to convince the self was a method utilized by the narrator of *HOMO;* to some extent, the child is involved in a version of the triangle relationships explored in *Ovntbroyt* and *Unter fremdn dakh.* In *Nakht, zay shtil tsu mir,* however, Glatshteyn employs these devices to indicate the very young age of the narrator, emphasizing his point by a clever approximation of language in the process of being learned. For example, the child knows that he wants to express the concept "repeat," but apparently he does not know the word for it; therefore he invents his own term based on the thought behind it: *iberibern* ("to over-over.)" The construction is ingenious since it incorporates the first part of the Yiddish word *iberkhazern* ("to repeat"), implying that the child has some familiarity with the word, although he cannot recall it precisely.

Similarly, the narrator has learned to use the command form *zay* plus adjective, as in *zay shtil* ("be quiet"). What he has failed to assimilate is that this pattern does not apply to verbs, which form their own imperatives; thus, he combines the two, creating such impossibilities as *zay kum* ("be come") and *zay kuk* ("be look"). Furthermore, since he knows that adjectives used predicatively in *zay* plus adjective may also occur attributively (e.g., *shtile nakht*— "quiet night"), he generalizes this as well, producing *shvayge nakht* ("silent night") [inadmissible in Yiddish] and *kuke nakht* ("looky night"). Without ever making an explicit statement, Glatshteyn thus reveals the narrator's level of development, managing thereby to cast new light on an old problem by shifting his perspective away from personal narrative.

In attempting to understand the genesis of relationships in earlier perceptions and experiences, Glatshteyn looked to social, as well as psychological, explanations of behavior. The narrator of *Tsu dir* ["To you"],[25] for example, addresses a sixteen-year-old girl who, in his estimation, has already been debased by American society. In one respect, the young woman is sophisticated, even somewhat glamorous. Her speech is the sharp, invincible repartee of a movie personality; she wears makeup in order to furnish external proof of her sexuality: *Af di lipn dayne ligt fet ongeshmirt dayn sofistikatsye.* ("On your lips your sophistication lies thickly smeared."). She has learned all the proper terms and acquired a theoretical understanding of sexuality.

Underneath the veneer of maturity and awareness, however, lies a personality devoid of spontaneity: the girl may be a vivacious talker, but she uses her talent in a studied way, coldly attempting to impress. For all her ostensible sexuality, she remains unmoved when faced with the reality of contact, calculating the length of a kiss by the tick of her wrist watch. Moreover, her general sexual attitude is colored, not by youthful fantasies of romance, but rather by an obsession with the sanctity of motherhood. In the view of the narrator, this narrow appraisal of relationships is damaging, robbing romantic and sexual unions of pleasure and tenderness, reducing people to commodities.

The sixteen-year-old's innocence is already lost; she is "pregnant," as the narrator says, *Mit oysdoyer far dem, vos vet bagildn dayn ere/Un dikh makhn far a mame.* ("With endurance for him who will gild your honor/And make you a mother."). *Ere*—"honor"—appears here ironically; unacceptable in the standard language, it recalls the German tinged vocabulary of Yiddish dime novels and the outlandish romances that characterize those works. The connection here of pregnancy, marriage, and honor is based on the traditional notion that a "fallen woman" can be saved only if a man is willing to wed her and provide her child with a name. In *Tsu dir*, however, the situation is reversed, since the girl's immorality lies precisely in her acceptance of a stereotyped marital future.

The man too gets sucked into this insidious syndrome. He is taught that, having married the woman and bestowed validity upon her, he may then view her as chattel, important to him only insofar as she retains her honor by remaining faithful and gratifying him sexually. Despite the fact that he feels no obligation to be loyal to her, he expects to receive . . . *dos bisl freyd zayns,/Vos darf vartn af im,/Ven er kumt a mider fun gesheft un fun zaytike eksperimentn.* (". . . his bit of pleasure,/Which must wait for him,/When he arrives, tired from business and experiments on the side."). He is even prepared to resort to violence in order to maintain his position. The narrator, contemplating the girl's acceptance of this kind of marriage, this kind of motherhood, concludes that he has come too late: *A gute nakht, ikh vel kumen/Farayorn.* ("Good night, I will come/Last year.").

VIII *The Artist's Heritage*

Throughout the 1930's, Glatshteyn continued to engage in controversies with members of the Yiddish literary world.[26] However, now he perceived his position within that environment differently: once the self-proclaimed renegade, he had come to consider himself part of a community and heir to a tradition whose leaders had given him special gifts for which he was grateful.

Both *Moyshe leybs kol* ["Moyshe Leyb's voice"] and *Shomer* ["Shomer"][27] are memorial poems, paying homage to a dead writer. In each work, Glatshteyn reveals that he has learned something from the artist about whom he is writing, at the same time setting them, and himself, within an American Yiddish milieu. The narrator of *Moyshe leybs kol* seeks to evoke characteristic aspects of Moyshe Leyb Halpern's poetic style as well as the complexity of the artist himself. The former is achieved essentially through language, and the latter mainly through content.

Halpern himself has played on the tension between narrator, character, and poet by employing a variety of distancing devices in his work, among them the incorporation of a persona named Moyshe

Leyb. The narrator of *Moyshe leybs kol* attempts to portray not only
the ostensible Moyshe Leyb—the wily ruffian whose veneer im-
perfectly conceals a core of sadness—but also the man behind all
the masks he dons: a man both angry and lonely, a man in conflict
with the quality and values of life in the United States. The poem's
action concerns one night in the life of a *mentshl* ("little person"),
trapped in a golden cage in the city of Tarshish. Tarshish is the
biblical city to which Jonah had fled, attempting to evade his God-
given responsibility as moral critic of humanity. The *mentshl*'s Tar-
shish is America and, just as Jonah had not been able to escape,
neither can the *mentshl* free himself from the golden cage of Amer-
ican life—an allusion to Halpern's own use of gold as a symbol for
existence in the United States.[28]

Although he pretends to be carefree and rambunctious—as epit-
omized by the disclosure that he *vayzt alemen a fayg* ("shows every-
one a fig"—a gesture signifying contempt)—the little person is
actually lonely and frightened; he feels comforted when a princess
comes to lull him; but no sooner does she leave than *di nakht iz
shrek* ("the night is fear"). Moreover, the man calls himself *Hots-
makh-tsingitang*, a reference to characters in two operettas by
Avrom Goldfaden, *Di kishef-makhern* (1893) and *Shulamis* (1883)
respectively. Hotsmakh is the stereotypical Jewish merchant,
whereas Tsingitang is so primitive as to be inarticulate. These op-
posites in Goldfaden's work have in common the fact that they both
operate as outsiders, while at the same time playing a crucial role
in the action of the plot. Thus they function as barometers of sig-
nificant events and conflicts; furthermore, as buffoons, they are
privileged to be truth-sayers.

The *mentshl* in his cage is isolated too, suspended between his
new society and the world of his tradition. For, the caged man is
not only a *mentshl*, but a *yidl* ("little Jew") as well, his isolation
evidently stemming from the perception that as a Jew in America
he is trapped. He maintains his traditional desires, exemplified by
the characteristically Jewish foods he eats in his cage—carrot *tsimes*
(a favorite Sabbath and holiday dish), *latkes* (potato pancakes tra-
ditionally eaten at Hanukkah), *khremzlekh* (Passover pancakes), to
name just a few. Yet when confronted by members of the assimi-
lationist *yidl-kristldiker khokhmes hayudaike* ("Judeo-Christianized
Wissenschaft des Judentums"),[29] he dances along with them, un-
derstanding them all too well. The intricacy of the *mentshl*'s conflict,

however, is emphasized by this dance, since, even as he dances, he again makes his contemptuous fig gesture yet, in an indirect appeal to his heritage, grabs a broom, shaking it towards them as if it were a *lulev* (used on the Jewish festival of Sukkoth, the Feast of Booths).

Nor can the *mentshl* accept the American version of traditional Jewish life; he sees that time honored values have been compromised when the Lower East Side comes to visit him, painting a grim picture of Jews intent upon gratifying their immediate desires. He cannot even flee to the non-Jewish world: . . . *kh'veys nisht vuhin men antloyft,/Kh'volt zikh gern draytsn mol getoyft,/Ven di goyim voltn oykh nisht gesarkhet*. (". . . I do not know where one runs to,/I would gladly be baptized thirteen times,/If the non-Jews did not stink also.").

Moyshe leybs kol concludes as morning dawns in Tarshish upon the *mentshl's* empty cage, an oblique reference to Halpern's death. In this context, however, the narrator comforts himself by implying that, for a man as tortured and deeply divided as Halpern, only death could provide an escape from the entrapment of living between two worlds.

For Glatshteyn, however, Halpern was more than a symbol of conflict in Yiddish poetry; his influence was such that Glatshteyn recognized it in his own work, particularly in the avoidance of distinct "poetic" vocabulary. He reveals this singular connection between himself and Halpern through the language of *Moyshe leybs kol*—in the list of traditional foods, for example, or the term *vayzn a fayg*. He copies as well certain other characteristics of Halpern's poetry: the latter's use of rhythm and fondness for refrains and, in an especially clever adaptation, Halpern's intentional confusion of poet and narrator in his work; according to the title, the narrator of *Moyshe leybs kol* is Halpern himself, since his voice is evoked. Yet the figure meant to represent Moyshe Leyb Halpern is not only the narrator, but the *mentshl* as well.

The illusion of Halpern as narrator is achieved by reference to the issues that were important to him. Ambivalence like that of the *mentshl* had been articulated by Halpern in such works as *Benk aheym* ["Long for home"] and *Zlotshev mayn heym* ["Zlotshev my home"];[30] his sometimes cavalier attitude towards death, epitomized by the poem *Memento mori*,[31] is echoed as well in Glatshteyn's poem, where death greets the *mentshl* with song and provides the implicit escape from a golden cage of cultural and religious conflict. The essence of Halpern emerges as well from the specific allusions to his poetry that appear within the body of *Moyshe leybs kol*, most notably in such expressions as *O lebn mayns, mayn blutik geveyn* ("O my life, my bleeding cry"), which closely resembles a line from Halpern's poem *Gingili* ["Gingili"]: *O gingili, mayn blutik harts,* ("O Gingili, my bloody heart,")[32] or *Mit der umru fun a volf un mit der ru fun a ber* ("With the turbulence of a wolf and with the calmness of a bear"), which harks back to the poem *Mayn umru fun a volf* ["My wolf-like turbulence"].[33]

Through these and other references, the narrator adapts Halpern's original contexts so as to focus on his own concerns. Specifically, *Moyshe leybs kol* enables Glatshteyn to return once more to the problem of the individual unreconciled to society and, in particular, to the difficulties faced by the immigrant in America. Clearly, Glatshteyn no longer felt threatened by the achievements of other artists.

Moyshe leybs kol is a powerful expression of the extent to which Glatshteyn felt connected to the older poet, especially to his poetic voice,[34] allowing himself to incorporate Halpern's language into his own, bending it to his needs. His attempt to reach the man at the center of his poetry further underscores the depth of Halpern's impact, the way in which his poetry moved Glatshteyn on both an explicit and an implicit level.

The poem *Shomer*, by contrast, is less an analysis of the artist and his technique than a comment about artistic function within society. In this work Glatshteyn establishes, as he had in *Moyshe leybs kol*, his sense of belonging to a community of writers that had experienced the enormous development of American Yiddish literature; he does so, however, not so much through analysis of Shomer's work *per se*—and not at all through an investigation of his personality—but rather by exploring Shomer's relationship to his audience.

Shomer (the pen-name of N. M. Shaykevitsh) had been a controversial figure in the history of Yiddish literature since 1888, the year Sholem-Aleykhem published a pamphlet in Barditshev entitled *Shomers mishpet* ["Shomer's trial"]. There he condemned the work of Shomer as cheap romantic trash that avoided depicting "real life," presenting instead a world of dreams and impossible happy endings. In opposition to Shomer, Sholem-Aleykhem placed writers like Sh.

Y. Abramovitsh (more popularly known as Mendele Moykher Sforim), whom he praised for not denying the ugly aspects of Jewish life. Sholem-Aleykhem's evaluation had a profound effect on the course of Yiddish literary history, establishing Abramovitsh as the respected elder and casting Shomer's work into disrepute.

With his loyal audience, however, Shomer fell out of favor not as a result of critical condemnation from on high, but rather because of changed circumstances among the readers themselves. His work had appealed, according to the narrator of *Shomer*, precisely to those for whom his stories were a welcome escape from the grim humiliations of "real life." These women, predominantly servants, worked to the point of exhaustion in homes where they were *Di farshtoysene, farshemte,/Fun balebos in der zaydener kapote,/In der fintster gekushte un getapte.* ("The repudiated and shamed ones,/Kissed and felt in the dark/By their boss in his long silk coat."). For these women, Shomer provided a Sabbath treat, a fantasy refuge from the drudgery of mundane life on the only day when they were privileged to rest. Through him, they could dream of "True Love," that magic which the exigencies of their lives would always deny them. Far from being a negative force, fantasy in fact aided these miserable creatures to endure their lot: *O treyst-geber, farvandler fun bidne teg un nekht,/Host farveyrukht tsholnt-luft un geeydlt di farklolete teg* ("O comfort-giver, transformer of wretched days and nights,/You incensed *tsholnt* [a baked dish of meat, potatoes, and legumes served on the Sabbath] air and ennobled the accursed days").

With the passage of time and mass immigration to the United States, however, Shomer's potential readership evaporated. The narrator, walking like a Shomer hero, finds that the servant women are no longer unhappy; they have married, and their daughters *varelibn zikh af griltsndikn english in di oytomobiln.* ("truelove in grating English in their automobiles."). Glatshteyn's earliest characters and narrators had needed fantasy to escape from an intolerable cosmos. In *Shomer*, Glatshteyn adopts a more distanced view of the function of fantasy, seeing it as a specifically literary refuge from a hostile world. However, as in *Fun undzer yokh*, where fantasy was increasingly unnecessary, here, too, Shomer's readers abandon his world as they move even further into the mainstream of American life. Shomer is therefore part of a dead heritage. Unlike Halpern, whose conflicts stemmed from spanning two worlds, Shomer is relegated to an ignominious burial for failing to meet a changing need. (Of course, the problem of vanishing readership, which Glatshteyn was able to treat relatively lightly in the course of *Shomer*, later became for him a much more serious and immediate matter in the wake of the Holocaust.)

The narrator shares Shomer's aversion to ugly naturalism: *Ikh hob oykh, vi du, gevolt antloyfn fun fishke dem krumen.* ("I, too, like you, wanted to run from Fishke the Lame.");[35] he finds, however, that his literary milieu is no more receptive to this approach than Shomer's had been. For the narrator, though, Shomer retains special value as an eternal Modernist, having sought, as does the narrator himself, to avoid the constraints of a political line and the pressure of societal values.

Glatshteyn does not incorporate Shomer's actual words into the lines of his poem, but rather plays goodnaturedly with the Germanic sounding catch-phrases and worn-out images of the latter's work. The very first lines of the poem parody—and show the narrator's distance from—Shomer's style, as they describe the moon shining with "True Love" upon a bit of sea, all the narrator can glimpse from his window. The obsolescence of Shomer's stereotypical world is emphasized later as well, when the narrator, discussing young women making love in cars, creates a verb, *varelibn zikh*—"true-love," out of the concept of *vare libe*—"True Love." They prefer to act rather than dream of a hero with a Shomerian *engel-reynem herts* ("angel-pure heart"). Through his ironic use of Shomer's supposedly elevated language, Glatshteyn is able to exhibit both affection for Shomer's purpose and amused criticism of his achievement.

IX   *Language Experimentation*

The poet of *Shomer*, who both evokes and ridicules Shomer's work, reveals himself as a master of his craft. In his hands, clichés and obsolete terms can come alive with innovative force, hackneyed prose be transformed into complex poetry. By this time, Glatshteyn had developed a unique poetic voice that, for all its singularity, was rooted within the heart of the language. Deep though his commitment to the literature of Yiddish may have been, his true passion lay in the realm of the language itself, and in his individual relationship to it. Yiddish was both the medium of his expression and his *raison d'être*. His fascination with the language led him to become intimate with its components, with its colloquial and formal styles, with its sound in the mouths of all sorts of individuals: children, intellectuals, old people, saints, rapscallions. Through diversified experimentations, he forged a language that, while composed of the basics known to every native speaker of Yiddish, became identifiable as his alone. It is a language of scintillating wit and consummate intelligence, displaying his ability to reconstruct the language after having reduced it to its skeletal elements. This is seen nowhere more clearly than in his invention of fusion terms— terms in which independent components are joined together to create a single new form. This associative technique is reminiscent of the one used by James Joyce, whose influence Glatshteyn explicitly acknowledged.[36]

Along with *Tsum kopmayster* ["To the head master"] and *Tsu a fraynt* ["To a friend"], the poem *Zing ladino* ["Sing Ladino"][37] is the culmination of Glatshteyn's experimentation. *Zing ladino* is unusual in Glatshteyn's repertoire in that its meaning emerges only as a result of deciphering its pattern of fusion. Upon reading *Zing ladino*, the very title of the poem is revealed as a hint of its focus; at first *Zing ladino* appears to be nothing more than a command to sing in the Jewish language, Ladino.[38] But as the poem unfolds, it transpires that *-ino* is employed more generally as a word ending, e.g., *tsoyberzhargonino* ("magic-jargonino"). *Zing ladino* must then be read both as Ladino, the name of the language, and as a nonsense name with an *-ino* ending. The result is, strictly speaking, a delayed reaction fusion: now, what was originally perceived as a unified, independent, and familiar entity suddenly appears as a form constructed by the narrator.

The poem itself seems at first to be a vehicle through which the narrator indulges in some highspirited joking about Jewish languages. However, by isolating all the points in *Zing ladino* where the ending *-ino* is used, a new understanding of the work is achieved, revealing a deep concern on the part of the narrator for the fate of Yiddish in Palestine. There are nine such lines in the poem, the fifth and therefore central one being *Palestino daberino* ("Palestine babblino"). The word *dabern*, from which *daberino* is formed, has a pejorative connotation in Yiddish, although its cognate in Modern Hebrew means simply "to talk." The independence of Yiddish from Hebrew is stressed by this distinction. The two lines following *Palestino daberino*, and referring to it, elaborate on the theme of

Yiddish in Palestine: *Undzer, undzer universladino/Blonder aladino zing.* ("Our, our universladino/Sing, blond aladino.") These lines present a dual fusion. *Universladino* is a combination of *universal* and *ladino,* a universal language of some sort. The next line supplies the *a* that was eliminated in forming *universladino;* at the same time, it fuses the remainder of the combination, *ladino,* into a word that sounds like "Aladdin" and implies thereby some sort of magical quality emanating from the Middle East. This allusion to magic indicates that Hebrew is the magic jargon, the *tsoyberzhargonino* but not, however, the same *zhargonino* that appears later in the poem as a term of contempt for Yiddish. The similarity between the two words sets up a connection between them: many speakers of *tsoyberzhargonino* are former speakers of *zhargonino,* that is, Yiddish, and it is Yiddish itself that is threatened by *Palestino daberino.*

X Concern for Jewish Life

Although its language is inimitable, the concerns of *Zing ladino* reflect a much broader attitude towards Yiddish than do such more self-centered earlier works as *Tirtl-toybn.* In this poem, which Glatshteyn's colleague Leyeles hailed as a "hymn to Yiddish,"[39] it is clear that Glatshteyn had come to an understanding of his role in the broad and continuing legacy of Yiddish literature and language. This was mirrored in a growing attachment to his Jewish heritage, a bond nowhere more forcefully expressed in the pre-Holocaust period than in his poem *Afn vaser* ["On the water"].[40] The narrator of this work describes himself as an old sailor—and his ship voyage is a clear metaphor for his journey into a secular world. As he moves with shaky certainty through life, he is sometimes angered, he explains, by a question: *Farvos bin ikh avek fun tatns hoyz,/Fun mames fartukh,/Fun der bobes tsoyberreyd?* ("Why did I go away from my father's house,/From my mother's apron,/From my grandmother's magic speech?").

The narrator-sailor feels guilty. While recognizing himself as a Jew, remembering his grandmother's wish that the gates of his heart be open to Torah, and acknowledging this as his Jewish baggage on the water of his life, he realizes that he has strayed from his heritage. Looking back, his motivations are clear to him: he had wanted to carve his own way, to reject the notion that, no matter what choices he made in life, his fate would be predetermined: *Tsu esn glik in krishkes/Shepn umglik mit a kvort.* ("To eat happiness by the crumb/To scoop up misfortune by the quart."). Now, however, he considers his adventurous, free life as a series of disconnected, rootless experiences, only incidentally raised above animal concerns: *Gefresn, gezoyft, gehulyet, getroyerikt un gelakht,/Getrakht, gefresn, gezoyft, gehulyet, geshlofn un gevakht.* ("Gorged myself, guzzled, caroused, was sad and laughed,/Thought, gorged myself, guzzled, caroused, slept and stayed awake."). And the narrator comes to the understanding that he must reevaluate his supposedly free life vis-à-vis the Jewish world he imagined he had left behind; he wonders what freedom actually means, *Az itst bin ikh mer tsu-geflantst/Tsum ashrey yoshvey, vi tsum gantsn vaserdikn lebn may-nem.*("When now I am more rooted/To the 'Happy they are that dwell' than to the whole of my watery life."). *Ashrey yoshvey* are the first words of a traditional prayer taken from Psalms (84,5) and recited three times a day. Established, all-encompassing Jewish life is thus contrasted with a secular existence that is thin and unmotivated. More than this, *ashrey yoshvey* refers to remaining at home, both religiously and culturally, since the verse, *ashrey yoshvey veytekhaw* ("Happy are they that dwell in Thy house"), implies both staying within the Jewish faith and literally staying home; the verse is also the basis of a Yiddish saying: *kenen vi ashrey*, literally "to know like *ashrey*," i.e., to know by heart. The narrator thereby acknowledges his heritage as his home, no matter how far he may have strayed in attempting to elude his identity.

With *Afn vaser*, it is clear that Jewishness had become a much more important element of Glatshteyn's poetry than he had intended it to be when he helped formulate the *In zikh* manifesto. His fourth volume, *Yidishtaytshn*, was the first in which the title itself reflected his new perspective. One of the longer poems of this volume, *Yosl loksh fun khelm* ["Yosl Loksh of Khelm"], marked the prewar peak in Glatshteyn's acceptance of an imperfect Jewish community and his recognition of responsibility to that world. It is with this work, too, that Glatshteyn inaugurated a series of persona poems that he would weave into his repertoire for the duration of his career. These poems became, in part, a forum for exploring the conflicting claims of public and private obligations, of faith and political reality.

The Khelm of *Yosl loksh fun khelm* is famous in legend as the home of fools, and Yosl Loksh—or Yosl Noodle as his name translates—is its tragicomic hero. Yosl's story, as well as his character, essentially simple: moved so deeply by human suffering that he challenges the workings of God's world, Yosl is given an unexpected opportunity to uplift Khelm when he finds himself selected as its leader, albeit against his wishes. Reluctant to accept this role because he senses in himself a lost soul ill-equipped to guide others, he attempts to gain his freedom by demonstrating that he is inept and lacking in answers: *Ver iz gerekht? der balegole? dos ferd?/ Oder gor di baytsh? vu ligt do der taytsh?* ("Who is right? the coachman? the horse?/Or even the whip? Where does the answer lie here?"). He goes even further: *Ikh zog aykh, kool, ikh bin a vilder nar* ("I tell you, people of the community, I am a wild fool").

But Yosl's protestations are to no avail; the public considers him a genius, the leader of his generation. Despite this adulation, Yosl's followers ignore his program for solving the major conflict of the world, i.e., the unequal distribution of wealth and goods. They continue to argue over the property he would have them share, calling on him to make decisions, exhausting him with their demands. They also bestow upon him a vicious wife who interprets his refusal to condemn any political group as sheer indecisiveness, for which she mocks him: *Tsitselistn,tsitsenistn,/Anakhristn, antisemistn,/Ale toters, ale kristn,/Nishto keyn yo, nishto keyn neyn./Nishto keyn tome, alts iz reyn.* ("Tsitselists, tsitsenists,/Anachrists, antisemists,/All Tatars, all Christians,/No yes, no no./No ritual impurity, everything is pure."). Finally, in desperation, Yosl flees to the bath-house, washes the filth of the town from himself and escapes to a meadow, to the free outdoors where he had first thought to challenge God. Despite their shoddy treatment of him, Yosl pities the fools of his community who waste so much of their time and energy in spiteful argument. Yosl sees this as a cosmic condition; he refuses to judge or castigate.

Yosl loksh fun khelm is a poignant description of a good man's futile attempts to deal with social responsibility in a sensitive and intelligent fashion. On one level, this is a general political statement. No "-ism" will be able to inspire change so long as individuals continue to abuse one another and refuse to recognize, individually, a common goal. On another level, this poem is intensely and complexly Jewish. At the outset, Yosl attributes the world's problems to an apparently weak or uncaring Jewish God. His final realization, however, is that God cannot be blamed for the stupidity of human beings who will not recognize what He offers them. In a way, *Yosl loksh fun khelm* transmutes the subject matter of Jewish jokes into the subject matter of tragedy. When its protagonist, a fool among fools, seriously attempts to confront irreconcilable conflicts, he concludes, not with a comic punchline, but with a cry of despair. The overall structure of *Yosl loksh fun khelm*, then, may be seen as a variety of double levels: it is both a joke and deadly serious; it reveals Khelm as a miniature of the entire world or of any part of it, yet at the same time renders the town quintessentially Jewish. It introduces a person who, while discouraged by the world, accepts it and his obligations to it.

Kredos and *Yidistaytshn* make the conclusion of Yankev Glatshteyn's first odyssey. Whether writing about personal relationships, society, literature or language, he had struck a balance between the responsibility to community and the claims of the self. This balance, however, was soon to be shattered by the awful events of the late 1930's and the 1940's.

CHAPTER 4

Take a Book of Records

I "Good Night, World"

I N 1938, Glatshteyn electrified the Yiddish-speaking world with the publication of A gute nakht, velt ["Good night, world"], his furious indictment of Western culture.[1] In this poem, the same Glatshteyn who twenty years earlier had insisted that his nature as a Jewish poet lay only in the fact of his Jewish religion and his use of Yiddish, now averred a total opposition between the essentially good and just life of Eastern European Jewry, and the complete corruption and evil of what he had accepted as the cultured modern world.

All the treasures of Western civilization disgust the narrator of A gute nakht, velt: a flabby system of democracy offers only kalte simpatye-kompresn ("cold sympathy-compresses"), instead of real equality; modern technological achievements have led to a pernicious elektrish-tsekhutspete velt ("electrically impudent world"). The narrator rejects as well the major ideologies of Western civilization, combining them into one negative concept, yezusmarkses ("Jesusmarxes"), and bemoaning the fact that these movements, even originating as they had in Jewish minds, nonetheless constituted a force seducing Jews away from their religion: Nem tsu di yezusmarkses, verg zikh mit zeyer mut./Krapir iber a tropn fun undzer getoyft blut. ("Take the Jesusmarxes, choke on their courage./Croak over a drop of our baptized blood.").

In opposition to this unclean and insidious framework, the narrator formulates his vision of Jewish values. Rather than rely on spineless democracies and alien ideologies, he can turn to: Mayne sheymes, mayn svarbe,/Mayne gemores, tsu di harbe/Sugyes, tsum likhtikn ivre-taytsh,/Tsum din, tsum tifn meyn, tsum khoyv, tsum gerekht, ("My sacred pages, my Bible,/My Gemorra, to my back-

breaking/Studies, to the bright Yiddish prayerbook,/To law, pro-
fundity, duty, justice,").[2] This new acceptance of traditional learning
and belief is accompanied by retreat from the brash technological
milieu of modern society; the narrator takes pleasure in thinking
of *kerosin, kheylevnem shotn, dribne shtern, hoykerdikn lamtern*
("kerosene," "waxy shadow," "tiny stars," "hunched lanterns,"), all
of which contribute to become the *shtiln geto-lekht* ("quiet ghetto
light").

This is not to say that the narrator overlooks the distasteful aspects
of the ghetto: he rolls in its garbage, covers himself with its dust;
he calls its way of life *tsehoykert* ("hunchbacked") and *farkoltnt*
("matted down"). Jewish existence has been beaten, it has become
a *troyerik yidish lebn* ("sad Jewish life"), but nonetheless it remains
gentle, untouched by the roughness and ugliness that has infected
Western culture despite all the latter's supposed sophistication.

A gute nakht, velt ends on a note of messianic hope: *S'veln nokh
royshn grine bleter/Af undzer boym dem farkvartn.* ("Green leaves
will again rustle/On our withered tree."). The narrator insists that
he wants no comforting; he is willing to wait for an apocalyptic
solution to the plight of Jewish life, since no cultural, political one
has been forthcoming. This poem, written before the Holocaust and
before the formal establishment of the ghetto referred to by the
narrator, was indeed touched by prophecy. Glatshteyn was later
chastised for not reverting to traditional ways as he had promised.[3]
But the ghetto as defined in *A gute nakht, velt* is in fact a metaphor
for Jewish life, not a geographical entity. The narrator talks in detail
of going back to ideas, to commandments, to a natural rather than
mechanical world, to a new identity; he does not concentrate on
physical return. The last lines of the poem emphasize this distinc-
tion: *Kh'kush dikh, farkoltnt yidish lebn./S'veynt in mir di freyd
fun kumen.* ("I kiss you, matted-down Jewish life./The joy of coming
back cries in me.").[4]

A gute nakht, velt was republished in *Gedenklider—Memorial
Poems,*[5] the volume that follows *Yidishtaytshn* in Glatshteyn's poetic
oeuvre and which, together with *Shtralndike yidn—Radiant Jews*
(1946), reveals the tortured darkness of his response to the Holo-
caust. In these two collections of the 1940's, Glatshteyn began to
confront the dread discovery that his people, the language of his
creative expression—in fact, his own literary immortality—were
being destroyed. The integrations that he had so painstakingly

achieved by the mid-1930's were abruptly shattered in the wake of
new, objective circumstances. Reality now made all the threatened
feelings that had plagued the Glatshteyn of *1919* seem pale by
comparison. This devastating truth was certainly all too clear to him
by 1946, if not absolutely so in 1943.

II   Gedenklider: *Struggle Against Despair*

Gedenklider is a mixture of hope and pessimism, much in the
manner of *A gute nakht, velt.* The volume is divided into two sec-
tions. The first, entitled *In midber blit a mandlshtekn* ["An almond
staff blooms in the desert"], contains a number of poems—at least
superficially sanguine and light in tone—in whose lines comfort is
derived both from recollections of a rich past and from visions of
a better future. The second part of the volume, *Nem a pinkes un
farshrayb* ["Take a book of records and record"], focuses much more
directly on contemporary issues and to a great extent undermines
the positive mood of *In midber blit a mandlshtekn.*

S'yidishe vort ["The Yiddish word"] (pp. 5–6), *Gedenklider's* in-
itial poem, begins with the image of Yiddish blossoming on a desert
almond staff, reminiscent of the staff of Aaron (Numbers, Ch. 17).
As with the new shoot hoped for in *A gute nakht, velt,* this flour-
ishing represents an auspicious beginning, a kind of return to Eden
without the prospect of negative consequences: the staff is sur-
rounded by sweet plants which, if eaten, make all hidden incom-
prehensibilities clear and cause all things to become meaningful.
The root of this blooming plant is *bobeshaft* ("grandma-ness"), the
institution of heritage. The narrator refers to the scene as a *getraye
landshaft fun amolikeyt* ("loyal landscape of past-ness"), and the
language he employs underscores the impression of reaching for a
bygone era: the use of *tut* in the lines *Yeder vort tut shmekn,* ("every
word smells,"), *Yeder vort tut trifn,* ("every word drips,") and in
the verb *"tut vekn"* ("awakens") is based on an antiquated form.[6]
The suffix *"-ekhtser,"* which functions as a means of forming cate-
gories, appears once in the word *kreytekhtser* ("herbs")—a term
traditional in translating Hebrew texts when the precise name of
a plant was not known—but occurs also in a neologism, *bataytekh-
tser* ("category of meanings"). The use of these words typifies the
poem's dual vision, its appeal to both past and future, encapsulated

in *bobeshaft*—a neologism whose meaning indicates age and tradition.

But, as enthusiastically as the narrator of *S'yidishe vort* may welcome the blossoming of Yiddish, his reaction is not universally shared. A traveler in the desert spots the staff and cries out into the night, awakening others with the message: *Hoy veygeshrign,/In der midber blit a mandlshtekn.* ("Lo, cry out a lament,/An almond staff blooms in the desert."). The implication of these lines is sobering: surrounding the flowering of Yiddish and the traditions of its speakers is a desert peopled by hostile individuals who, although travelers themselves, cannot bear to see the rooting of this language in their midst. Although like Aaron, Yiddish has been chosen, the privilege means attendant danger.

S'yidishe vort reveals the depth and complexity of Glatshteyn's ties to Yiddish: it celebrates the continued spirit of the language and its vivacity, also unfolding through its structure and vocabulary some of the charm and intelligence that make Yiddish so wondrous in Glatshteyn's eyes. In the midst of crisis it is a solace, affording him optimism and satisfaction and granting a direct route back to the past out of which it was formed. At the same time, however, this work represents Glatshteyn's most direct expression so far of the fact that his beloved tongue is struggling for survival.

In *S'yidishe vort, A kholem* and other poems in the first part of *Gedenklider*, the awful implications that accompany the subject matter are held in check by a certain playfulness of spirit. In *Nem a pinkes un farshrayb*, however, the tone changes. The works themselves are arranged like a *pinkes*, a "book of records"; many of them are dated, providing an account of the terrible progression of history and its effect on the despairing poet. Here too, as in *In midber blit a mandlshtekn*, the Yiddish language assumes a position of primary importance. But where the first section of *Gedenklider* begins hopefully with *S'yidishe vort, Nem a pinkes un farshrayb*—and thus the entire volume—ends poignantly with *Undzer tsikhtik loshn* ["Our tidy language"] (pp. 82–84), whose narrator asserts that Yiddish is too beautiful to be defiled by employing it to describe German atrocities.

The poem is divided into three sections, each pointing out a different aspect of the language and its speakers, and each constructed so as to stress that point. In the first section, the narrator explains the formation of Yiddish as stemming from a gentle re finement and elevation of German. The musicality of Yiddish is emphasized by the liberal use of rhyming words, both within and at the ends of lines. On several occasions, the rhymed phrases are images of purification, as in the narrator's analogy that links the development of Yiddish and the traditional Jewish manner of adapting and uplifting a melody: *Vi di gute yidn fun amol,/Vos flegn oysleyzn un derkvikn/A volvlen nign,/Imlaytern un gebn tikn-Un dervaytern fun der tume*—("Like good Jews from the past,/Who used to redeem and refresh/A cheap melody,/Purify it and grant it redress/And remove it from sinfulness—"). In a wry barb directed at German, the narrator concludes his comments on the growth of Yiddish by contrasting the latter's momentum with the former's *baykhikn/Verden vurden zayn*. ("bulging/Will be-were-to be."), its overblown and ponderous essence.

But Yiddish is no longer being used. The narrator speaks metaphorically of *s'vareme fidele yidish* ("the warm fiddle Yiddish") hanging mutely on a willow tree, an obvious allusion to the biblical dispersion of Jews from Babylonia (Psalms: 137). Now, however, Jews are no longer permitted to mourn; rather, in the tens of thousands, they *Faln op un feln* ("Fall away and are missing"). As the people and their language are threatened, the poem's rhyme diminishes. In its place, Glatshteyn employs a chiasmus to depict the trapped back and forth motion of the refugees, among whom the narrator includes himself: *Der koyler tseylt un yogt undz,/Un der tseyler koylet,* ("The slaughterer counts and chases us,/And the counter slaughters,"). In such a desperate period in the history of Yiddish-speaking Jewry, the sprightly rhymes of the first section can no longer be valid.

In the final section of *Undzer tsikhtik loshn,* the narrator angrily declares that only the German language itself can properly express the horrors of its people's crimes: *Nor du aleyn af dayn blut-vursht shprakhe,/Kenst oysrevn vi du host genumen/Daytshe, meshugene rakhe,/Fun dershrokene, umbashitste, shvakhe.* ("Only you in your black pudding [literally: blood-sausage] language,/Can roar out how you took/German, insane revenge,/On frightened, defenseless, weak [people]."). By describing the German language as one of *blut-vursht,* Glatshteyn manages in one term to combine a condemnation of German culture, a contrast between German fondness for pork and Jewish prohibition of it, and an allusion to the bloodthirst of the Germans. These same lines contain a virtuoso coupling of content and expression of content, since two of the three rhyming words are German rather than Yiddish: *shprakhe* instead of *shprakh* or *loshn; rakhe* rather than *nekome.* But the *shvakhe,* the innocent victims of German cruelty, are described in Yiddish.

Confronted with the enormity of the Holocaust, Glatshteyn began, in *Gedenklider,* to concentrate on thoughts of God. Glatshteyn's God was no source of consolation, however, but variously a projection of impotence and a target for rage. In *Got iz a troyeriker maharal* ["God is a sad Maharal"] (pp. 68–69), for instance, he depicts a God incapable of prevailing over the wickedness of humanity. Playing on the legend of Rabbi Judah Loew of Prague, known as the Maharal, and his creation of a golem,[7] Glatshteyn constructs a view of God forced to witness the final demolition of His creation because it has become so monstrous. The entire world is seen as a golem, formed in the hope of resultant good, in the desire to preserve life. But unlike the Maharal, who was the agent of his golem's destruction, God is merely a passive spectator to the annihilation of the world. As a shophar sounds in the forest, announcing the end of day, God becomes *farshemt un kleyn in gemit,/Vi yeder dershrokener yid.* ("ashamed and small in spirit,/Like every frightened Jew."). He slips into synagogue and, as if He were a penitent, wraps Himself in a prayer shawl, rending the heavens with his weeping.

At the conclusion of *Got iz a troyeriker maharal,* the narrator returns to his earlier evocation of the forest, focusing now on its individual components: *A vint git a harbstikn tsiter./A boym git zikh a tsevig./A blat git a fal./Got iz a troyeriker maharal.* ("A [gust of] wind quivers autumnally./ A tree sways./A leaf falls./God is a sad Maharal."). The form *gebn a* refers to action performed only once, and its use here reflects the extent to which nature operates actively yet without any guarantee of continuity. The autumnal quality of the images, especially the third one, which acts as a force for closure, raises the prospect of death and perhaps even cosmic finality. Juxtaposed with these three lines, the poem's last line— having already appeared three times earlier in the body of the work as well as in the title—assumes a new urgency and tragic aspect: while His forest trembles in what may be its last moments, God can only observe. Whereas earlier, the line *Got iz a troyeriker maharal* had indicated an active need to destroy a malign creation, now it underscores the ultimate helplessness of God.

The final position of God as Maharal serves to intensify the expression of the Jewish plight. The question: To whom is God praying? yields to the questions: What good is there in hope and prayer when God himself has been dethroned? If God is like a defeated Jew, then how is it possible to have faith? Most important, how can a Jew be called upon to act in, and understand, a world where even God has had to admit confusion and impotence?

In *Letartsat* ["To 5699 [the Jewish calendar equilvalent of 1938–1939]"] (pp. 43–45), the sense of threat and abandonment that had distinguished *1919* returns, this time with national ramifications. In the earlier, secularly oriented work, time was calculated according to the Western, Christian calendar. For *Letartsat*, in contrast, Glatshteyn employs the traditional Jewish calendar so as to emphasize the parochial nature of the poem's topic and perspective. In this work, Jewish history is rewritten and age-old beliefs reversed, beginning with a foreshadowing of doom that plays ironically on the biblical blessing of Jacob's tents in the desert (Numbers: 24,5). Now this tent has been cursed; the Jewish people are under attack.

The nature and extent of this Jewish disaster unfolds in a version of the Exodus story that departs from the original in both its order and its final outcome. It begins at the end, but now the Jews in flight do not manage to elude their oppressors. There is no miracle of the Red Sea; instead, their attackers come upon them, saying: *Ot iz di shuld fun ale plogn.* ("Here is the guilt of all plagues."). As time moves backwards, the Passover night is still to occur. The narrator envisions it, not as *peysekh*, the Hebrew-Aramaic origin Yiddish term, but rather as *zeyer yontev fun iberhipn* ("their holiday of passing over"). During this night, the Jewish doorposts will be marked as a sign of doom: it is their homes that will be struck. God's abandonment of His people is thus revealed in its awful totality: *Mir, di pkhoyrim, muzn shtarbn.* ("We, the first-born sons, must die."). Nor has God disregarded His people through forgetfulness or the cosmic detachment that had apparently motivated the *oyberhar* in *1919*. The Jewish God has capitulated, depositing the power of the world into evil hands. As the narrator says, in a parody of Psalm 115: *Der himl iz himl tsu got,/Di erd hostu ibergeentfert in roshe's hant,/Er zol shaltn un valtn.*("The heavens are the Lord's heavens [literally: the heaven is heaven to God],/The earth You have surrendered to the villain's hand,/That he may have complete authority.").

The narrator's final plea indicates a recognition that his people are not destined to be liberated. He implores God to open a crack in the heavens to help the Jews as they await their inevitable destruction. Meager though it might be, such a crevice would nonetheless represent a merciful semblance of freedom to lives in which no other options exist: *S'vert undz orimer dos lebn un klener di velt,/Es vert undz enger di velt.* ("For us, life is becoming poorer and the world smaller,/For us the world is becoming narrower.").

Through *Letartsat,* Glatshteyn began to confront the realization that his entire Jewish world was imprisoned and collapsing. Reality had outrun the paranoia of his earliest poems. In *Milyonen toytn* ["Millions of deaths"] (pp. 80–81), he looked directly into that reality, contemplating the special interpenetration of life and death wrought by the Holocaust.[8] The narrator of this poem explains that from the death that has been absorbed into the earth new but tainted life will emerge: *Az men vet akern un zeyen toyte erd,/Vet zi gebn fintstere broytn,/Nor s'vet veyts und korn eybik shmekn/Mit milyonen toytn.* ("When they plow and sow dead earth,/It will yield dark breads,/But wheat and rye will forever/Reek of millions of deaths."). In the face of this eventuality, the narrator charges someone, whom he addresses as *du* ("you [familiar form]") to compile a register of the dead: *nem a pinkeṡ un farshrayb* ("take a book of records and record").

The task of the *du* is to register—with dry reserve—the death of the entire Jewish people. Even the living have been sacrificed: *eybik vet undzer lebedik folk/Zayn toyt mit milyonen toytn.* ("eternally our living people/Will be dead with millions of deaths.").[9] Indeed, the person who attempts over time to forget the dead will be cursed. At all costs, the memory of sacrifice must be kept alive.

Thus the living have an awesome responsibility: they must become *pinkeysim,* books of record, attesting to the murder of their own people and, as such, of themselves as well. In another statement of paradox, the narrator sums up the ambiguous yet symbiotic relationship of dead and living Jews, telling the *du* to note down— and meaning, therefore, that all the living must record this within themselves: *nisht zey zaynen geshtorbn far undz,/Nor farmishpet zaynen mir tsu lebn far zey,* ("they did not die for us,/Rather, we are condemned to live for them,"). Death will flow as a powerful force through the living; the survivor must keep alive the death of all those who have perished, so that the world will constantly encounter and be horrified by its murderous deeds.

As in *Undzer tsikhtik loshn*, Glatshteyn contrasts German and Yiddish in *Milyonen toytn* to emphasize the atrocity of the Holocaust. Of 1943, which he refers to in its equivalent Jewish calendar form, he says: *zeyer merderlikher tag/Iz gevorn undzer nakht fun ale nakhtn*. ("their murderous day/Become our night of all nights."), using German in *tag* rather than *tog*, and approximating it in *nakhtn* rather than *nekht*. The narrator cautions: *Un gedenk—mir hobn nisht keyn verter/Far dem umglik*. ("And remember—we have no words/For the misfortune."). Significantly, the narrator uses the bland and, under the circumstances, neutral word *umglik* ("calamity", but more usually "accident; misfortune"), in his comments, eschewing even such a term as *tragedye* ("tragedy"). No words are strong enough to capture the truth.

III   *The Artist's Dilemma*

Clearly, Glatshteyn was tormented by the inadequacy of art and the impotence of the artist in dealing with the Holocaust. In the poem *Tsum tatn* ["To my father"] (pp. 63–65), his distress is plainly visible. As the title suggests, this work is addressed to and concerns Glatshteyn's father, Itsik Glatshteyn. The narrator relates that he had been imbued by his father in very early childhood with a love of Yiddish language and literature. Perceiving immediately that his son would grow up to be a Jewish writer, Itsik Glatshteyn had responded with delight. In a reference to the binding of Isaac, the narrator recalls how his father had sacrificed him to the life and duties of a Jewish writer: *Gey, du shnek, tsu dayn folk*. ("Go, you little shrimp, to your people."). And with the passage of time, the elder Glatshteyn had remained joyful in the hope that his vision would ultimately become reality.

Now it is the father's holiday, for the narrator has indeed become a respected Jewish writer, fulfilling the expectations implicit in his father's desires and fueled by his own ambition. But he cannot celebrate, because his father is trapped in the ghetto of Lublin, unable to occupy the seat of honor prepared for him. Sick at heart, the narrator reports: *Ikh zits gantse teg umzist baym bortn./Mayn bisl glik dergreykht nisht tsu dayn harberik/Un s'kumen nisht keyn shifn fun dortn.* ("I sit whole days by the shore in vain./My bit of happiness does not reach your haven,/And no ships come from there.").

Ironically, it is Itsik Glatshteyn who, true to his name, has become the Jewish sacrifice, transcending his parental role as he achieves a higher calling: *Du bist nisht nor tate./Bist a yid in geto mit a geler late.* ("You are not only father./You are a Jew in the ghetto with a yellow patch."). However, in one sense the father is more secure than the son, for he maintains his faith, his belief in a heavenly father. Thus, although they are apart, the younger man continues to benefit from the older one's wisdom and learns that connections of the spirit need not be broken, even when physical ties are ruptured. Comparing his father's sacrifice to his own, and faced with the agonizing meaning of Jewishness at this time in history, the narrator realizes—even at the moment when he finally attains it— how meaningless his artistic goal has become. At this point, he wants only: *Tsu geyn a nit-dershokhtener korbn,/Mit farblutikte un geshvolene fis./Tsu dir af yener zayt toyer./Ahin, tsum fintstern lublin.* ("To walk as an unslaughtered sacrifice,/With bloodied and swollen feet./To you on the other side of the gate./To there, to dark Lublin.").[10]

Feeling alternately overwhelmed by his inability to comprehend and discuss the Holocaust yet charged with the awesome duty of recording it, Glatshteyn felt tempted at times to run—not towards his heritage, but away from the responsibility of being a Jewish artist. Through six short poems collectively entitled *Gezangen* ["Songs"] (pp. 74–79), he discusses his wish to forget the horror and despair bombarding him at every turn and to devote himself, naively and thoughtlessly, to beauty. A shifting narrative perspective reflects this ambivalence: sometimes the voice is immediate, emerging in the first person; at other times it is omniscient and distant, as if the first-person narrator of the other sections were now talking about himself in the third person. These variations in narrative outlook notwithstanding, the poems of *Gezangen* all represent some aspect of a struggle between two forces clashing in one man. Part of him is Little Yankev, who wants nothing more than to be made *onseykhldik sheyn* ("witlessly beautiful") and to sing praises to sunshine and morning. The other part is Big Yankev, a committed Jew who bears the weight of historical Jewish misery and who attempts to burden Little Yankev with the same load. The last of the six poems reveals the unification of the two sides and marks the acceptance by the narrator/Little Yankev of his ineluctable obligations.

From the beginning, however, this conclusion is foreshadowed, when Little Yankev, who in his childish imagination has become a rooster, is described as "not yet a Jewish one." In another poem, the narrator manages to evade the attempts of Big Yankev to encumber him with the collective yoke of his people. Big Yankev, also called Yankev-Yisroel ("Jacob-Israel," i.e., the Jewish people), is described both as a *zoger* ("announcer") and a *zinger* ("singer"). (This is a play both on the notion of poet as singer and on the Yiddish idiom *hobn tsu zingen un tsu zogn*,—"to have no end of trouble.") Singing from his sleep, he seeks to trap the narrator within his restless, troubled dreams, as a spider catches a fly. The narrator eludes Yankev, anxious to avoid the latter's waking perceptions: *S'hilkhn im hilkhers in di oyern,/Fargiftn, farnikhtn,/Fartilikn, farhungern, umbrengen,/Koylen, shekhtn, oysmordn,/Oysrotn, oysvortslen,/Paynikn, fargazn.* ("Loudspeakers resound in his ears,/Poison, annihilate,/Decimate, starve, kill,/Slaughter, slaughter, murder off,/Exterminate, eradicate,/Torture, gas."). However, at the same time as he rejects taking upon himself a full recognition of Jewish suffering, the narrator is aware that his life is miserable and cheap, that it is *Faresikt far der tsayt* ("Soured prematurely").

Eventually, the narrator realizes that he has no choice but to become a Jewish rooster. The burden attaches itself to him like a painful hump on his back; he senses that he will never have the chance to be as carefree as his non-Jewish neighbor, whose cheerful good-morning crows out through an automobile horn. The two are essentially different: *Der shokhn iz a goy a mentsh,/Un ikh a yidisher hon.* ("The neighbor is a non-Jew and a human being,/And I am a Jewish rooster."). The chasm between them is ultimate, because it involves their very identity as human beings; the nice English-speaking neighbor can sympathize with the plight of Jews, and then just as casually dismiss the matter, having viewed Jewish disaster as no more than an interesting news item. The narrator, in contrast, although he may speak English and thereby appear to communicate freely with his neighbor, now knows that underneath his public response lies a more basic, entirely Jewish perception that separates him from his neighbor: *So long! entfert a yidisher hon.* ("So long! answers a Jewish rooster.").

A Jewish rooster does not have the luxury of heralding dawn with stupid and beautiful singing; his is the hoarse voice of urgency, crowing out an awful message. The last poem of *Gezangen* is based on a series of rhyming couplets, emphasizing not only the final unity of the narrator and Big Yankev as they sing a duet, but also the compulsive need of the dual narrator to express his despair, one line after the other helplessly tumbling out. He is a *kreyendiker idyot* ("crowing idiot") but not, this time, by choice; now he is also a *troyeriker idyot* ("sad idiot"), unable to make sense of a world that is *Blut un blut un blut un blut./Taykhn shlekhts un kvorim gut.* ("Blood and blood and blood and blood./Rivers of evil and graves of good."), a world in which life and death have become indistinguishable: *Kep dos lebn. leb dem toyt.* ("Behead life. Live death."). The narrator of *Milyonen toytn* had explained to his interlocutor the special position of the Jewish artist: *Gib a feygele a boym,/Un tsum himl narish zingt es,/Ober du nem a pinkes un farshrayb* ("Give a little bird a tree,/And it sings foolishly to heaven,/But you take a book of records and record"). Little Yankev of *Gezangen* has been forced, despite his ambivalence, to reach the same conclusion.

IV   *Reb Nakhmen of Bratslav*

Gezangen are among the earliest of Glatshteyn's poems to deal with what was to become a major conflict in his career: the rival claims of poetry as public outcry and poetry as more personal and idiosyncratic expression. Here, the latter has necessarily been rejected in favor of a voice that Glatshteyn invests with the stridency of a loudspeaker, an announcer. Yet, during this period Glatshteyn did manage to find a middle ground between the bald cry of anguish and the untenable song of escape. By adopting a traditional mask—that of Nakhmen, the colorful and enigmatic Bratslaver *rebbe*—he was able to retreat into the past, thereby achieving a healing distance from the haunting presence of the Holocaust while at the same time speaking as one for whom responsibility to the Jewish community was of consummate significance. In the series of five poems, *Der Bratslaver tsu zayn soyfer* ["The Bratslaver to his scribe"] (pp. 7–16), Glatshteyn explores aspects of the Bratslaver's personality, using as the superficial basis of his portrayal characteristics popularly attributed to Nakhmen: a sense of friction between his intellectual and mystical leanings; his intense and unusual love of nature; his

practice of fasting; his struggle with sexual temptation; his convic-
tion, mixed as it was with self-doubt, that he was the leader of his
generation.[11] With these traits as a backdrop, Glatshteyn's Nakhmen
emerges as a gentle, hopeful, yet lonely man attempting to come
to terms with conflict—a fuller version of the Yosl Loksh persona.
He is a man whose greatest wish is to overcome the complexity of
his soul by willing a cosmic unity into which he can be integrated.

The first of the Bratslav poems centers around Nakhmen's desire
to obliterate thought, to lose himself instead in praise-giving. In
this mood, he contrasts intellectual engagement with living, telling
his scribe Nosn: *Kh'vel dir derlangen a frask,/Oyb vest haynt oys-
kvetshn a gedank./Krank bistu haynt tsu lebn?* ("I'll give you a
powerful smack,/If you squeeze out a thought today./Aren't you
capable of living today?"). To avoid concerning himself with matters
of the mind, the Bratslaver fantasizes returning to a peasant way
of life, imagining it to be simple, earthy, imbued with holiness. The
goodness of this life stems in part from its involvement with song—
not songs with words, which would be too intellectual, but *nigunim,*
the simple melodies that are an essential part of worship among
Hasidim.

Reb Nakhmen wishes to overcome all ambition in this poem. He
is uninterested in reaching heaven; he does not even want to dream.
His only goal is to be able to awake in the morning with a *nign*
("melody") on his lips. Nakhmen seeks to shut off his intellect so
that, by clearing his mind, he may arrive at a perception of the
unity of all things. In a charming play on *ekhod,* signifying both the
Hebrew translation of Yiddish *eyns* ("one") and also the last word
of the *shma-yisroel* (the credo "Hear, O Israel, the Lord is our God,
the Lord is One"), Nakhmen tells Nosn that, as peasants who cannot
count even until two, they will be able to understand that everything
is one: *Eyns un bazunder eyns/Iz alts ekhod* [itself a play on *alts
eyns* ("all the same")],/*Un nokhamol un videramol ekhod.* ("One and
separately one/Is all one,/And again and once again one."). This
realization frees him to find full expression in the *day-dane-day*
("La-da-da") of his *nign* and renders more complicated messages
unnecessary. The simplicity of the melody needs no interpretation;
by itself it says everything.

The theme of the contemplative man attempting to reach for a
more basic and mystical life is explored further in the second poem
of *Der bratslaver tsu zayn soyfer,* in which Nakhmen speaks out

against hypocrisy. Commenting that many people believe in study and the externals of religious behavior as synonyms of piety, he explains that, on the contrary, these outward signs may hide a bitter truth:

> *Zey lernen zikh oys sheyne verter,*
> *Zey zaynen oyle regl tsu di heylikste erter.*
> *Nor zol kumen a nedove betn a mentsh a farshmakhter,*
> *Blaybt zeyer hant farmakht*
> *Un s'harts farmakhter.*

> They learn beautiful words,
> They make pilgrimages to the holiest places.
> But if a languishing person comes begging alms,
> Their hand remains closed
> And the heart even more closed.

This is only an apparent contradiction, Nakhmen reveals later, for: *Trakhtn iz vi notn tsu gezangen,/Un di gezangen voynen in lev.* ("Thinking is like notes to songs,/And the songs live in the heart."). The significance of melody as implied in the first poem is here made more explicit: real religiosity, like pure music, originates in the heart, not in the mind. Therefore, it is impossible to arrive at goodness through reason and intellect. Rather than concentrating on brilliant interpretations of sacred texts, Nakhmen advises the savants of Jewish life to look at *Breyshis* ("In the beginning"), the first word of the Bible, and to discover there what is truly important. Playing on the grammatical possibility that *breyshis* can function as a noun as well as an adverbial phrase, he continues: *Breyshis hot bashafn.* ("Breyshis [In the beginning] created.").[12] His interpretation resembles *eyns iz ekhod* in that, here too, he seeks strength in simplicity. But whereas *eyns iz ekhod* concentrates on unity, *breyshis hot bashafn* focuses on the essence of creation. It suggests that these first letters of Genesis—rather than the sea of knowledge available to the mind—contain the secret of life. And the way to absorb and celebrate this awesome understanding is through song. As Nakhmen says: *Un lomir zingen—/Breyshis hot bashafn veltn.* ("And let us sing—/Breyshis created worlds.").

Nakhmen of Bratslav was famous for his love of nature and belief in its importance, and the third of Glatshteyn's Bratslav poems is a brilliant exposition of this affection and regard. Nakhmen relates how, going out into the forest one morning, he had discovered creation in a sullen mood, unwilling to form itself into a new day: the trees turned their backs on him, the birds did not answer his greeting, even the drinking water in the spring refused to have a blessing made over it. The Bratslaver explains that he had not attempted to puzzle out the reason for this abdication, choosing to apply some simple psychology: *Veys ikh dokh, az di velt iz tsu a mentsh geglikhn./Vayl alts vos vakst un alts vos flit,/Un alts vos tut krikhn vil nebekh zayn.* ("Now, I know that the world is like a person./Because all that grow and all that fly,/And all that crawl, poor things, want to be."). Thus he had pretended to believe that creation was merely an illusion, and in so doing shocked the forest out of its malaise by forcing it to assert its existence: *Mit a koyekh a farborgenem/Hot der gantser vald genumen zayn/Un zikh morgenen.* ("With a hidden strength/The whole world began to be/And become morning."). The forest world, affirming its presence, had become cheerful, childlike, paradisiacal.

The poem's final point is once again a statement of simplicity expressed through song: *Velt, du bist do.* ("World, you are here."). The forest, assuming its own collective voice, made up of twitterings and loud cries, had announced *Mir zaynen dododo./Mir zaynen dododo.* ("We are hereherehere./We are hereherehere."), as the Bratslaver himself stood in the middle of the forest, allowing his voice to sound out like a shophar. By telling this story about creation, Nakhmen points out that even the most regular of natural occurrences may never be taken for granted, but must be observed and cherished.

In the fourth poem of the Bratslav series, Nakhmen reveals still more of his relationship to creation, an intimacy resulting finally in cosmic union of the two. Nakhmen explains that he had fasted until he achieved an understanding of his soul in which thought was secondary to body: *Kh'bin gegangen un mayn guf iz gegangen mit mir,/Un s'iz nisht geven keyn eyn gedank,/Vos hot nisht durkhgeshtralt mayn hoyt-un-beyner.* ("I walked and my body walked with me,/And there was not a single thought,/That did not shine through my flesh and bones."). Because of his fast, he reached a point of nothingness from which he was able, in the words of the first Creation, to recreate himself: *Un ikh hob mayne tunkele glider/Bafoyln: yehi or.* ("And to my dark limbs I/Commanded: Let there be light."). Becoming part of the daily renewal of nature,

Nakhmen attained fusion with the awaken ng day itself: and he relates how, in the moment of total cleaving, the two had recited the morning prayer together: *Un beyde hobn mir gedavnt afn kol—/Vi gut zaynen dayne getseltn.* ("And both of us prayed out loud—/How goodly are your tents.").

Thus Nakhmen, who wants neither dreams nor thoughts, is able for once to lose himself in his surroundings. As opposed to the narrators of Glatshteyn's earliest works, who feared relinquishing control and instead attempted to incorporate the cosmos into themselves, Nakhmen feels blessed by his release. But in a life filled with inner strife, such moments are not only rare but tenuous. The final poem of the Bratslav series depicts the powerful reassertion of Nakhmen's individuality. In this work a different Bratslaver emerges; no longer the ethereal individual who finds fulfillment in a realm of song and simplicity, he is lonely, longing for sexual closeness and tormented by these desires. Discussing the life that exists between the earth below and the awe inspiring heavens above—a life that involves thoughts of sexuality—Nakhmen discloses that he tries to purge himself of such thoughts when they arise. But at the same time, he realizes that the *yeytser-hore,* the "evil inclination"—sexual passion—is not so evil after all: *Un vos iz den oysn der yeytser hore?/Khedve. basheyd fun freyd. treyst geyert fun troyer./Geveyn fun aleyn fartsveyt.* ("And what then is the point of passion?/Bliss. Solution of joy. Comfort fermented from sorrow./Lament of alone doubled."). In previous poems, song was used to represent and express simple faith and the understanding of nature; here, sexual longing and the *yeytser hore* itself become song. Now the Bratslaver does not want to overcome mind in order to gain spirituality and a union with metaphysical forces. He wants to give in to body, to achieve oneness through sexuality. The evil inclination means: *Fayer un flamen in gots geflekht fun tsvey./S'meynt vayb.* ("Fire and flames in God's entwining of two./It means woman.").

The Bratslaver is lonely. He realizes that Nosn is tired and evidently not able to empathize fully with his master's passionate description of wonders implied by the *yeytser hore:* as Nakhmen talks of strength, desire, *Un glid-glid fun heylikn flam/Un dos likht fun irs un zayns vos vert eyn.* ("And limb-limb of the holy flame/And the light of hers and his that becomes one."), Nosn's eyes are closing with fatigue. Nonetheless, fearful of being left alone with thoughts that overwhelm him, the great *rebbe*, able to cajole all of creation on other occasions, is finally reduced to begging his scribe not to abandon him in the night.

In the language of the Bratslaver poems, Glatshteyn succeeds in emphasizing the peculiar duality of Nakhmen the visionary poet and Nakhmen the down-to-earth, tormented individual. Through the use of repetition, rhyme, assonance, consonance, and sound similarity, he suggests Nakhmen's striving for a rhythmic, songlike simplicity that is more basic than speech. Sometimes the technique is so subtle that only a vague impression of musicality is imparted, as in the juxtaposition of *farmish* and *efsher*, where the consonants of *efsher* occur also in *farmish*; or in the juxtaposition of *poyerimlekh* and *milkh*, where all the phonemes of *milkh* are contained in *poyerimlekh*.

In contrast to his evocation of Nakhmen's spirituality, Glatshteyn chooses to reflect the Bratslaver's earthiness in the homey colloquialisms with which his speech is peppered, for example: *Kh'vel dir derlangen a frask* ("I'll give you a powerful smack"), *Kh'vel dir brekhn a beyn* ("I'll break one of your bones"), or *Di beymer shteln zikh mit di zaytzhemoykhls tsu mir* ("The trees turn their rear ends on me"). Moreover, the Bratslaver's individuality is stressed by his use of neologisms, as in his description of the forest beginning to *zikh morgenen*, literally "to morning", or his desire for a little *fargenakhes*, a combination of *fargenign* ("joy") and *nakhes* ("satisfaction").

But perhaps the most exciting aspect of the Bratslaver poems, and of Glatshteyn's use of Reb Nakhmen as a poetic mask, emerges from a consideration of what the persona means in Glatshteyn's poetry at this juncture. Indeed, the function of these poems is as significant as their aesthetic worth. To be sure, the use of Nakhmen as a persona is, on one level, simply a convenient distancing device, one of two faces that Glatshteyn repeatedly assumed during the course of his career. The other, that of the Chinese poet Li Tai Po, allowed him to step outside his tradition and historical framework, while at the same time retaining his identity as an artist. The Bratslaver provides Glatshteyn with an imaginative opportunity both to remove himself from his own environment and remain tied to it, to deal with public issues as well as struggles of the self. Reb Nakhmen's complex psyche, representing conflict within a framework of tradition and belief, is an ideal model for the modern secular Yiddish poet who nonetheless feels deeply bonded to his past.

One of the most striking elements of these poems is that, in them, Nakhmen conveys a secure and deep religious faith—yet he never mentions God; the closest he comes to referring to God is his comment that *Breyshis hot bashafn veltn.* ("Breyshis created worlds."), which is an ambiguous statement. Given Glatshteyn's general mood in *Gedenklider,* but taking into account the hedged optimism of its first section, Nakhmen's outlook is expressive of an overall problem: how to maintain some sort of Jewish faith in a confusing environment that militates against it. The Bratslaver poems mark the fullest communication of Glatshteyn's wish—explored as well in *A gute nakht, velt* and *Tsum tatn*—to return to the basics of Jewish life. Nakhmen offers simplicity that is, however, not simplistic. At the same time as he feels weariness and even despair, he is able to derive joy from the most basic gifts that the world has to offer. Moreover, through Nakhmen, Glatshteyn is also able to concentrate on sexuality and the desire of individuals for human companionship. This theme, to which he consistently devoted himself both at the beginning and at the end of his career, is conspicuously absent from the poetry he composed during the Holocaust years, when his obsession with annihilation and isolation evidently left him little taste or energy to contemplate fruitfulness and constructive human interaction.

But there is another, veiled reason why Glatshteyn may have chosen the Bratslaver as a mouthpiece during the miserable and crucial period of the Holocaust: the relationship between Nakhmen and his Hasidim centers around a delicate fusion of life and death—an important motif in Glatshteyn's work from this time until the end of his long poetic career. Nakhmen is the *rebbe* of the *toyte khsidim* ("dead Hasidim"), so-called because, when Nakhmen died, they refused to recognize an heir to replace him, preferring instead to defer to him as their master. In a paradoxical way, they follow a dead leader but view him and respond to him as if he were living, thereby creating within themselves a closeness to death. In this way, Glatshteyn exploits not only the contradictory nature of Nakhmen's faith, but the very duality of his interrelationship with his followers: in death he lives; their lives encompass the dead. Glatshteyn is thus able to construct a foundation that is traditional yet in congruence with the entirely new historical situation of the 1930's and 1940's.

This framework is complicated by the figure of Nosn the scribe, the intermediary through whom much information about Nakhmen, his biography and tales, has been conveyed and preserved. In

Glatshteyn's poems, Nosn becomes the listener, not the transmitter. He is the writer taking down what is said to him; he is the chronicler, a companion to the person who is told to *nem a pinkes un farshrayb*, to make a record of destruction and death. Nosn thereby comes to embody one of the artist's roles at this point in history. He must note down, as if it were still alive, the great heritage of the dead, recognizing all the time that this heritage does in fact survive, because it exists at the core of those who live. After all, it is not Nosn's recollections of Nakhmen's comments that emerge from these poems, but rather the words of a vibrant Nakhmen.

Thus, the creative force behind the Bratslaver and his scribe is a dual yet connected one. It is that of the artist who is free to express a variety of moods, to follow anything to the extent of its meaning for him; at the same time, it is that of the devoted archivist who does not have unlimited choices, but who has been charged to commit to paper the thoughts and passions of a dying world so that it may continue to live.

V   *A Moribund Legacy*

The relationship of life and death and particularly the issue of literary immortality is the subject matter of another poem in *Gedenklider: A kholem* ["A dream"] (pp. 22–25). Glatshteyn plays here with two famous poems, Khayim Nakhmen Bialik's *El hatsipor* ["To the bird"] and Edgar Allen Poe's "The Raven." In each of these works, the narrator addresses a bird that has come to him; so too in *A kholem*, where in fact the same bird that visited Bialik now taps on the window of the narrator.

Glatshteyn's use of his literary models is ironic, but the form of this irony is not the same for both works. In the case of *El hatsipor*, the source of amusement is the environment of the original: Bialik's bird possesses some typical characteristics of a turn-of-the-century, enlightened Jewish intellectual. He is ceremonious, sports a monocle, frequents spas, and speaks Hebrew. The original poem is evoked even more pseudo-realistically by the disclosure that the bird, having appeared to Bialik so long ago, is now old, bald, and blind in one eye. He is also an *odeser* ("from Odessa"), a tongue-in-cheek reference to the fact that, although *El hatsipor* is a Hebrew poem, it nevertheless derives from Bialik's own Eastern European framework and imagination. Glatshteyn's use of this poem, then, is direct and thematic. In contrast, his reliance on Poe's "The Raven"—which some years later he admitted to parodying here[13]— is indirect and formal. The narrator mentions Poe's bird only once, saying that he is relieved not to have the raven visiting him. On a number of occasions, however, the form of "The Raven" is adopted; the characteristic metrical and rhyme scheme of Poe's poem—trochaic octameter containing a caesura and rhyme between the two halves of the line—is copied in the lines: *Foygl kluger, ikh dermon zikh./Liber foygl ikh derkon dikh.* ("Clever bird, I remember./Dear bird, I recognize you."), and approximated in the line: *Makht tsurekht der alter foygl mitn fisl dem monokl* ("The old bird fixes his monocle with his little foot"). Furthermore, the famous reply of Poe's raven is echoed in *A kholem,* once again in form rather than in content. Like that bird, Bialik's bird restricts its answers, although it has two replies rather than one: *Tshepezikhop.* ("Leavemealone."), before the narrator has discovered its identity, and afterwards in Hebrew, *Ani hatsipor shel bialik.* ("I am Bialik's bird.").

Glatshteyn's use of formal elements from Poe's "The Raven" is an indication of the underlying metaphor of *A kholem,* namely that the visit of the bird represents a contact with the realm of the dead. In *El hatsipor,* the time was spring, the bird was coming from a land that had been fruitful in the past and that could revive again at any moment; the mood was hopeful. *A kholem* is set in autumn. Bialik's bird, whose importance centers on his relationship with a dead poet, is close to death himself, and hails from a dying world. In the end, the narrator is left desolate, without promise for the future. Underneath the humor of the poem, then, lies the realization that the occupation of the narrator is not with future and life, but rather with death.

This perception of death, and the concomitant urgent need to somehow prevent it, is at the heart of Glatshteyn's work. The narrator says: *Farvor, farvyanet groz is itster dos folk,/Un dos hot er dokh gezogt demolt,/Ven yidish lebn iz nokh geven lebedik un kvalik.* ("Verily, the nation is wilted grass,/And, as you know, he said that then,/When Jewish life was still lively and gushing."). Bialik had worried about Jewish existence and survival at a time when to do so was not a dire necessity. At that point, the bird had helped Bialik by transmitting a message that enabled the poet to support his people, to be both a comfort to them and a warning voice awakening them. Now the misery described by Bialik is no longer an over-

reaction: destruction is imminent. The narrator of *A kholem* begs
the bird to bequeath him some similar advice, so that he too can
assume a responsible and life affirming position as an artist in the
select society of Jews: *Ikh vel a bloz ton dem lebedikn otem/Af dem
gantsn goles,/Af dem gantsn lebn undzers,/Vos iz itst azoy farum-
glikt,* ("I will blow the living breath/On the entire diaspora,/On our
entire life,/Which has had so much misfortune,"). But soon the
narrator realizes that his hopes are in vain, for this bird is *on ge-
zangen* ("without song"), he can utter nothing to guide and soothe
the Jewish people. Their situation is already beyond hope: they are
doomed to remain *on a yerushe-vort un on freyd.* ("without a word
of inheritance and without delight."). The narrator sees that even
Bialik, who has continued to live in and through his work, will now
die as the readership responsible for his existence perishes. Cer-
tainly Bialik will not be able to help the narrator, who is condemned
to absorb and reflect the death of his entire people.

Despite his attempts at cheer and wit, then, Glatshteyn's mood
was grim in 1943. Everything was doomed: his people, his tradition,
his language, his artistic freedom, his chances of contributing to a
continuing literature. Even his awesome responsibility as the chron-
icler of the last days of Eastern European Jewry was infused with
ironic futility: in anguish, he would *nem a pinkes un farshrayb*—
but who would read it?

VI   Shtralndike yidn: *Glatshteyn's Holocaust*

Shtralndike yidn—Radiant Jews—was published in 1946,[14]
amidst the rubble of what had so shortly before been a thriving and
energetic culture. Like *Gedenklider,* this volume centers around
Glatshteyn's responses to the Holocaust and contains some of the
most powerful poetry in his repertoire. Now his expressions of
mourning were even more raw, direct, and immediate than those
of the earlier collection. His mood alternating between unprotected
grief and intense fury, Glatshteyn struggled to come to terms not
only with the general, collective Holocaust of his people, but also
with an assortment of private, personal holocausts.

The anger that had marked Glatshteyn's earliest work reasserts
itself in *Shtralndike yidn;* this time, however, the target of his
attacks is neither society nor an abstract cosmos, but the Jewish

God. *Nisht di meysim loybn got* ["The dead do not praise God"] (pp. 12–15) and *On yidn* ["Without Jews"] (pp. 37–38), two of Glatshteyn's most famous poems, express this anger while probing the broadest ramifications of the Holocaust, its significance with respect to Jewish history and to all of contemporary Jewish life.

The title *Nisht di meysim loybn got* is a reference to Psalms 115,17. The narrator takes the words of the psalm literally in his poem, asserting that for the dead it is impossible to praise God and explaining that the covenant of chosenness between God and Israel has come to an end. Basing his comments on a midrash which claims that every Jew born in the world—no matter where or when—was present on Mount Sinai at the giving of the Torah,[15] the narrator goes on to say that all these Jews were again present, this time at Lublin, for the termination of the covenant.

The narrator addresses a little boy who is a special witness to the fate of the covenant because he has experienced all of Jewish history, including its aftermath.[16] This child is an important participant in the collective Jewish tragedy, for he is finally introduced as the Torah itself: *Dos bistu dokh geven, di shtile, kleyne, elnte,/Opgegebene toyre.* ("That was you—the still, small, forlorn,/Returned Torah."). Earlier, the narrator had described the position of the little boy, i.e., the Torah, in Jewish life:

> *Yidish yingele, ongetseykhnt iz dayn lebn*
> *Afn oysgeshterntn yidishn himl,*
> *Host keynmol nisht gefelt,*
> *Host nisht getort feln.*
> *M'hot dikh oysgehoft un oysgebetn,*
> *Alemol ven mir zaynen geven, bistu oykh geven.*
> *Un ven mir zaynen gevorn oys,*
> *Bistu mit undz nisht gevorn.*

> Little Jewish boy, your life is traced
> In the star-studded Jewish heavens,
> You were never absent,
> You were not permitted to be absent.
> You were hoped for and pleaded for,
> Whenever we were, so were you too.
> And when we vanished,
> You vanished along with us.

This section of the poem provides a rough precis of the work as a whole, alluding to the covenantal promise that Jews would be mul

titudinous as the stars of heaven and referring as well to the fact—
emphasized throughout the poem—that Jewish history had until
the present been a succession of seeming ends followed by new
beginnings. But the language of these lines reveals that the end in
Lublin, while it may look the same as others, is qualitatively dif-
ferent because it marks the obliteration of the Jewish people. All
that can remain of its heritage is the useless and abandoned Torah,
rising above the gas chambers to cry endlessly into a dead world.
The use of *oys* as an adverbial complement and thus as a simple
intensifier in the words *oysgeshternt* ("star-studded"), *oysgehoft*
("hoped for"), and *oysgebetn* ("pleaded for") switches abruptly in
the seventh line, where it functions, much more centrally, as an
adverb meaning "no more; through." Similarly, *nisht* ("not"), used
as an adverb in lines three and four, combines with *vern* ("become")
in the last line to signify the verb "to vanish."

Glatshteyn retains an element of particularity in *Nisht di meysim
loybn got*, even as he deals with the fate of his entire people. He
chooses Lublin, the city of his birth, as the locus of the Holocaust,
and invests it with the importance of Mount Sinai; the destruction
of Lublin means for him the end of Jewish life. Moreover, the little
boy, who as witness and victim also embodies the canonical history
of his people, reflects Glatshteyn's feelings about his own role as
an artist; like him, the child is a singer. At Sinai, he had been a
zing-foygl ("songbird") who added his voice in acceptance of the
covenant; at Lublin he becomes a dove, stretching out his neck for
slaughter. Thus, if the Jewish people is murdered, its poetic voice
becomes a sacrifice as well.

The harshest irony of this poem lies in its allusion to Psalm 115.
There, the dead are those who are blind to the sovereignty of the
Jewish God. Here, in contrast, the ones who die are precisely those
who had assumed the covenant in good faith. The juxtaposition of
midrash and a far more unbelievable tale of annihilation in the *gaz-
kamern fun lublin* ["gas-chambers of Lublin"] simply underscores
the magnitude of God's abandonment of His people, the emptiness
of His promise, and the irrelevance of His commandments.

The realization of *On yidn* is even more extreme. In this poem,
the narrator explains that the destruction of the Jews will result not
only in the violent conclusion of God's covenant with His chosen
people, but in His own disappearance. The reason for this, and the
major point of the poem, emerges near its beginning: *Un mir hobn*

dikh gefuremt in undzer geshtalt. ("And we formed You in our image."). If Jews are responsible for the existence of God, He will cease to live when they do.

In *On yidn*, formal devices used to create an ironic impression of order and control clash with the poem's content. Thus, rhyme, repetition, anaphora, consonance, and anagrammatic repetition are all employed to portray a world that has fallen apart. Fittingly, however, some of the most important lines in the poem stand alone, not conforming to this framework. One instance is the very first line of the poem: *On yidn vet nisht zayn keyn yidisher got.* ("Without Jews there will be no Jewish God."), a stark comment that in fact encapsulates the remainder of the work. Furthermore, even when a basic scheme is established, its effect is finally jarring: either the pattern is unexpectedly broken with a shocking statement or the harmonious form collapses beneath the weight of meaning. The section following the initial line of *On yidn* is a striking example of Glatshteyn's technique. Essentially end-rhymed (except for one instance of linked rhyme), it serves to emphasize the harshness of the two lines that come after it, explaining why there will be no Jewish God in future: *Itst tseyln zikh in di milyonen/Undzere toyte kep.* ("In the millions now, are numbered/Our lifeless heads."). Towards the end of the poem, another series of tightly connected lines occurs. Here, although anaphora as well as rhyme and a metrical mesh unify the sequence, they nonetheless manage to reflect discord. Indeed, these lines communicate growing agitation, the tortured understanding of the narrator, who knows the answers to his rhetorical questions:

> *Ver vet dikh kholemen?*
> *Ver gedenken?*
> *Ver vet dikh leykenen,*
> *Ver vet dikh benken?*
> *Ver vet tsu dir, af a farbenkter brik,*
> *Avek fun dir, kedey tsu kumen*
>   *tsurik?*

> Who will dream you?
> Who remember?
> Who will deny you,
> Who will yearn [for] you?

Who will to you, on a yearning
   bridge,
[Go] away from you, in order to
   return?

VII   *Life Among the Dead*

Nisht di meysim loybn got and *On yidn* are urgent and compelling
outcries of anger at God for allowing the Jewish people to be de-
stroyed. But *Mayn bruder binyomin* ["My Brother Binyomin"] (pp.
99–100), a poem that contributes to Glatshteyn's private version of
the Holocaust, represents an indictment no less severe for its poig-
nancy and tone of resignation. Now God is accused of toying with
and depreciating the life of one human being—the narrator's broth-
er. The message of *Mayn bruder binyomin* is hauntingly clear: why
did God create Binyomin if He planned to let him die, at age forty-
four, in a concentration camp? Through the formulation of this
question, the narrator provides a touching portrait of Binyomin, at
the same time exposing his own intense pain.

The poem begins quietly: *Shenk mir nokh-nisht oysgeveynte vert-
er,/Got, kh'hob nisht keyn koyekh tsu sheltn* ("Send me uncom-
pletely cried words,/God, I have no strength to curse"). The
subsequent verbal assault on God belies this elegiac opening. Bin-
yomin's entire life had been abject, the narrator asserts. He had
suffered not only material need but also the loneliness of God's
neglect, His refusal to grant Binyomin any happiness in life, with
the single exception of a son: *Zayn lakhndik shtikl freyd/Mit di
pekh-shvartse zunen.* ("His laughing bit of joy/With the pitch-black
suns."). Binyomin was simply God's *narishn vits* ("foolish joke").

Just as in *Nisht di meysim loybn got* and *On yidn*, formal con-
struction underscores the meaning of *Mayn bruder binyomin*. Here,
line length is used in order to summarize and produce a jolting
effect. For example, in the middle strophe of the poem, interspersed
among longer lines, are four nonconsecutive short lines that together
describe the essence of Binyomin's life and death: *Mayn bruder
binyomin?; Un oykh mir gelebt,; Tsum koymen.; Oremkeyt.* ("My
brother Binyomin?"; "And lived not much of a life,"; "To the chim-
ney."; "Poverty."). The last of these also ends the strophe, echoing
the central characteristic of Binyomin's existence.

The final lines of *Mayn bruder binyomin* are arranged in an en-

velope pattern of two long lines containing three shorter ones. In
this instance, the alternation of line length serves not only to provide
a synopsis but also to startle:

> *Host davke gevolt az er mitn vayb zoln derlebn*
> *Freyd af aribertsushoymen,*
> *Tsu firn dem eyntsikn zun*
> *Tsu der khupe fun koymen,*
> *Und dort hostu zey alemen farbrent.*
>
> You wanted no less than that he and his wife
> should live to experience
> The overflowing joy,
> Of bringing their only son
> To the chimney canopy,
> And there You cremated them all.

The outer lines contrast life and death, while the three intermediate
lines build to the horror of the poem's conclusion; beginning op-
timistically, they swiftly reveal the narrator's irony. *Mayn bruder
binyomin* grinds to a halt, its final line rendered all the more ar-
resting by the rhythmic incompatibility between it and the lines
directly preceding it. This abruptness is accented further in that,
whereas each line except the last terminates in a continuant, the
second syllable of *farbrent*—as well as receiving stress—ends with
a stop.

In addition to the use of line length as a formal device in *Mayn
bruder binyomin*, Glatshteyn employs a separate technique, the
ironic adaptation of traditional terms, in order to mirror his partic-
ular disgust at God's perversion of Jewish life; thus, instead of *big-
dey-shabes* ("Sabbath garments"), Binyomin was dressed in *bidgey
konsentratsye-lager* ("concentration-camp garments"); Binyomin's
son is led, not to the marriage canopy, but to the *khupe fun koymen*
("chimney canopy"). Rather than asking *May ko mashme lon?*
("What does it mean to us?") as a detached intellectual question,
or even, as Avrom Reyzen had done in his famous poem by the
same name, in order to question a path of religious life, the narrator
asks, searching once again for the purpose of Binyomin's life: *May
ko mashme mayn bruder binyomin?* ("What does my brother Bin-
yomin mean?"). But, as in *On yidn*, the grieving narrator knows the
answer to his question only too well. In his poem *Yisker* ["Yisker

(a prayer commemorating the dead)"] (pp. 10–11), Glatshteyn had declared: *Umzistik iz der toyt fun yokhed un narish./Der martirer-toyt fun milyonen iz legendarish.* ("Vain is the death of the individual, and foolish./The martyr's death of millions is legendary."). In the memorial to Binyomin, however, he illustrates that, although individual death may appear insignificant amidst the enormity of the Holocaust, at times the immediacy of one person's suffering can cause this perception to be reversed.

Like *Mayn bruder binyomin, A yidishe kroyn* ["A Jewish crown"] (pp. 93–94) reflects personal bereavement—the narrator's loss of his father. However, although the poem's perspective is individual rather than collective, the death of this one man also symbolizes the destruction of Jewish tradition much as it had in *Tsum tatn.* When his father had turned forty, the narrator of *A yidishe kroyn* explains, he had voluntarily assumed the mantle of old age and become a grandfather. This leap into superannuation did not endanger the old man's life, though, for his advanced years were: *bashitst kegn toyt/Un farpantsert akegn moyre,/Mit toyznter morgns fun avoydes haboyre.* ("protected against death/And like a tank against fear,/With thousands of mornings of prayer."). By believing so strongly, the narrator's father had managed to remove himself from historical time and place; his faith had been as tangible to him as Palestine—and he himself could be a shepherd, rather than a Lublin merchant.

Despite this seeming immunity to death, however, the last strophe of *A yidishe kroyn* reveals that the aged Jew is dead after all.[17] The narrator, admitting that he has difficulty enough simply being a father, realizes that he is unable to assume the additional yoke of becoming a grandfather, as his own father had done. Thus, the institution of Jewish "grandfatherness"—the total and loving acceptance of history and commitment— must die along with the old man. In the absence of this established continuity, the narrator attempts at least to maintain contact with his father: *Kh'baklog un baveyn dikh, tate,/Un du lebst in mir.* ("I lament and mourn for you, father,/And you live in me."). But the connection between the two is tenuous, as the narrator comments—echoing from a distance the words and sentiments of *Tsum tatn: Kh'kush di trit fun mayn benkshaft nokh dir.* ("I kiss the steps of my longing for you.").

In *Kh'tu dermonen* ["I remember"] (pp. 109–21) the narrator's reconstruction of his past takes the form of a dream vision in which he follows his own chronological, intellectual and emotional development, simultaneously seeing within it all of Jewish history and tradition. The departure point for his recollections is his parents' home, the center of his childhood world. The narrator arrives there by following a *kholem-stezhke* a "dream path," moving back in time and space through countries, streets, and houses to reach *dem eyntsikn,/Sharfn un freydikn shnit,/Fun dem kholem stezhke,/Vos hot geheysn heym.* ("the only,/Sharp and joyful section,/Of the dream path,/That was called home."). Now this path has been destroyed. Although the destruction may be unimportant in a larger scheme, the narrator comments that for him it is a private holocaust and therefore he must memorialize it.

The narrator is obsessed with the individuality of his experience, regarding both things destroyed and destruction itself. Talking about his initial learning experiences, the introduction to Jewish heritage, he recalls his own little Bible in which the matriarchs and patriarchs had actually lived. This world was as real to him as his historical present and provided him with the model for incorporating the totality of the Jewish fate within himself: *Farvos iz mir bashert geven/Ontsuheybn fun same onheyb/Un dergeyn tsum same sof,/Vi tsu a bazunderer eygener tliye?* ("Why I was destined/To begin from the very beginning/And to arrive at the very end,/As to a separate, individual gallows?").

With the study of Rashi and the unfolding of Jewish history, the narrator begins to be aware of those around him, starting with his teacher and continuing to a perception of his parents. At this point, his reactions reflect a discerning, although narrow, perspective: he notices his *rebbe's* eyes, which hold the key to the *rebbe's* entire disposition. He concentrates on his mother's mouth, voice, and songs, in which he has found the central part of her personality and the source of her impact on others. To his father, the narrator attributes a more abstract, though no less pivotal, characteristic, for it was he who—out of his own total involvement as a Jew— had selected the boy's special Jewish world for him and provided the child with a private interpretation of chosenness.

It is only later that the narrator describes his mourning with a fuller understanding of the broad cultural implications that accompany personal loss. When he visits his dying mother, with whom he feels he has almost caught up in terms of age and sagacity, he suddenly realizes that where once only her family had trusted and depended upon the wisdom of her words, now it is the whole

Yiddish language and its culture that will be extinguished with her death. To the outside, the narrator's mother is a representative of *mame-loshn* ("mother tongue"), the Yiddish language. To him, however, she is quite literally his *mame-loshn;* thus the general theoretical consequence of the cumulative deaths of people like the narrator's mother, who are repositories of the culture, is linked with—and in a way, a pale reflection of—the importance of his particular bereavement and impoverishment.

The same sense of a deeper significance to his very specific memories and suffering is made clear by the narrator at the conclusion of *Kh'tu dermonen,* where he recalls the death of his father and brother. Now, once again, the end of his family and his people is inextricably fused:

> *Dort, mitn folk zaynen zey gegangen mit trit,*
> *Vos hobn zikh getseylt, vi zamd baym yam,*
> *Ober far mir zaynen zey geven,*
> *Bazunderdike trit,*
> *Vi eygene harts-klep.*

> There, they walked with the people, with
>   steps,
> As numerous as sand by the sea,
> But for me they were,
> Individual steps,
> Like my own heart-beats.

Kh'tu dermonen is unusual among the poems of *Shtralndike yidn* in its length (twelve pages) and in that, along with *Lublin, mayn heylike shtot* ["Lublin, my holy city"], it is conspicuously lacking in rhyme and in structured meter. *Kh'tu dermonen* is constructed as a series of catalogues, achieving its unity through this device rather than any other. All the small holocausts that the narrator wishes to remember provide the foundation for his discussions; but within these subdivisions are lists that form a kind of narrative inventory. There is an air of compulsiveness about these catalogues, as if to omit a detail would be to consign it to perpetual oblivion. So, for example, the poet describes Lublin's Jewish quarter: *Di bsomim-gesheftn,/Di kashe-un-mel-kromen,/Di hering-gevel blekh,/ . . . Di mandlen, taytlen un faygn,/Dos frishgebakene zoyer-broyt, /Di mon un getsiblte pletslekh* ("The spice stores,/The cereal and flour stores,/The little herring shops,/ . . . The almonds, dates and figs,/The freshly-baked leavened bread,/The poppyseed and onion crackers"), or at another point, he discusses his teacher's eyes:

> *Parnosedike, vokhedike oygn,*
> *Daygedike, atsvesdike oygn,*
> *Kheyune-zukhndike, fartrerte oygn,*
> *Ziftsndike drimlendike,*
> *Zeltn menukhedike, shabesdike, ganeydndike oygn,*
> *Shver un tif gefregte un mit a nign*
> *Farentferte oygn.*

> Subsistence, workaday eyes,
> Worrying, morose eyes,
> Livelihood-seeking, tearful eyes,
> Sighing, dozing,
> Seldom restful, Sabbath-like, paradisiacal eyes,
> Heavily and deeply asked and with a melody
> Explained eyes.

The lists of *Kh'tu dermonen*—and other descriptions as well—are structured as lengthy clauses or sentences; the effect of this technique is to signal a mood of breathless urgency, a need to reach the end of each construction without pausing. Punctuating these fast-moving sentences are much shorter ones—sometimes merely exclamatory clauses—that summarize the larger descriptions and occasionally emphasize the destruction of the remembered past, for example: *Heym. S'yingl iz gekumen tsurik aheym.; Der gantser himl lesht zikh.; A gants land vert khorev.* ("Home. The little boy has come home again."; "The entire sky is extinguished."; "A whole land is annihilated."). The form reinforces the poet's assertion, both at the beginning and at the end of *Kh'tu dermonen*, that the little holocausts in him had become ripe for discussion and that therefore he was compelled to talk about them.

Shtralndike yidn concludes with a work that is unprecedented in Glatshteyn's volumes of poetry: *Lublin, mayn heylike shtot* ["Lublin, my holy city"] (pp. 122–23), is arranged as prose.[18] In light of Glatshteyn's comments elsewhere, this special form may be seen as a striving for intelligibility and clarity.[19] Here, it is the Holocaust itself—and not private holocausts—that claims the narrator's attention. As in *Kh'tu dermonen*, the former life of Lublin is evoked: its Jewish market existence, its smells and textures. But in addition, the foment of the pre-World War II era—which would be apparent to the adult, though not to the child of *Kh'tu dermonen*—emerges in all its complexity: the economic and political class struggle, the development of secular interests and loyalties, the excitement over new literature in juxtaposition with devotion to old values and respect for traditional masters. And where life in *Kh'tu dermonen* ended in metaphoric striding toward oblivion, there is a geographic specificity to death in *Lublin, mayn heylike shtot:* Maidanek Forest.

Like *Kh'tu dermonen, Lublin, mayn heylike shtot* relies heavily on catalogues as a structural device for noting down the past. Although these lists occur in paragraph construction, they are not what could be called traditional prose. The first four paragraphs do not begin with sentences at all, but are rather exclaimed apostrophes to the city of Lublin. Moreover, the lists themselves become anaphoric in the latter two of these four paragraphs and never form sentences. Thus, they sound similar to the inventory of *Kh'tu dermonen* although the visual effect is much different:

Lublin, mayn heylike shtot fun bildung-dorshtike yunge-layt un yunge meydlekh, fun dem ershtn bez-aromat fun yung-hebreish un fun der batamtkeyt fun shtoltsn yidish, . . . fun undzer gekeytlter benkshaft keyn odes un keyn varshe, vu mir hobn getsitert iber bialik, frishman, mendele, perets, sholem-aleykhem, reyzen.

Lublin, my holy city of education-hungry young men and young women, of the first lilac aroma of young Hebrew and of the tastiness of proud Yiddish, . . . of our longing linked to Odessa and to Warsaw, where we quivered over Bialik, Frishman, Mendele, Perets, Sholem-Aleykhem, Reyzen.

However, *Lublin, mayn heylike shtot* concentrates proportionally less on cataloging the vibrance of the past than does *Kh'tu dermonen*. Instead, the last part of the work is devoted to the city's deathly present. This shift in emphasis is paralleled by the introduction of more proselike language. In the description of Lublin's ruination, the narrator's references to the city change. In the lists it is "Lublin, the city of . . .," whereas later it becomes, for example: *Heylike shtot mayne, dos hostu oysgebetn di skhie far zikh . . .* ("My holy city, it is you who, by pleading, won the privilege . . . "). Furthermore, in the end it is evident why Lublin is holy: the city has become the cemetery of the Jewish people. For this reason, although the world may begin to rebuild and reconstruct itself, Lublin—as the symbol for the cultural and spiritual world—can never exist again. Hence, what was seen in *Kh'tu dermonen* as the ripping apart of an individual dream of the past, looms here as general destruction, the impact of which extends forever into the future.

VIII   *Life Among the Living*

No matter how strongly he empathized with the death of his family and of Eastern European Jewry, however, Glatshteyn's duties in *Shtralndike yidn* were broader than those attendant upon the chronicler of a murdered world; for, the Holocaust had taken a toll on the lives of American Jews as well. In *Kh'davn a yidish blat in sobvey* ["I pray a Yiddish newspaper in the subway"] (pp. 81–87), he focuses on the difficulties of the Jew living in America, surrounded by non-Jews who cannot understand his plight and are unsympathetic towards him.

It is morning in a New York City subway, where the narrator is reading a Yiddish newspaper. For him the paper carries the weight of a sacred document: the word *blat*, which means "newspaper," also pertains to a page of Talmud. The narrator goes on to say, moreover, that in reading the newspaper he is praying the daily morning service; elsewhere he elaborates: *Dos davn ikh azoy./Kh'zog tfiles, kines.* ("I am praying this way./I say prayers, laments."). What appears to be a mundane activity, then, is actually a means of reaffirming Jewish ties and turning every day into a day of mourning.

For the narrator's non-Jewish neighbor, in contrast, the newspaper is a source of relaxation, from which he can extract *dem honik/Fun der khronik* ("the honey/Of local news"): politics and sports. He can enjoy his reading, a luxury denied the Jew. The narrator, in a real or imaginary conversation, challenges the non-Jew's ostensible tolerance, suggesting that the advice: *Biy ey men, riyd ameriken* ("Be a man, read American") is in fact based on the belief that Jews are *a fremder element* ("an alien element").

Jews are considered an alien element everywhere, the narrator asserts. He dismisses as legend the enlightenment fantasy that there could be something called an international Jew, going on to label it a *bayke* ("nursery story; fib") that has been burned to ashes. Though he may possess a variety of passports, the Jew is stateless. Rather, it is the American non-Jew who is international, free to travel wherever he wishes and join whatever causes he finds desirable, without having to fear repercussions. The narrator reveals that he has never been comfortable in America: *Shoyn bald fertsik yor vi ikh vander,/Vi di yidn in midber,/Mit a dershrokenem passport in keshene.* ("For almost forty years I have been wandering,/Like the Jews in the desert,/With a frightened passport in my pocket."). The subway ride now takes on symbolic proportions—it is a journey toward a different, hoped-for America, where the narrator and all other Jews will be safe.

Yet another change wrought by the Holocaust, Glatshteyn felt, was in the very nature of his own poetry. Suddenly he found himself with an obligation to a weakened and grief stricken readership, an obligation that had to transcend aesthetic concerns. In *Fun a briv* ["From a letter"] (pp. 57–59), Glatshteyn explores the conflicts caused by this realization. Discussing the present situation of Yiddish literature, the narrator reminisces to a colleague: *Eybik hob ikh gebenkt,/Nokh petite minutn, shtile, eygene—/Nokh kleyne lider.* ("Perpetually I have longed,/For petite minutes, quiet, individual—/For small poems."). Now, however, because of the tragedy of his people, he is no longer permitted the luxury of writing introverted and incomprehensible poetry. Rather, he and other writers must accept—however reluctantly—the burden of writing clearly and accessibly. In a wry comment on their condition, the narrator tells his colleague that they have become *farfolkt* ("folkized"), a neologism that not only signifies the concept of total involvement with one's people but also suggests the near-homonym of *farfolkt: farfolgt* ("persecuted"). Thus, the Yiddish writer is doubly victimized, beaten down not only by historical circumstances but by his own milieu as well.

A separate aspect of the survivor-narrator's dilemma is the feeling that, as the unwilling mouthpiece of his people, he is compelled to transmit that which he does not necessarily believe. *Fun a briv* concludes ironically; the narrator describes reading about a group of Holocaust survivors who, joyful to be alive, are confident that their survival is an act of God. He asserts that he and his colleague should also *gebn/A knip in dem bahaltnstn shtik lebn,/Az di farb zol shteyn./Un lomir oykh loybn un hopken,/Hopken un loybn,/Un, leeys breyre, gloybn.* ("pinch/The most hidden bit of life,/So that the color rises./And let us also praise and hop,/Hop and praise,/And—there is no choice—believe."). By forcing himself to assume religious faith, the narrator reaches the extremity of capitulation to the requirements of a public voice.

IX   *The Trials of Reb Nakhmen*

Quite different from the discussion of public memory and responsibility that marks *Kh'davn a yidish blat in sobvey, Fun a briv,* and *Lublin, mayn heylike shtot* are those poems in *Shtralndike yidn* in which Glatshteyn again employs the persona of Reb Nakhmen of Bratslav. Just as before, he uses the Bratslaver as a vehicle for exposing and attempting to untangle his literary conflicts. Earlier, he had found in Reb Nakhmen a means of resolving his contradictory need to both escape from and delve into his feelings about the Holocaust. Now Glatshteyn used the Bratslaver to question his dual role as chronicler of a murdered Eastern European Jewish life and comforter to its few survivors. Moving from a political realm into a spiritual one, and from externalized perception to introspection, Glatshteyn aired his doubts, fears, feelings of inadequacy and resistance to this position of community responsibility. *Der Bratslaver in a nakht fun yeride* ["The Bratslaver in a night of descent"] (pp. 25–32) is a twelve-poem cycle recording the events of a night in which Nakhmen defines his inner strife, experiences it fully, and—with the arrival of morning—comes to terms with it.[20] The poems are connected, not only through their subject matter, but also through imagery; their number, furthermore, implies circularity of time, the sense of a fresh start—and this impression is reinforced by a reversal in the last poem of certain images from the first one.

In the first poem, Nakhmen declares his inadequacy to be spiritual leader of his people. Far from living in a state of closeness to God, he fears he is dangerously removed from Him: *Kh'hob zikh dir tsufil gevorfn in di oygn,/Getoptshet in a blote/Un gemeynt, az kh'bin gefloygn.* ("I was too conspicuous to you,/Plodded in mud/And thought I was flying."). Feeling that he can offer nothing to his people, he therefore begs God to silence him. Nakhmen's problem, however, is complicated in that he is indeed special, set apart from his community, both in goals and in personality. As he explains in the second poem: *Toyznt yidn zukhn takhlis/Un ikh—zikh aleyn./Toyznt yidn meynt khedve./Un ikh—meynt geveyn.* ("A thousand Jews search for results/And I—for myself./A thousand Jews means bliss./And I—means weeping."). He thus feels obligated to play some important role but knows neither what to say nor how to say it. In the third poem, however, he does come to the realization that in order to be a leader, he must first gain insight into his community and consider its—and his own—position in a hostile world. This is something that he had been too high-flown to do previously: *Ikhele, nem aroys a noztikhele,/Vaks frier uf un vaks arayn,/A yid tsvishn yidn.* ("Little I, take out a little handkerchief,/First grow up and grow into,/A Jew among Jews.").

The next six poems comprise the core of this Bratslav cycle, as Nakhmen faces the center of his conflict. The first and last of these poems employ the term *yeride,* which does not appear elsewhere outside of the title, thereby providing a subtle boundary for the process. Like the Bratslav poems in *Gedenklider,* these reveal Nakhmen attempting to return to a more basic type of Jewish life. Now, however, he does not search for unity with the cosmos or for the melody of life; rather, he seeks to make himself into the kind of simple Jew who, he believes, is the foundation of his community and its proper representative before God. At first, he approaches the discrepancy between what he is and what he would like to be in an oblique fashion, viewing it in terms of the distinction between body and soul. Playing on the custom of *shiraim,* wherein Hasidim eat the remnants of the *rebbe's* food as a means of unifying themselves with him and with each other, Nakhmen—as body—identifies with the flock rather than with its leader: *Di shtraymldike neshome varft tsu shiraim,/Dem guf, dem prostn khay vekayem.* ("The *shtrayml*-like soul [*shtrayml* refers to the fur-edged hat worn by Hasidic Jews on the Sabbath and holidays] pitches *shiraim*/To the body, the lowly common man.").

The metaphoric equation of body and simple Jew becomes a concrete one by the beginning of the next poem in the cycle, as Nakhmen asserts that he wishes to be a man *mit a fargrebt kepele,/Nor mit a veykh hertsele.* ("with a boorish little head,/But with a soft little heart."). But despite this desire, he continues to be drawn in the direction of separateness and the need to be superior. Is he a simple Jew or an elevated leader? He cannot come to terms with his position.

Un mayne brider zaynen voyle yidn,
Farvos shray ikh zey rak ariber?
Kh'veys, az kohols tfile
Iz ongeleygter un liber.
Kh'veys, kh'makh fun zikh a blazn,
Vos ikh gorgl zikh mayse khazn.

And my brothers are good Jews,
Why do I keep outshouting them?
I know that the community's prayer
Is more welcome and more
    pleasing.
I know that I make a clown of
    myself,
When I trill like a cantor.

Nakhmen's perception of contradiction casts him into the depths of his crisis in the ninth poem of *Der bratslaver in a nakht fun yeride*. Before, this conflict had been implied by the juxtaposition of contrasting but separate statements; now Nakhmen no longer divides them. He is paralyzed by the opposing claims on him: *Kh'vil epes zogn, nor s'hot nisht keyn haft,/Kh'vil betn, nor mayn gebet iz farshtumt,/Kh'vil loyfn fun zikh, nor mayn veg iz farkrumt—*. ("I want to say something, but it does not hold water,/I want to beseech, but my plea is mute,/I want to run from myself, but my path is twisted—."). It is little wonder that he would like to escape from himself, but this too is a futile effort. All he can do is pray that God will grant him strength in his hour of need.

Ironically, Nakhmen's mood begins to change after he realizes that he is not only isolated from his community and from God, but also from his wife, the person who is closest to him. He sees that she is distanced from him as well. They move about, passing in darkness, never able to reach one another: *A vint fartrogt dayne verter,/Nokh eyder kh'hob zey farshtanen.* ("A [gust of] wind carries your words away,/Even before I've understood them."). Nonetheless, she is a comfort to him: *Dayn bazundernish iz a gebentshter gortn/Antkegn mayn vistenay.* ("Your separateness is a blessed garden/Compared to my aridness."). Nakhmen thus begins to understand that the division within him between separateness and responsibility to a collective is natural and legitimate.

The final poem of *Der bratslaver in a nakht fun yeride* reflects the resolution of Nakhmen's conflict. Joyfully addressing God in the light of day, the Bratslaver asserts that: *S'harts vakst in mir un ot/Krig ikh fligl un fli*. ("My heart grows in me and presently/I receive wings and fly."). He is willing to try again—gone is his earlier feeling that flying is actually a misinterpreted wallowing in mud. The difference now is that Nakhmen can fulfill his lonely leadership role while at the same time understanding—and actually being—a simple Jew. He does not want to become too elevated; he rejects any ambition to be a healer or a great scholar; he does not want to be saintly. But this is not the same longing for simplicity that had informed his musings before. It is true that he will only rest when he hears a *baskl* ("oracular voice") from God, saying *Fun ale kleyne, proste mentshelekh,/Bistu, bratslaver, der prostster un der klenster*. ("Of all small, lowly little people,/You, Bratslaver, are the lowliest and the smallest."). But at the same time, he tells God: *Kh'nem on ale dayne khsodim./Af alts vos du basherst mir bin ikh kapabl*. ("I accept your favors./I am capable of all to which you destine me."). It is this new synthesis that enables him to find fresh meaning in his existence.

X   *The Survivor's Nightmare*

Just as he worked out Nakhmen's fusion of roles in *Der bratslaver in a nakht fun yeride*, so, too, did Glatshteyn continue to search for ways of unifying his own public responsibility as survivor and memorializer with his need for private expression. The epitome of this effort is his series of four poems, collectively entitled *Nakhtlider* ["Night poems"] (pp. 48–53). At the same time, this work represents Glatshteyn's most sophisticated exploration of the interrelationship of life and death that symbolized the result of the Holocaust for him as a Jew and as an artist.

Nakhtlider progresses from a perception of darkness as general and total within the narrator's self—though unconnected to history—and moves to an internalization of the Holocaust that is finally externalized and viewed as an active historical force. In the first poem, the narrator asserts that he intends to turn down his lamp and extract nights from his days. He longs for the comfort of his brother as he retreats into the *mindstn tirl* ("least little door") of his life, there to save up his days and nights. At first he is not even sure that he is alive. As he puts it: *A simen ikh leb—ikh trakht,/Vel ikh zikh narn mit dekartn.* ("A sign that I live—I think,/So I will fool myself with Descartes."). Later he reveals that his sense of life stems from denying certain daytime attackers who hurl abuse and insult at him. His response is to turn his lamp even lower and bid the outside world good-night—not, as in *A gute nakht, velt,* to return to some imaginary other life, but rather to turn into himself, since this seems to be the only safe place for him and his loved ones.

In the next two poems, the narrator describes the complex landscape and population of his inner world, explaining the confusion over whether or not he is in fact alive, and providing a statement of purpose for his internal existence. In the first of these works, millions of hands stretch out to the narrator, asking to be buried within him, because they have been deprived of any other resting place. They are not content, however, to be buried and forgotten. On the contrary, they demand: *Leb undzer toyt, derheyb im iber ale freydn.* ("Live our death, raise it above all joys.") They intend their cries to fill his dreams with fear but they are not motivated by any sadistic desires. Their purpose, rather, is a poignant wish to achieve continuity through awakening a sense of urgency within the narrator. He is their only hope: they have no other means of being remembered. The poem ends with a plea from the millions that the narrator become *der mayver yabok tsvishn lebedikn eyn-ikl/Un farbrentn zeydn.* ("The *mayver yabok* [a book containing prayers recited by a dying person as well as those said for the person after death] between the living grandchild/And the cremated grand-father."). Thus, as the physical repository of mourning for an extinguished generation, the narrator transmits life to the dead and death to the living.

But what happens when that living witness himself dies? This is the problem faced in the third poem of *Nakhtlider,* in which the narrator continues his internal study of the Holocaust and deepens his perception of the paradoxical coalescence of life and death. Here the fusion of life and death is complete: *Dos halbe lebn in mir iz toyt./Lebedik in mir iz der halber toyt.* ("Half of life in me is dead./Living in me is half of death."). This is a function of the narrator's inner life only: superficially, he appears normal, socially adept, calm and polished. No one, to look at him, would guess that at home he possesses *a beys-oylem in miniatur* ("a miniature cemetery"), that he can walk all night long among the graves of the entire destroyed Jewish world. In the previous poem, the dead had made demands on the narrator; here, it is he who seeks something from them: *Lozt mikh maseg zayn un onen/Dem khurbn fun milyonen.* ("Let me comprehend and conjecture/The Holocaust of millions."). Endeavoring to grasp the catastrophe that has befallen Eastern European Jewry, the narrator requests the dead within him to become like his family. Only through a personalization of death, the reduction of enormity to manageable scope, can he begin to fathom the meaning of extermination.

The narrator wants to keep the inhabitants of his inner world dead within him so that, paradoxically, he will be able to understand and thus hold alive the memory of their sacrifice. The narrator prides himself on possessing perhaps the only private cemetery of the Jewish people. This creates a special problem, however, because at some point he too will die, and they will no longer be able to live their death through him. The poem ends with a complex question: *Ver vet arbn mayn kleynem beysakvores,/Un dos likhtike geshank,/Fun a ner-tomedik yortsayt likht,/In eybikn getsank?* ("Who will inherit my little cemetery,/And the bright gift,/Of an eternal memorial light,/Eternally flickering?"). The fragility of keeping alive the memory of death is underscored in these lines; the memorial candle which is customarily lighted only on the anniversary of death must be like an eternal light, because of the sheer numbers of the dead and the magnitude of their annihilation; yet the eternal nature of the light rests also in the fact that it is continually about to burn out, extinguishing even memory.

The first three poems of *Nakhtlider* gain their richness from the complexity of the concepts they probe. The fourth poem of the series is distinguished from the others in two ways: the narrator looks outward, away from himself, and permits himself to see a ray of hope. The subject of the work is funerals—the seemingly endless funerals of millions of dead Jews. There are so many of these that Jews cannot in this period be seen as a race, a people, or even a belief; rather, they are merely a sect of mourners. The poem's rhythm reflects its mood; it is dirgelike and plodding:

> *Mir geyen pamelekh un farvoglen di gasn.*
> *Mir zaynen di gedenkers,*
> *Mir kumen dermonen,*

Mir firn, mir firn milyonen.
Tsu der letster levaye iz nokh vayt,
Vi vayt.
Mir hobn tsayt, mir hobn tsayt.

We walk slowly and make the streets
   homeless.
We are the rememberers,
We come to remind,
We lead, we lead millions.
The last funeral is still far off,
How far off.
We have time, we have time.

The sect of mourners brings its funerals before the public even
though more direct evidence of death may already be obscured. Its
mission is to insure that every funeral act as a reminder to the
world. As the narrator explains, again blurring the lines between
life and death: *Zeyer gantser toyt muz oysgelebt vern.* ("Their entire
death must be lived to the end."). Only through paying tribute to
this totality of death, he argues, can life begin to elevate itself once
more.

In this poem, the narrator allows for a possibility denied in the
rest of *Nakhtlider*, namely that there may be a conclusion to mourn-
ing, an end to the preoccupation with death. Through the arduous
act of living out millions of deaths, of grieving for an entire people,
it may happen that the final lament will be completed, whereupon
night will fall. Implying that the world is now in a state comparable
to the void preceding creation, the narrator concludes that only
after this new night will there be day: *ershter tog* ("the first day").

In this work, then, Glatshteyn offers a hint of his weariness with
mourning and a prelude to his future conflict about discussing the
Holocaust. *Gedenklider* and *Shtralndike yidn* are Glatshteyn's most
tortured collections. Nevertheless, these volumes contain some of
the finest poetry he ever wrote. But the desire to avoid a subject
that aroused so much of his passion and intelligence would in itself
soon become a source of difficulty for Glatshteyn.

CHAPTER 5

A Shadow on the Snow

WITH *Dem tatns shotn—My Father's Shadow—*(New York, 1953),[1] Glatshteyn moved into a new stage of his career. In this volume,[2] almost all direct references to mourning the victims of the Holocaust have disappeared. For, Glatshteyn had integrated the catastrophe of his people into his life. Even as he contemplated continuity and rebirth, the tragedy of history was a grim shadow that hung over almost every aspect of his consciousness, affecting his expression of private as well as public concerns and presenting distressing implications for his future as a Yiddish poet and bearer of a tradition.[3]

Moreover, Glatshteyn had become aware that the future of his heritage was being increasingly and constantly threatened. In the two parts of the world where the Yiddish language and its literature could still flourish freely, it was being stamped out, the victim of hostile attitudes in Israel and of gradual assimilation in the United States. Thus, Glatshteyn perceived that not only Eastern European Jewry, but *yiddishkeyt* itself, was being obliterated.

I Continuing Reflections on the Holocaust

Despite this new general perspective, a few poems in *Dem tatns shotn* hark back to the themes Glatshteyn had pursued in *Gedenklider* and *Shtralndike yidn. Do lign* ["Here lie"] (pp. 144–45), for example, centers on the martyrdom of Jews who perished during the Holocaust. But although the subject matter is familiar, Glatshteyn emphasizes a new issue here: the death of remembrance. The narrator of *Do lign* rejects the possibility of perpetuating the dead. Their memory, which in previous poems had assumed an element of eternity through the intercession of the living, is now revealed as ephemeral after all: *Zeyer shterblekhkeyt iz fargenglekh./Di kritsungen zaynen farshtendlekh/Un klor,/Bloyz far eyn dor fun libshaft.* ("Their mortality is transitory./The engravings are comprehensible/And clear,/For only one generation of love.").

The form of *Do lign* underscores the futility of any attempt to thwart the ravages of time. The poem is constructed so as to evoke a cemetery: each strophe consists of a one-word line followed by longer lines, and the effect resembles a series of monuments protruding from the earth. Indeed, the very title *Do lign* is itself a tombstone inscription. But just as the memorial stones lack foundation, since many of the dead have no physical remains—*Zey hobn zikh ufgeleyzt vi roykhn.* ("They have dissolved like smoke.")—so too, do the first strong words of each strophe yield to a statement of weakness and defeat. In *Shtralndike yidn,* the narrator of *Nakhtlider* had preserved a cemetery within himself so that he could constantly commemorate the dead. The narrator of *Do lign* can find no comparable solace. Instead he concludes: *Gey gikh aroys fundanen./Zukh a lebedikn mentsh un heys im/Gloybn in tkhies hameysim.* ("Leave here quickly./Find a living person and tell him/To believe in resurrection of the dead.").

During the 1940's, the Jewish God had begun to figure as an object for Glatshteyn's expressions of anger, desperation, and sense of betrayal. In *Dem tatns shotn,* Glatshteyn continued to reduce Him to manageable proportions through a combination of compassion and deprecation. His objective in this volume was somewhat different than in the earlier ones, however: now that the Jewish fate had been sealed, Glatshteyn was searching simply for ways to maintain a relationship with God.

The narrator of *Onhoyb* ["Beginning"] (pp. 60–62) is sympathetic to God. The two of them, he suggests, should make a new start together: *Zoln mir efsher onhoybn kleyn un vigldik/Mit a kleyn folk?/Mir beyde farvoglte tsvishn felker.* ("Should we perhaps begin small and cradlelike/With a small people?/We two, homeless among peoples."). The narrator of *Der guter yid taynet zikh oys* ["The good Jew [or: Hasidic rabbi] presents his arguments"] (pp. 123–25), in contrast, is full of anger at the God in whom he nonetheless believes. This work is constructed as a monologue in which a *guter yid* ("good Jew [or: Hasidic rabbi]") explains the intricacies of his faith to an evidently skeptical young man. Initially, he admits that because of the Holocaust (although he does not name it directly), he cannot in good conscience defend God: *Af dem vos er hot derloybt biyameynu,/Iz nishto keyn farentfer./Un oyb s'shtekt afile in dem a tifer sod,/ . . . Tor oykh azoy a folk nisht opgeyn in blut.* ("For what He allowed in our days,/There is no excuse./And even if there's a deep secret involved in this,/ . . . Even so a people must not abate in blood.").

As angry as he is, however, the *guter yid* refuses to act as God's prosecutor; such a role, he claims, would be beyond his powers. Nonetheless, in his own fashion, he does try God, and this process becomes the poem's focal point. The *guter yid* is a simple man and his rebellion more intuitive than theoretical. As he puts it: *Kh'davn, kh'bentsh,/Kh'lern a blat gemore,/Ober alts broygezerheyt.* ("I pray, I say benedictions,/I study a page of Talmud,/But all of it sullenly."). He feels justified in his anger, for attempt though he may, he can never free himself of misery and doubt. Only a humble mortal, and an unsophisticated one at that, he is incapable of contriving a refined justification for the horrors of the Holocaust: *Getlekhe soydes zaynen far di himlen,/Un ikh baveyn mayne milyonen toyte/Af der erd.* ("Divine secrets are for the heavens,/And I mourn my millions of dead/On earth."). Thus the *guter yid* has constructed a *modus vivendi* for his interactions with God, but it is clearly an uneasy arrangement, since neither he nor God can derive satisfaction from his half-hearted acts of devotion.

The utter loneliness of struggling to make peace with God and of endeavoring to endure a life emptied of joy after the Holocaust can be seen with particular clarity against the backdrop of close personal associations. In *Gedenklider* and *Shtralndike yidn*, when he was overwhelmed by the magnitude of historical events, Glatshteyn had avoided discussing relationships between men and women. With *Dem tatns shotn* he returned to this subject, but could not escape the inevitable presence of the Holocaust.

The poem *A getselt* ["A tent"] (pp. 174–76) harks back to the type of union depicted in *Fun undzer yokh:* it is deeply committed, based on sharing the smaller as well as the larger incidents in life. Understanding has gone beyond the need for words: in *Fun undzer yokh*, the narrator had wished to learn what his woman's eyes would say; the narrator of *A getselt* comments that *Zi hot nisht geredt, nor getrakht tsu mir.* ("She did not speak, but rather thought to me."). The man and woman of *Fun undzer yokh*, while no longer young, had exuded a healthy ripeness; this couple is weary and seems older.

Despite these significant similarities and apparent continuities, however, there are definite differences between the earlier and the later relationships. The woman is more assertive now, even though she does not speak, and the narrator describes the fact that he often quarrels with her thoughts. More important is the position of the narrator himself. In *Fun undzer yokh*, he had spent his time shingling the roof of his house to protect himself and his woman. There was an aura of safety, permanence, and elevation about this symbolic act. Now, the narrator lives in a tent; completeness and stability are gone. In the earlier poem, the narrator had allowed himself to be alone with his thoughts, those private musings and developments that for him constituted the essential isolation in every individual. Here, he is set apart again, but the reason is very different: he is constantly with God. This is both the source of his arguments with the woman and the reason why she cannot reach him.

The woman views the man's preoccupation as an act of expiation for the sin of having survived the Holocaust and suggests that he is punishing himself unduly. But the narrator explains that there is nothing symbolic about his behavior. As he says, contradicting the sentiments expressed by the narrator of *Do lign: Ikh aleyn bin umshterblekher khurbn.* ("I myself am immortal Holocaust."). He is irrevocably bound to God by an ultimate, if paradoxical, realization: *Der eybiker khurbn iz getlekh./Di groyse tseshterung/Iz azoy eybik vi bashaf.* ("The eternal Holocaust is divine./The great destruction/Is as eternal as creation."). If Glatshteyn's men and women had previously been separated by their own limitations and by the inevitable boundaries of secret thoughts and dreams, now the impenetrable barrier had become the Holocaust, which weakened even the deepest of relationships.

II   *The Threat to Yiddish*

A mood of hopelessness is never far from the poetry of *Dem tatns shotn* and the hard-won closeness of a shared life was not the only secondary casualty of the Holocaust. The Yiddish language, which from the very earliest of Glatshteyn's poetry had been a source of comfort and support for him, was itself facing imminent demise and could no longer provide him with the emotional sustenance of an earlier time. In *Mayn tate-mame shprakh* ["My parental language"] (pp. 150–51), Glatshteyn attempts to convey the extent to which Yiddish is the nucleus of his existence and the way in which it merges past and present for him. The narrator asserts that Yiddish is not only the language of his parents and a vehicle for commemorating them, but has in itself constituted a parental figure as the medium of his intellectual nourishment.

One of Glatshteyn's achievements in *Mayn tate-mame shprakh* is to connect the humble, work filled lives of Eastern European Jews with the earthiness of Yiddish. To underscore the beauty of ordinary existence, Glatshteyn employs the imagery of *havdole*, the ceremony that marks the conclusion of Sabbath holiness and the commencement of a mundane week. The narrator, however, elects to blur this distinction. For him there are two kinds of holiness: the quiet one of Sabbath, and the talkative one of every day. Alluding to the use of wine in celebrating both the beginning and the end of Sabbath, the narrator comments that his father's *havdole* is actually a *kidesh* [the benediction said when ushering in the Sabbath] welcoming and blessing a week of Yiddish. Moreover, he recreates the end of Sabbath by recalling his father's Yiddish *gitvokh*, a dialect version of *gut vokh* ("good week") and his mother's *Got fun avrom*—the prayer "God of Abraham"—which is recited in Yiddish. By implication, then, their daily tongue becomes as holy as Hebrew, the sacred language of Sabbath and of prayer.

But Yiddish does more than remind the narrator of his parents: it is also the language in which he had received his education. The religious texts he studied may have been Hebrew-Aramaic in origin, but translations, explanations, and examinations were all in Yiddish. It was the language not only of his traditional teachers and of those who, like the Baal Shem Tov and Reb Nakhmen of Bratslav, comprised what the narrator refers to as a *malkhes-khsidish* ("Hasidic kingdom"), but also of those nonbelievers and enlighteners who influenced him.

Like the narrator's parents and instructors, however, Yiddish too has been relegated to the domain of memory. As he says: *Bist mir nisht bloyz keyn mutershprakh,/Keyn shprakh fun vigl,/Nor der zigl fun ale mayne gedekhenishn.* ("To me you are not only a mother tongue,/A language of the cradle,/But the seal of all my recollections."). The rhyme *vigl/zigl* ("cradle/seal") is important here, because it emphasizes the narrator's understanding that one level of his association with Yiddish is ending. What the cradle had initiated, the seal on his memories now renders final. His parental language has assumed a new role: described as *Foterlekher gitvokh undzerer, blitslomp fun undzer lebn,* ("Our fatherly good week, extra-bright lamp of our life,") and transmitted through his mother's prayer, Yiddish has been reduced to a comfort for the narrator. Aware that the previous function of the language—as a living link to the simplicity and warmth he had experienced with his parents, and as a provider of intellectual and spiritual succor—is obsolete except in his mind, the narrator turns to Yiddish as an aid in overcoming the pain caused by the death of what it itself once symbolized.

The disappearance of Yiddish was also being hastened by circumstances not directly connected to the obliteration of Eastern European Jewry. Had the Holocaust never occurred, anti-Yiddish trends in Israel and the United States would have been bad enough—as Glatshteyn had implied years earlier in *Zing ladino*. Now these blows seemed fatal. In *Dem tatns shotn*, anger at the depreciation of Yiddish is expressed with particular vehemence in the poems *Tsvishn minkhe un mayrev* ["Between minkhe (the Jewish afternoon prayer) and *mayrev* (the Jewish evening prayer)"] (pp. 54-56) and *Yidish* ["Yiddish"] (pp. 127-30).

The narrator of *Tsvishn minkhe un mayrev* describes Yiddish in Israel not as *mame-loshn* but rather as *zeyde-loshn*, ("grandfather language"). The central conflict in this poem is between Yiddish or *zeyde-loshn* and Hebrew, encapsulated in the word "shalom." The former is personified as a grandfather, the latter epitomized by the Hebrew University. Although the University bestows its cheerful greetings on the grandfather, it will not allow him to respond. The problem is stated so clearly that it borders on the simplistic: the younger generation—or at least a generation that has gone away from Yiddish to Hebrew and away from plainness and traditional piety to dull intellectualism—gains a good deal from contact with its Yiddish-speaking forebears, but wishes to deny that connection. At the conclusion of the poem, the narrator pleads for the grandfather and for Yiddish:

> *Lozt im efenen s'moyl un zogn,*
> *Tsvishn minkhe un mayrev—*
> *Got helf! Oder, gut yor!*
> *Oder, a lebn af dayn kop,*
> *Yunger shalomtshik,*
> *Vos du gist op koved a zeydn.*

> Let him open his mouth and
>   say,

> Between *minkhe* and *mayrev*—
> Hello! or, good-bye!
> Or, bless you,
> Young *shalomchik*,
> For honoring a grandfather.

Far more interesting than the purely thematic message of the poem, however, is Glatshteyn's way of contrasting Yiddish and Hebrew—both through the vocabulary he uses and through his choice of orthography. Yiddish terms and idioms incorporating the Hebrew-Aramaic element abound: *harbe kashe* ("baffling question"), *mafsek zayn* ("interrupt"—especially a prayer), *vern aroys fun di keylim* ("lose one's temper"); the merged Hebrew term *moneshekh* ("either or"); the words *moshl* ("example") and *terets* ("justification"). In contrast to the richness of Yiddish, the Hebrew University has only one response: *shalom*. Significantly, this term appears, not in the orthography customarily used for Hebrew-Aramaic words in Yiddish, but rather phonetically, as if it were not of Hebrew-Aramaic origin. Thus, the form of *Tsvishn minkhe un mayrev* emphasizes its thematic point: by undercutting Yiddish and by refusing to show respect for the older and more fertile tradition from which the language derives its life and complexity, speakers of Hebrew reveal their naivete and spiritual poverty.

The circumstances of the poem *Yidish* are very different from those of *Tsvishn minkhe un mayrev* but its message is similar.[4] This work, set in New York rather than Israel, concerns a recently widowed Jew from Venezuela who has come to the United States, in part to do business but with the added hope of finding a new wife to take home with him. Aided by well-meaning friends and relatives, he is brought together with a woman who is not only *oysbrakirt* ("rejected") but none-too-young, since she is *bald . . . azoy alt/Vi ir mame vos hot zikh bishtike oysgeveynt di oygn*. ("Almost . . . as old/As her mother, who surreptitiously cried her heart out.").

The problem with the businessman is that he speaks Yiddish—not in an offhand, casual manner, but rather: *Vi dos volt nisht geven af der vayl,/Nor gor af takhles*. ("As if it were not for the time being,/But indeed a serious business."). The girl and her parents vary in their responses to the Jew and his language, but none of them are positively disposed. The father's reaction is the mildest;

sighing, he decides *az s'iz alts taluy bimazl.* ("that everything depends on luck."). The mother is deeply affronted, hurt that her daughter, the American-born child of a United States citizen, should suffer the indignity of being approached by one who speaks like an immigrant. The daughter, who has little desire to marry in any case, recoils from the would-be suitor with the greatest anger and contempt, because he reminds her of the Eastern European heritage that she has spent years attempting to evade. The Venezuelan, having become so intoxicated by his own speech that he imagines the match already settled, could not be more mistaken. His Yiddish, which both connects him with and sets him apart from the faded and depressed family into which he has wandered, signifies his rejection in the end. Because the widower's world of Yiddish is perceived by the woman as old-fashioned and impotent, it becomes her reason for dismissing him as a marriage possibility: *zi hot gor itst ufgeshmeykhlt in zikh a frage:/Vi azoy hot an amerikaner meydl/ Kinder mit aza man, vos redt yidish?* ("she smiled a question to herself even now:/How can an American girl have/Children with a man who speaks Yiddish?").

The abiding problem of Jewish assimilation in America, upon which Glatshteyn had touched in *Moyshe leybs kol* and *Shomer*, assumed especially ominous gravity in the wake of the Holocaust. The narrator/protagonist of *Monolog in driter perzon* ["Monologue in third person"] (pp. 130–34), however, refuses to see the dangers to Jewish continuity implicit in the weakening of cultural and religious ties. In this poem, an old candystore owner who has worked his way up from such ventures as pushcart peddler and milkman (*A brukliner tevye der milkhiker*—"A Brooklyn Tevye the Milkman") muses contentedly about his life. He revels in being a full and committed Jew and does not worry that his three sons, whom he has forced to accept a Jewish education, no longer have time for Jewish matters— and had never wanted to be concerned with them in the first place. Rather, they have achieved what would seem to be a second-generation dream, but which the old Jew appears to regard with some measure of regret: *vi af umistn/Zaynen ale dray gevorn dentistn.* ("as if on purpose/All three became dentists."). But their father is not worried; pleased that he has tricked his sons into absorbing some *yiddishkeyt,* he remains confident that they will one day appreciate the good deed he has done for them:

Itst hobn zey nit keyn tsayt, m'rayst tseyn.
Nor ay hot dos a koyekh.
Af der elter veln zey ersht onhoybn farshteyn
Un derfiln dem tam derfun.

Now they have no time—they're pulling teeth.
But oh, does that [*yiddishkeyt*] have power.
When they are older, they will begin to understand
And sense the taste of it.

In the meanwhile, the father enjoys his own *yiddishkeyt*, convinced that he has discovered its true meaning: *Yidishkeyt iz tuevdike gutskeyt* ("Yiddishkeyt is active goodness"). In his dotage, the old Jew makes a vocation of being fully Jewish, just as previously he had dedicated himself to his candy store.

The mood of *Monolog in driter perzon* is cheerful and accepting without being resigned. The father does not consider his sons assimilated, merely uninterested at present. And he is perfectly at ease with the English that has crept into his own Yiddish: *storke* ("little store"), *vokayshon* ("vocation"), *lalipap* ("lollypop"), *flors* ("floors"), *kontriy* ("country"). It mixes well with his folksy tone—reminiscent of the simple and intimate speech of Reb Nakhmen—in which a variety of informal terms are incorporated for emphasis and clarity: *nebekh* ("unfortunately"), *abiy* ("as long as"), *tsurik-geshmuest* ("on the other hand"), *mamesh* ("literally"), *mishteyns-gezogt* ("alas"), *opgeton . . . af terkish* ("play a dirty trick"). The old Jew's vocabulary is emblematic of the integration he has made in his own life and which he evidently expects to see perpetuated in his sons: a comfortable adjustment to America that is simultaneously anchored in a deeply committed Jewish orientation.

But this is a monologue related in third, rather than first, person, suggesting that the old Jew is distanced from himself. In his calm satisfaction with his existence, he overlooks the obvious dangers to Jewish religious and cultural continuity in America. His richly comprehensive Jewish perspective, revealed both in his speech and in the ideas he expresses, makes assimilation impossible for him, but says nothing about what will happen to his sons. In *Dem tatns shotn*, *Monolog in driter perzon* occurs directly after *Yidish*, where intensely hostile feelings towards Eastern European *yiddishkeyt* were described. When these two poems are juxtaposed, what at first appear to be opposing views are revealed as complementary, for each describes an East European Jew blissfully unaware of the contempt in which his identity is held.

III   *Literary Evaluation and Reevaluation*

For Glatshteyn, the issue of incorporating traditional Jewish values into a secular framework reverberated everywhere. At the same time as he was bemoaning the demise of Yiddish and the progressive corrosion caused by assimilation, he expressed his admiration for two poets who, while eluding parochial constraints, had nonetheless functioned as important models for their Yiddish literary successors. Now, as the language of their communication was fading, Glatshteyn sought to commemorate their achievements, and he did so in a specifically Jewish fashion, since both *Dovid Edelshtat* ["Dovid Edelshtat"] (pp. 179–81) and *Yortsayt lid: M.L. Halpern* ["Yortsayt poem: M.L. Halpern"] (pp. 189–90) are *yortsayt* ("anniversary of death") poems. The importance of Edelshtat has emerged in retrospect, the narrator of *Dovid Edelshtat* explains. Only now, when intricate language and sophisticated ideas may seem useless and superfluous, do modern Yiddish poets seek comfort in the banalities and clichés of this revolutionary elder. Assuming for them the religious elevation of a *tsadek*, a saint, Edelshtat epitomizes the dignity of writing simple words in order to encourage and move a suffering audience: *Mir, vos hobn gekletert af verter bravadish,/Veln zukhn remozim in dayn poetisher klor,* ("We, who scaled words with bravado,/Will search for hints in your poetic clarity,").

Unlike his newly discerned appreciation of Edelshtat, Glatshteyn's respect for Moyshe Leyb Halpern was one of long standing. As early as the 1930's he had acknowledged his own special debt to Halpern. The narrator of *Yortsayt lid: M.L. Halpern* praises the earlier poet's contribution to an entire generation of Yiddish writers. As the symbol of Yiddish bohemian life, he had introduced a new literary perspective into his milieu, insisting upon fighting Jewish battles from outside the typical paradigm:

> *Bist geven meylekh fun a yidisher melukhe,*
> *Gants on yidishe shrekn.*
> *Host zey getribn fun zikh mit a goyeshn shtekn,*
> *. . . In milkhome mit yidishe problemen*
> *. . . Bistu keynmol nisht gefaln keyn dershepter.*

You were king of a Jewish state,
Completely without Jewish fears.
You chased them from yourself with a non-Jewish stick,
 . . . In [the] war against Jewish problems
 . . . You never fell exhausted.

Glatshteyn was not interested in Dovid Edelshtat and Moyshe Leyb Halpern purely for the sake of memorializing them, however. As he had done in the past, he was looking to his precursors as sources of inspiration in dealing with the complexities of his own role as a post-Holocaust Yiddish poet. During the early and mid-1940's, Glatshteyn's duties had been obvious and inescapable, even if he felt uncomfortable that his subject matter had been restricted and his voice necessarily public. Now his position was less well defined. The sense that he must be as clear and socially committed as an Edelshtat warred in him with the desire to be true to himself in the manner of Halpern. To persist in using the style and substance of his Holocaust poetry seemed unwarranted; moreover, Glatshteyn feared for the quality of his art.

The narrators of *Yidishkeyt* ["Yiddishkeyt"] (pp. 137–38) and *A briv tsu zikh* ["A letter to myself"] (pp. 105–06) criticize themselves for having allowed sentimentality and predictability to creep into their work, thereby cheapening what remained an unspeakable catastrophe. *Yidishkeyt* begins as a general condemnation of nostalgic impulses in Jewish life, the desire to flee to a world that no longer exists and perhaps never did. The central object of the narrator's disapproval, however, is not the Jew in general, but rather the Jewish poet, who has compromised his sense of art. The narrator worries that the influence of maudlin feelings will reduce poetry to folksong, which tugs at the heart and *gist on mit varemen honik/Fun dermonung di gederem* ("fills the intestines/With warm honey of remembrance"). The poet, by becoming a honey gathering bee, is guilty of contributing raw material to the downfall of productive *yiddishkeyt*. He thus renders himself no more than a *meshoyrer*— a choirboy in a synagogue—who follows a derivative Jewish path and performs in an artistic mode but is not a true artist himself. Having been coopted by a general negative mood, he satisfies himself *Mit an omeyn in khor fun untergang* ("With an amen in the chorus of decline"), and avoids his artistic responsibility. By harping on the past instead of progressing, the poet unwittingly participates in the destruction of his own culture.

Yiddishkeyt based on longing is not only unsophisticated and automatic, the narrator declares; it is a limp soporific, providing fodder for old people who must consume their *khale*—the Sabbath bread that is a mark of their connection with tradition—in pap form. And he challenges himself and his colleagues: *Zoln mir tsushteln di veykhe krishkes,/Di verter oysgelebte un hoyle,* ("Shall we provide the soft crumbs,/The lived-out and hollow words,")?

In the poem *A briv tsu zikh,* Glatshteyn approaches the same dilemma from a perspective more aesthetic than cultural. The narrator warns himself that he is becoming a *balebatisher rebel* ("genteel, comfortable rebel"), that although he may appear to be an *enfant terrible,* in reality he conforms to the expectations of others. Using imagery reminiscent of that in *Yidishkeyt,* he asks: *Ober vifl teplekh honik kenstu fartrogn?* ("But how many cups of honey can you stomach?")—How much sweet reward for yielding to authority can be absorbed? In fact, the narrator has lost what he knows is most important for him: his sense of artistic loneliness, his mark of individuality and integrity. He thinks back onto his past, when he had rejoiced in his literary iconoclasm, his true rebellion: *On moyre bistu geshvumen/Antkegn ale gegramte shifn.* ("Without fear you swam/Against all rhymed ships."). His poetry may have been obscure, but it was an honest representation of his intense relationship to language.

Now he has abandoned earlier sensitivities and strengths to embrace a more acceptable mode of writing. In a word, he has become clear. In *Fun a briv,* this clarity was rationalized as necessary because of historical circumstances; here it is merely the result of weakness. As a denial of the narrator's deepest artistic needs, it is an abdication rather than the salutary restructuring of aesthetic priorities in the service of a shattered community. Though the devastation wrought by the Holocaust may be the underlying cause of his new approach, the narrator views it as illegitimate: *Host zey akegngetrogn gantse koyshn klorkeyt./Dayn valdik gemit iz nokh itst farplontert./Ober afile du aleyn kumst dort nisht arayn/Host moyre far dayn eynzamkeyt.* ("You have carried towards them entire baskets of clarity./Your forest-like spirit is still tangled now./But even you do not enter it/You're afraid of your loneliness."). In fulfillment of one obligation, a communal, historical one, he has failed to live up to another—his artistic commitment to himself.[5]

The narrator proceeds to define the nature of his problem more explicitly: by concentrating on meaning, he has lost his delight in pure language. Inasmuch as he has confronted and survived the essence of death, his response is understandable, but it remains suspect. Hence the narrator's loneliness takes on a new dimension. No longer rooted in aesthetic individuality, it stems from the dread of obscurity. He needs his shrunken audience as much as it needs him. Thus he imagines that the ordeal of Eastern European Jewry and, by extension, of the Yiddish language, has directly reduced the quality of his poetry. Moreover, to the degree that the communal role he has adopted is based on selfish motives, his work is demeaned still further. The narrator accuses himself: *Bistu der troyer-marshalik,/Der aplodirter kloger,/Der forzoger fun a gantser eyde shtume leftsn.* ("You are the sadness-jester,/The applauded mourner,/The spokesman for an entire community of mute lips."). He challenges himself to crow as he longs to do—not the communal warning of *Gedenklider*'s *Gezangen*, but rather the personal statement that he has stifled. He need only return to the *fartsvaygtn, mokhikn plonter* ("branched, mossy tangle") of the forest that still lies within him. Like Yosl Loksh and Reb Nakhmen, the narrator translates his idea of freedom into images of nature.

But a return to the realm of deeply personal expression requires the courage to relinquish centrality. The crucial question for the narrator of *A briv tsu zikh* is whether he has become so dependent on the prospect of being acclaimed and remembered that he can no longer tolerate the loneliness of individuality and independence. He answers this question at the conclusion of the poem by implying that he will not reenter his forest: *Neyn? vest nisht? vorn ikh dikh, fundestvegn, afn oyer./Faran in dir an eygener,/Nisht nor a koolsher troyer.* ("No? You won't? I warn you confidentially nonetheless./There is in you an individual,/Not only a public sadness."). This tension—between recognizing the need for personal poetic loyalty and feeling the charge to write publicly, despite an inherent toll on artistic quality—underlies much of the poetry in *Dem tatns shotn*.

IV   *The Birth of a Jewish State*

One public issue that Glatshteyn could not avoid was the emergence of Israel, which occupied his attention in the series of nine

short poems collectively entitled *Gezangen* ["Songs"] (pp. 70–74).
Exuding a sense of new beginning and growth, these works also
define Israel as a final resting place for the victims of the Holocaust.
The land is a refuge for everyone: as the narrator inventively com-
ments, it is *farmaynikt* ("made mine") for his own body, which has
been *farpaynikt* ("tortured"); Israel is a place where survivors can
revitalize themselves and participate in the building of a fresh new
realm. Here, too, those who have not survived may nonetheless be
brought together: *Oyb nisht undzer lebn,/Zol do ayngezamlt vern
undzer shtarbn.* ("If not our life,/Let our death be gathered in
here."). The narrator envisions a kind of messianic dream state, in
which prophets or punishers will no longer be needed because evil
will have disappeared. And all this can occur without waiting for
a future age: *O, dos vet geshen in undzere eygene teg.* ("Oh, this
will happen in our own days.").

As he constructs and transmits his positive concept of Israel, the
narrator realizes that it is fashioned more out of inherited knowledge
than experience. Conceding that he is not very familiar with the
actual geography of Israel, he goes on to say, in the last poem of
Gezangen—which plays a summary role not only by its position but
by the overview nature of its content—that he can nonetheless reach
and perceive it through the shortcut of religious texts: *Mit a kapitl
tilim/Ken ikh dikh glaykh dergreykhn.* ("With a chapter of Psalms/I
can reach you directly."). Finally, then, the weight of tradition is
revealed as more important than immediate events in the narrator's
understanding of Palestine and the new state of Israel.

The validity and significance of this Eastern European perspective
is the central point of another poem, *Fort a yid* ["A Jew travels"]
(p. 48). The title is interesting; not only does it foreshadow the
poem's first line: *Fort a yid keyn erets yisroel,* ("A Jew travels to
Palestine,"), but it can also mean "still a Jew," hence underscoring
the insistence on maintaining a particular idea of heritage. This Jew,
whose family has been tortured and killed, experiences a mixture
of emotions as he approaches Palestine. The closer he gets to the
gate, the less he feels he can allow himself to live: *Veynen in im ale
freydn.* ("All his joys cry in him."). Confronted by a hero with a
bared sword who threatens to attack him if he cannot express his
joy in song, the refugee continues to cry. But the hero does not
carry out his threat; instead, he joins the Jew who has suffered so
greatly: *Veynt der giber un er leygt di shverd in sheyd,/Un beyde*

tantsn veynendik durkhn toyer. ("The hero cries and places the sword in its sheath,/And both dance through the gate weeping.").

Two matters are at issue here. One is the possibility of disagreement between Jews over how to act with respect to Israel; the other is the question of physical force, the use of weapons as a Jewish response to danger or disobedience. In *Fort a yid*, the traditional Jew prevails, and there is no violence. But in other works, Glatshteyn explores Israeli divergence from Eastern European values, symbolized for him in part by the new nation's dependence on military might. In the poem *S'redt der alter yid* ["The old Jew speaks"] (pp. 63–66), Glatshteyn gently takes to task those who would argue that Jews died in the Holocaust like sheep, emphasizing that cowardice—not only historically, but in the present as well—is a necessary and valuable Jewish trait. The poem is preceded by a dedication to the heroic endurance and clever prowess of the fighters in Palestine, and its first line reads: *Heylik iz di yidishe gvure, heylik.* ("Jewish heroism is holy, holy."). Thereafter, the narrator begins subtly to undermine and withdraw this praise, indicating that the only reason Jews are alive to take risks today is that for two thousand years they have been apprehensive: *In yeder dor darf zikh undzer folk/Abisl shrekn,/Kedey tsu lebn.* ("In every generation our people must/Be a bit fearful,/In order to live.").

Far from being a cause for embarrassment, however, this Eastern European Jewish characteristic is a proof of strength, since survival in a dangerous and precarious world requires courage. The narrator declares that he would rather live timidly than die in glory and admires his ancestors for having done the same. He reaches the kernel of his argument when he defends those Jews who suffered the penalty of death because they could not escape their enemies. There is no shame in the fact that *afile in toyt/Zaynen zey geven vi shof—/Vi in lebn.* ("even in death/They were like sheep—/As in life."). If their lives as cowards were meaningful, then their deaths are also worthy of respect.

Indeed, that Jews now have a *shlakht-feld* ("battlefield") instead of an *antloyf-feld* ("escape field") is due to the fact that individual Jews, by managing to stay alive, had also succeeded in maintaining a continuous Jewish tradition. The narrator concludes by blessing the brave Jewish fighters but hoping as well that they will run away *fun nayn shlakhtn mit khokhme/Kedey tsu gevinen di tsente shlakht fun lebn.* ("from nine battles with wisdom/In order to win the tenth battle of life.").

V *Recapturing the Past*

Despite its promise, Israel remained for Glatshteyn a place where Eastern European Jews who insisted upon upholding their values and outlook risked the disdain of those around them. Nor did the United States seem any better a substitute for the world that no longer existed. As if to counteract his sense of estrangement, Glatshteyn attempted to rediscover the essence of the past that had encompassed his only true home. In a number of poems, he sought to create that period anew, as if it were the present, and to eternalize it in his art.[6] At the same time, from the safety of this realm, he managed to find some respite from the burdens of his self-imposed public yoke.

In the poem *Kh'vel zikh ayngloybern* ["I'll believe into myself"] (pp. 38–39)—which achieves the private, ambiguous expression longed for by the narrator of *A briv tsu zikh*—Glatshteyn discusses this reconstructive process and points out the difficulty of revivifying a past that has no reflex in the present. The narrator begins by stating that he will compel himself to believe in a little speck of wonder that blurs his sight as far back in time as he can see or dream. His darkened vision picks up the bright fragment of a star that has managed to survive destruction. This salvaged bit of planet, reaching him from the past, enables the narrator to be reminded of a flourishing world without having to face his present bleak situation. He recalls a place *Vos hot amol gehat lebn,/Grine shefe, pashedike zet.* ("That once had life,/Green abundance, pastureful plenty."). Now, however, the sky is one of *eybikn untergang* ("eternal sunset"), advancing unremittingly towards death. Nature is no longer thriving: *Di bleter . . . vign zikh vi gleker,/Batoybte, on klang,/Af fun keynem-nisht-gezeene beymer/In a leydiker velt.* ("The leaves . . . sway like bells,/Deafened, without sound,/On trees seen by no one/In an empty world.").

The image of the speck of wonder gains depth as the narrator declares that he will plant himself in a wonder-surrounded night of his own invention. Claiming a tiny spot in space, *Vi a flig di groys,* ("The size of a fly,"), he will construct his vision, *mit gvald* ("by force") and *af ale tsaytn* ("for all time"). Thus, the speck that had initially allowed the narrator to dim his perspective now functions as a container for the images he wishes to animate. At the center he puts a cradle and a child, continuing: *Araynzingen in dem a kol/Fun a drimlendikn tatn,/Mit a ponem in kol,/Mit libshaft in kol,* ("To sing into it a voice/Of a dozing father,/With a face in his voice,/With love in his voice,"). The sound-filled spectacle expands around the cradle to include a Jewish city, complete with a synagogue and a wakeful God who guards it in all its poverty and fear. It is an anxious community lacking in glamour, but at least it is alive.

In the end, however, the narrator realizes that his attempt to elude pain by rigidifying former days in a loving vision is doomed to failure. He cannot forget that the past, in which his only happiness is preserved, also contains the horrible destruction of that happiness; he is forced to acknowledge that the loud and lively Jewish world of old has been silenced, *Un in maydanek veldl/Mit etlekhe shos fartilikt.* ("And in Maidanek Grove/Exterminated with a few shots.").

In the poem *Tsayt* ["Time"] (pp. 16–17), Glatshteyn attempts to reattain his origins in a different way, this time seeking to distinguish between events recollected in memory and those literally relived by an act of moving backwards in time. The incident recalled by the narrator is a simple one: as a child, returning home from school on a wintry evening, he had experienced the comfort and pleasure of placing his freezing hand in his father's warm one. Years later, the narrator discovers that to return to that precise point and to find his father alive within it would require incalculable effort, not only because the moment continually recedes further into the past, but also—and chiefly—because it had originally occurred in the life of a little boy for whom *A tog un a nakht zaynen geven sezonen.* ("A day and a night were seasons."). The expanse that would have to be covered is therefore qualitative as well as quantitative, as the narrator stresses:

> *Avade iz gring tsuriktsutrakhtn,*
> *Ober tsuriklebn meynt poshet tsurikshpanen,*
> *Nemen af zikh dem ol*
> *Fun voglen un durkhshnaydn*
> *Eygene midboryes un sambatyens.*

> Of course it is easy to think back,
> But to live back means simply to stride back,
> To assume the burden
> Of wandering and traversing
> Individual deserts and Sambations.[7]

The image of the desert implies many arduous years, while the Sambation signifies distance and unrest. Clearly then, the way back—its importance underscored by the triple use of *tsurik* ("back") as a verbal complement—is lined with the difficulties of personal history.

Another source of obstruction is revealed as the narrator continues: *Az ikh zol onkumen punkt tsu yenem baynakht,/Darf ikh durkhgeyn, ver veyst,/Vifl khurbones.* ("In order for me to arrive exactly at that night,/I must go through who knows/How many Holocausts."). Once again the Holocaust intrudes as a destructive barrier between present and past. Finally, the narrator is forced to admit that he lacks the agility for the journey he contemplates: he is simply too old. He and his dead father may look back in memory but they cannot reach back in time. The poem concludes with the narrator's comment that, for those who are able to block out certain periods in their lives, time may indeed fly *Vi in di farbenkste folks-lider.* ("Like in the most yearning folk-songs."), but it cannot do so for him, because he refuses to eliminate any part of his experience: his existence cannot be telescoped. By insisting on facing the totality of his past, the narrator remains confronted with the same problem as the narrator of *Kh'vel zikh ayngloybern:* he is stymied as he endeavors both to be historically faithful and to avoid the impact of the Holocaust. The narrator of *Kh'vel zikh ayngloybern* had failed in his attempt to recreate a lost world through imagination. Here, the narrator is no more successful in his struggle to regain a bygone period through recaptured time.

The impulse to use childhood events as a basis for reflecting on, and giving extra meaning to, adult occurrences was not new in *Tsayt*. Already at the outset of his career, in *Tirtl-toybn*, Glatshteyn had explored his earliest years. In *A vort* ["A word"] (pp. 20–21), he returns to *kheyder* years and to a word. But this poem, although it may be outwardly similar to its earlier counterpart, is radically different in both form and function. *Tirtl-toybn* deals with the narrator's private musings about a specific word that had affected him

at one point in his childhood. Additionally—perhaps more signifi-
cantly—its primary concern is the narrator's associative process. In
A vort, as its title suggests, fundamental importance does not lie
in the particular definition or sound of a word, but rather in the
warm memories it can arouse. For the narrator, recollection leads
to thoughts of the childhood relationship he had enjoyed with his
parents, and the word is crucial only because it allows him to create
this mental connection.

There is another way as well in which *A vort* differs from Glat-
shteyn's earlier poem. Not only does the narrator remove himself
from the center of the work—a stance that would be inappropriate
to the egocentric and associative narrator of *Tirtl-toybn*—but he
turns his attention outward, to an audience: *Ir vet es ale derkenen/Un
ir vet zikh zetsn varemen/Arum dem likhtikn vort*, ("You will all
recognize it/And you will sit down to warm yourselves/Around the
bright word,"). This word brings to the narrator's mind the fears
and revelatory wonder of his first day in *kheyder*, when his father
had tossed raisins and almonds onto his *talis* [prayer shawl]-covered
head to symbolize the hope that Torah study would always be sweet
for him. Describing his satisfied response to life at that period and
referring again, as in *Tsayt*, to the child's special perception of time,
the narrator remarks to his audience:

> *Derfiln vet ir dem heyvn*
> *Fun kindisher, varemer eybikeyt,*
> *Fun zikhern shlof,*
> *Fun ersht-geefnte oygn.*

> You will sense the yeast
> Of childish, warm eternity,
> Of secure sleep,
> Of just-opened eyes.

This is not so much a poem about a word, then, as about the
narrator's early realization of separation from, and connection to,
his parents. Here, Glatshteyn's investigation of time as a means of
remembering the past without cheapening it results in a novel so-
lution. For the subject matter of *A vort* parallels its intention: on
a narrative level, it concerns a child's simultaneous closeness to and
growing distance from his parents within a time span which at that
point was experienced as eternal, but is now related from the per-

spective of an adult looking back; on another level, however, its purpose is to maintain an eternal bond with the past while at the same time recognizing and accepting its irrevocable remoteness.

The examination of time as a phenomenon, and the tendency— evidenced in *Tsayt* and in *A vort*—to memorialize early childhood moments, reach their pinnacle in a series of four short poems collectively entitled *Shneyike shnitn* ["Marks in the snow"] (pp. 17–19). In one poem of the group, the narrator communicates his desire for permanence, stating as his aim the wish to write for eternity. He reveals why early episodes are especially important to him:

> *Oyb shraybn far der eybikeyt*
> *Meynt shraybn vi m'volt aleyn geven eybik,*
> *Volt ikh zikh farleygt af a kleynikeyt,*
> *Vider un oberamol volt ikh tsurikgekumen*
> *Tsum zelbikn:*
> *Mestn in tsayt fun a dervoksenem*
> *Di freyd fun a tog kindheyt.*

> If writing for eternity
> Means writing as if one were eternal
>   himself,
> I would set my heart on a trifle,
> Again and again I would come back
> To the same thing:
> To measure in an adult's time span
> The joy of a day of childhood.

Previously, the narrator had explained that for a child, something as simple as running after a butterfly could contain a year's worth of meaning and require even longer than that to retell. Now the narrator knows that although it is possible to recall experience, he will never be able actually to relive it; at most, he can hope to recapture intensity. Hence he quips wryly, greeting a cow from his immortal past: *Mu tsu aykh fun a bintl beyner,/Mu tsu aykh fun mid fleysh.* ("Moo to you from a bundle of bones,/Moo to you from tired flesh.").[8] Memory is not the same as movement back into the past, but by transmitting a sense of what time itself has signified to a young mind, the impression of eternity may be evoked.

The final poem of *Shneyike shnitn* centers on the image chosen by Glatshteyn to represent his entire 1953 volume: his father's shadow. In this work, the narrator once again laments the futility of attempting to revive the past. He begins by commenting:

> *Shoyn bald tsayt tsu zukhn takhles.*
> *Shoyn bald tsayt tsu gefinen khotsh etlekhe verter,*
> *Vos zoln zayn azoy doyerevdik,*
> *Vi der shotn fun tatn*
> *Af dem frish-gefalenem shney*

> It's almost time to search for substance.
> It's almost time to find at least a few words,
> That will be as durable,
> As my father's shadow
> On the freshly-fallen snow.

The irony of these lines is at once sharp and poignant in its complexity. The narrator's choice of transitory phenomena to indicate permanence subtly exposes his helplessness and underscores his bitter comprehension that the effort to sustain recalled experience through art must ultimately fail. For, as the product of a mortal and changing mind, memory itself is fleeting, slipping away almost at the point of contemplation. Indeed, *Shneyike shnitn* concludes with the narrator's revelation that his father's shadow—which was to symbolize the eternity of a moment—has disappeared, yielding a past lacking in reflection even as it is remembered.

In a sense, Glatshteyn's attempt to immortalize his father's shadow signifies as well the tragedy of his ties to all of Eastern European Jewry, whose existence had proved to be equally ephemeral. Moreover, the narrator understands that even the creation of an eternal verbal recollection—were it possible for him to achieve—would not in the end be meaningful, since the very language that could regain the past had perished along with its speakers. This realization lies behind the narrator's peculiarly ambivalent comment that he must *bald* ("soon") search for expression: while urgently enjoining himself to capture an elusive vision, he admits at the same time that he is already too late. In the search for his father's shadow, then, Glatshteyn is able to indicate both his private misery and the agony of post-Holocaust Jewry.

VI   *The Bratslaver Reconciled?*

In *Dem tatns shotn,* as in earlier volumes, Glatshteyn assumed the voice of Reb Nakhmen of Bratslav, using the simple eloquence of the Hasidic master to explore his innermost conflicts and come to some apparent resolutions. *Der bratslaver zingt nigunim* ["The Bratslaver sings *nigunim* (melodies)"] (pp. 77–82), is comprised of five short poems. In the first of these, the Bratslaver declares that his apparent pride and conceit is in fact due to a deep understanding of how small he actually is—and this insight paradoxically imbues him with some sense of greatness. His is a pride based on belief in God.

Nonetheless, Nakhmen is uncertain about how good a Jew he is, or even what being a Jew, let alone a good one, signifies; these thoughts occupy him in the third poem of *Der bratslaver zingt nigunim*. Of all the *nigunim*, this work is most closely constructed to resemble a Hasidic melody; its lines, peppered with *tshiri boms*— meaningless syllables used instead of words in the *nign*—contain a good deal of anaphora as well and thereby approximate a lively song rhythm. The poem is cheerful in its message, stressing warmth and simplicity as the ideal qualities of a good Jew:

> . . . *kule gutskeyt,*
> *Kule hartsikeyt,*
> *Kule libshaft,*
> *Kule frumkeyt,*
> *Oy s'meynt dokh zayn a yid.*

> . . . Complete goodness,
> Complete sincerity,
> Complete love,
> Complete piety,
> Oy, that means being a Jew.

The poem ends on a note of doubt, however, with Nakhmen assuring himself that he is a good Jew, then immediately questioning his own assumption.

This insecurity about his Jewishness appears in a somewhat different form in the next *nign*, where the Bratslaver begs God not to shield him from the miseries endured by other Jews. In Nakhmen's interpretation, it is a privilege to suffer—a sign of God's attention rather than a punishment. Hence, he feels cheated and ignored because he is not subjected to the same trials as they: *Farvos zolstu mikh nisht shlogn,/Mit alts tsubislekh baloynen,/Fun dayn umendlekhn shtrof-khesed?/Fun dayn groysn shtrof-shpaykh-*

ler? ("Why shouldn't you beat me,/Reward me little by little with everything/From your endless punishment-grace?/From your great punishment-storehouse?").

The poems of *Der bratslaver zingt nigunim* are not only an investigation of Nakhmen's battle with faith and ideas, but summarize as well the historical struggles of Yankev Glatshteyn. Tradition as a positive means of facing death and annihilation (but perhaps too difficult to maintain precisely under the conditions that demand it most), guilt at surviving the Holocaust, reevaluation of his own position as a Jew—all these conflicts are encapsulated here. So, too, is the issue of coming to terms with Israel. The Bratslaver's *nigunim* end on a note of messianic hope and trust: Nakhmen relates a prophetic vision in which he had started out alone, walking towards Palestine. Soon he was joined by one Jew, and then by many: *a gantse velt mit yidn* ("a whole world of Jews"), and together they continued their jubilant march. Palestine, impatiently awaiting their arrival, had come to meet them. Suddenly, all the walking sticks used by the wanderers had turned into rifles and swords. But there is a happy ending; having served as weapons, the sticks had been transformed again, this time changing into *freylekhe grob-ayzns* ("cheerful digging instruments") singing *hallel*, a hymn of praise. Thus Nakhmen predicts a contented and peaceful future for Israel: this is his way of reconciling the anxieties of the preceding *nigunim*.

Nakhmen's ability to achieve a measure of equilibrium by the end of *Der bratslaver zingt nigunim* is seen as well in other poems of which he is the narrator, but in these the focus is much narrower, alternating between two problematic areas: the question of how to respond to mourning and suffering, and the difficulties of the artist attempting to react to tragedy. In the first part of *Davnen minkhe* ["Praying the afternoon prayer"] (pp. 82–84), Nakhmen discusses two separate, although connected, themes. On one level, as the title suggests, he describes the beauty of the afternoon service and the joy of prayer; but his comments reveal that he is concerned with far more than *minkhe per se:* for Nakhmen, this prayer is a link with eternity. As he describes it, although human beings cannot participate in creation, the afternoon prayer enables the worshiper to accompany a day to its rest. And, in doing so, the individual sees that days do not disappear, but rather remain forever, forming their own sort of eternity. Nakhmen's mood is quietly optimistic. He does not fear the arrival of night; rather, he accepts the end of day without associating it with finality. On the contrary, night implies immortality to him. Through Nakhmen's concrete, nature oriented perceptions, then, Glatshteyn achieves the link with eternity that had escaped him in the more abstract realm of memory.

Juxtaposed with the first section of *Davnen minkhe* is another section, also about the afternoon service, but with an entirely different perspective and message. Nakhmen relates that once, while praying *minkhe* after a stint of fasting, he had heard his grandfather's voice asking why he so enjoyed mortifying his flesh. What had he done to deserve such punishment? From his grandfather's words, Nakhmen had understood that when submitting himself to orgies of fasting, he was in fact seeking to inflate and elevate himself. His suffering was a perverse form of pleasure and self-aggrandizement rather than exactly the opposite. Nakhmen explains that at that point he had learned the meaning of humility: *mit mayne kleyntshike aveyres/Darf ikh zikh nit groysn./M'darf zayn a mentsh/Un zikh aleyn kenen fargebn.* ("About my tiny sins/I don't have to boast./One must be a human being/And be able to forgive oneself.").

The issue of self-indulgence versus true misery is explored more fully in *Faran aza gekekhts vi hunger* ["There's such a dish as hunger"] (pp. 87–93); Nakhmen's comments in this work are catalyzed by a poor man's request for help in finding work. Moved by the abject circumstances of his fellow human being, Nakhmen contemplates the ease of his own existence, realizing that for him fasting is not a way of life but rather a hypocritical act of self-denial that he is free to enjoy because he engages in it by choice. In contrast, the one who truly suffers while fasting is the poor man for whom hunger is unavoidable. In an allusion to the way in which art trivializes misery, Nakhmen declares: *Moykhl, zing mir nisht keyn lider./Mentshn hobn sholem gemakht mit di lidlekh,/Zey ongenumen far lib,/ Yenems hunger, yenems noyt,/Gramt zikh mit eygn broyt.* ("No thanks, don't sing me any songs./People have accepted the little songs,/Put up with them,/That one's hunger, that one's need,/Rhymes with one's own bread."). *Noyt* and *broyt* may rhyme, but the empathy that occurs through art is spurious because it is not motivated by experience. Here, Glatshteyn hints at a concern he would later state explicitly: because he has been spared the horrors of the Holocaust, perhaps he has no right to agonize as if he had actually undergone them.

The task of a Nakhmen, therefore, is not to chastise himself for imaginary deviations from the path of righteousness, and not to believe that he is afflicted when he is not, but rather to perceive where the true misery of the world lies and devote himself to its eradication. In this way, through the persona of Nakhmen, Glatshteyn aired his need to avoid what had become self-serving punishments and to concentrate instead on grappling with the many immediate problems entering his awareness.

Glatshteyn attempted to resolve another of his artistic difficulties—the sense that popularization was compromising his authenticity—in the poem *Der bratslaver git aroys a tshuve* ["The Bratslaver issues a reply"] (pp. 84–86). Here, Nakhmen addresses a writer who, by becoming famous, has lost his self-respect and sense of responsibility. The disavowal of poverty, anonymity, and the right to be silent has resulted in his abuse by others: they have stripped him, shamed him, and finally failed to appreciate his work. Nakhmen's advice to this individual is: *Barakh, antloyf fun zey./Zaml tsurik on azoyfil gezang,/Vifl s'iz dir nokh bashert.* ("Escape, run away from them./Reclaim as much singing,/As is still given to you.").

Throughout his career, Glatshteyn had connected his devotion to literature with the specific issue of language as a force possessing an almost tangible energy. Significantly, the last poem of this Bratslaver series—*Her un shtoyn* ["Hear and be amazed"] (pp. 93–97), which occurs after the references to literary role contained in *Faran aza gekekhts vi hunger* and *Der bratslaver git aroys a tshuve*, is a revelation of Nakhmen's passionate commitment to speech. Inasmuch as this poem provides an oblique reference to the life of a modern poet, speech becomes a metaphor for poetic language and a metonym of communication in general. Nakhmen begins his tale by giving Nosn its moral: he will sacrifice anything in order not to lose his *shenste kroyn—dos vort* ("most beautiful crown—the word"). He proceeds to explain how he had once been thrown while riding a donkey; subsequently confronted by a supernatural creature who informed him that he was now *altsloz af der velt* ("all-less in the world"), Nakhmen relates how his greatest mortification had come as he realized that he could no longer speak. He had been taken to paradise, had seen his great-grandfather, and had learned that he was destined to remain mute. In response to this fate, Nakhmen had caused such commotion that his speech had been returned to him.

Of course, Nakhmen concludes, it had all been a dream, but one that had taught him a lesson: he can have no interest in paradise if he must be silent there. Rather, he prefers his present life, for it allows him: *Do af der zindiker velt—/Reydn un reydn un reydn.* ("Here in the sinful world—/To talk and talk and talk."). In *Her un shtoyn* then, Nakhmen has decided to stay amidst difficulties and discuss them, even if that means postponing—or never reaching at all—tranquility and acclaim. The Bratslaver, whose entire world had revolved around his desire to elevate himself, now rejects that in favor of remaining active.

The use of Yiddish in this series of Bratslav poems reflects an attempt to render it living, to make hackneyed language take on new vitality. In the first of Nakhmen's *nigunim,* he refers to the expression *odem a mentsh katshke rir zikh,* literally "Adam a man, duck move yourself" [said of a petty person who tries to seem important, or of a do-nothing who makes the pretense of high attainment], calling himself *katshke rir zikh:* the essence of failed endeavor, of nothingness. Although *katshke rir zikh* does not exist by itself in Yiddish, its meaning is clear, as is its implication of Nakhmen's great humility. In *Faran aza gekekhts vi hunger* the rhyme *noyt/broyt* ("need/bread") graphically expresses the clashing of two world views.

In *Her un shtoyn,* metaphorical expressions take on literal significance. Nakhmen relates how the mysterious being he encounters says to him: *Atsindert bistu der khokhem balayle,* ("Now you are the sage of night" [a man of doubtful wisdom]."). But he goes on to connect this term with the actual darkness around him: *Un du, nosn, host badarft zen a balayle,/A shtokfintsternish . . .* ("And you, Nosn, should have seen that *balayle,*/A pitch-blackness . . ."). The Hebrew-Aramaic of "night" would be simply *layle;* the addition of a preposition keeps the word within its metaphorical framework while at the same time allowing its literal meaning to emerge. Similarly, when Nakhmen describes entering paradise, he explains that he had been kicked through the gates with such force that, as he puts it: *kh'hob derzen dem elterzeydn./Iz dokh dos a vertl—ha?/Ober mayn elterzeyde iz befeyresh epes mer vi a vertl.* ("I saw my great-grandfather./That is just a saying, eh?/But my great-grandfather is clearly something more than a saying."). Here, Nakhmen is playing on an idiom—analogous to the English "to see stars"—that describes perception after a particularly sharp blow. But, although he acknowledges his use of a common figure of speech, he stresses that he is not speaking rhetorically; he actually had seen his great-grandfather as he entered paradise. By renewing terms that have ceased to be perceived literally, Nakhmen illustrates the fruitfulness of his active involvement with Yiddish. Through him, moreover, Glatshteyn is able to express the immense importance to him of a living and changing Yiddish language.

VII   *The Emergence of Li Tai Po*

Although in this series of Bratslav poems, Nakhmen appears to have reached a point of resolution about his role as a committed Jew, he has a new conflict: that of the artist who is uncomfortable with compromise and seeks a means of avoiding it. But as a mouthpiece for Glatshteyn's undisguised aesthetic concerns, Reb Nakhmen of Bratslav was not totally convincing. Indeed, in *Her un shtoyn*, he seems to achieve a reconciliation with the necessities of public involvement that is not consonant with other of Glatshteyn's writings on poetic responsibility. Significantly, the Bratslaver fades from center stage after *Dem tatns shotn*, to be replaced by a persona who, like Nakhmen, was an historical figure but whose province, in contrast, was more purely that of literature: the Chinese poet Li Tai Po. By selecting for his new voice not only a poet, but one who is totally removed from his own cultural milieu, Glatshteyn openly—as much as possible within the framework of a distancing device—emphasizes his desire to concentrate on art, to exist in a realm apart from the world of Jewish causes. But *Tsen umgeklorte gezangen fun yungshaft* ["Ten unclarified songs of youth"] (pp. 26–32) are not merely interesting because they introduce Li Tai Po, for Glatshteyn also uses these poems to comment on his interest in personal relationships and incipient old age, and to address his deepest feelings about life as a poet.

Tsen umgeklorte gezangen fun yungshaft consists of ten poems plus an introduction explaining that Li Tai Po had drowned five years previously. The body of the cycle probes the question of how much clarity an older poet, with the weight of years and sadness upon him, is required to incorporate into his work. This conflict is presented in the introduction: the narrator recounts that, in old age, Li Tai Po had grown immensely sorrowful and, with the vision of his advanced years, deemed his earlier, arcane poetry inappro-

priate and therefore unacceptable. Although at times able to over-
come his sorrow with the help of wine, *der troyer hot im
ibergekligt,/Zikh geshtarkt,/Un zayne fartunklte lider zaynen im/Mer
nisht geven tsum hartsn.* ("grief outwitted him,/Grew stronger,/And
his obscure poems/No longer appealed to him."). Before his death,
he had asked his friend Tshu Tshin to destroy this evidence of poetic
excess; the latter, however, although aware that the poems are
unclear, nonetheless finds them immediate and meaningful re-
minders of the great artist who had been his friend; to him, Li's
poetry resembles cloudy wine. He therefore does not destroy it but
sets it to music instead, thereby validating and accentuating its
aesthetic value.

The ten poems that follow the introduction are, like the Bratslaver
poems, an attempt to recreate a voice quite unlike that of Glat-
shteyn's narrators elsewhere—although Chinese poetry, with its
richness of suggestion rather than explicit statement, had been a
source of interest to Glatshteyn very early in his career as a member
of *In zikh.*[9] Now, however, the use of Li Tai Po as a model stems
from Li's fascination with personal, rather than social or historical,
themes. By this time the Holocaust had so permeated all of Glat-
shteyn's writing that the only sure escape for him into purely in-
dividual and artistic concerns was through a figure who would be
ahistorical and acultural for both himself and his readership. The
poems themselves are all brief, made up of short and almost entirely
unrhymed lines. They are replete with nature imagery—a charac-
teristic distinctly foreign to Glatshteyn's work—and these images
are central to meaning rather than peripheral.

Tsen umgeklorte lider fun yungshaft can be divided into two basic
groups: those poems which explore relationships in a manner rem-
iniscent of the youthful subject matter and attitudes of Glatshteyn's
earliest work, and those in which Li Tai Po reflects on the process
of aging and on his feelings about youth. Most of the poems about
romantic relationships describe a battle arena, a scene of dis-
appointment. In one poem, Li Tai Po relates how he had fought
with the father of a woman he was attempting to see and had fled
without reaching her. His unfulfilled hope that she would break
through all barriers and come to him despite her father only adds
to his feelings of defeat. Various situations are potentially destruc-
tive and humiliating for him. In another poem, for example, he
describes how a woman's grace falls from a window. His response

is to ask whether he should look up *A farshemter,/A farvunderter,/A farvundikter?* ("Shamed,/Astonished,/Wounded?"). In an even greater expression of self-abnegation, the narrator goes on to comment that he will bring goodness born of suffering to his woman, spreading it like flower petals at the threshold of her house; then she will be able to choose whether to trample his gift or use it to adorn her hair.

An interesting aspect of this work is that it interweaves not only early, but also later, perceptions of the world as Glatshteyn saw it. Thus, one poem reflects a thematic continuation of the union set up in *Fun undzer yokh* and elaborated upon in *A getselt*. Once again, man and woman are equals. Moreover, two seemingly contradictory tendencies that emerge repeatedly in Glatshteyn's work— the poet's urgent need for speech and the lover's ability to communicate without it—are united here as the narrator describes his relationship: *Dayne oygn/Veln blitsn/Vi kluge gli-flign,/Ful mit dankbarkeyt/Far mayn gezang.* ("Your eyes/Will flash/Like clever fire-flies,/Full of gratitude/For my song."). In this way, each person appreciates the other in a quiet, understated manner.

Although the idea of youth is stressed in the title of this cycle, it is the subject of only two poems; in both of these, the narrator looks back from a later period in his life, evaluating his feelings about youth and its relevance for the present.[10] In each instance, Li Tai Po declares that he has never yearned to be young again, although in one poem he does admit that his childhood is "longed into" him, with its year-long days and lengthy winter dreams, images reminiscent of the childhood described in *Shneyike shnitn*. In the second work, the narrator states unequivocally in the very first line that he does not miss his youth, continuing: *Di tsayt shotnt mikh vi an eplboym./Der zoyerer vayn kilt mayn gumen.* ("Time shadows me like an apple tree./The sour wine cools my palate."). Rather than look backward, Li Tai Po would like to move forward into nothingness, a state that, in the last poem of the cycle, emerges as unhoped-for release from the entrapments of life.

The dual themes of *Tsen umgeklorte gezangen fun yungshaft* would appear to be unrelated, were it not for one section that combines the two and grants a view of what is at the root of all the other poems. Here, as elsewhere in the work, a troubled relationship is sketched: the narrator declares that if he could, he would write vicious poems and disrupt the peace of the person he is ad dressing. As he puts it: *Ven ikh volt gekont,/Volt ikh baleydikt dayn harts,/Ufgezukht dayn bahaltnstn khisorn.* ("If I could,/I would insult your heart,/Find your most secret fault."). He dreams of attack even though he knows he would never win the battle but would instead be dragged off and devoured by his adversary. But his angry wishes cannot in any case come true, for he is incapable of writing unkind words: his writing is measured and quiet.

An elliptical phrase provides the crucial clue to the concern underlying the narrator's impotent resentments: *Nisht altkeyt, nor tsugeteylte genugshaft.* ("Not old age, but allotted sufficiency."). Here, by taking a defensive stance and insisting that it is satiety and not decline that renders him powerless, Li exposes the conflict between his urge to write the poetry of a younger man and his refusal to acknowledge any desire for youth. He worries that he is slipping, losing the ability to write with the passion of an earlier period, yet he knows that he cannot accept the role of an old man in his poetry. Questions thus arise that were to gnaw at Glatshteyn—in subsequent Li Tai Po poems and elsewhere—for the remainder of his long career: Does writing with the clarity of old age limit the scope and depth of a poet's art? Do advancing years restrict the subject matter of the poet or the intensity with which he expresses it? Darkest of all looms the fear: is he sinking as a poet—is he headed towards nothingness?

CHAPTER 6

The Silver Crown of Yiddishkeyt

W ITH advancing years, Glatshteyn's desire for renewed poetic independence, already clearly visible in *Dem tatns shotn* and implied particularly through the figure of Li Tai Po, assumed a more distinct form. In two collections of the 1960's, *Di freyd fun yidishn vort—The Joy of the Yiddish Word*[1] and *A yid fun lublin—A Jew from Lublin,*[2] he openly displayed his intention to pursue a diversity of artistic concerns, to expand his vision beyond the contemplation of a shattered and shrinking Eastern European Jewish existence and embrace numerous other social and personal issues. To be sure, these books contain poems rich in grace, intelligence, and wit, particularly as Glatshteyn returned to one of his favorite topics: relationships between men and women. Nonetheless, as integrated volumes, they are irregular in quality: even the best poems seem anticlimactic at times, after the intense and riveting works that had emerged in reaction to the Holocaust.

I The Older Man, the Aging Lover

Like his persona Li Tai Po, Glatshteyn now viewed the world through the eyes of an older man struggling with the reality of his own impending end and the disintegration of his milieu. Indeed, in this period, aging itself became a subject for reflection and discussion. At times exposing his determination to cull from life those pleasures still available to an older person, Glatshteyn would on other occasions view the problems of advancing years with gentle resignation. The narrator of *Alte beyner* ["Old bones"],[3] for example, talks of the comfortable narrowing of existence that comes with passing time, describing it as a cozy framework of little islands that are *Di leng un breyt far eyn mentsh.* ("The length and breadth of one person."). The chilling prospect of living as if already in a coffin does not faze him; on the contrary, he calmly interprets his increasing confinement as a healthy process of withdrawal from life. Much as one would overcome an addiction, he is learning to adjust *Tsu kleyne un klenere goblekh lebn.* ("To small and even smaller little gifts of life.").

Understandably, not all of Glatshteyn's poems evince such sanguinity about deterioration. The narrator of *Inderfri* ["In the morning"][4] views growing older not as a comfortable waning, but rather as an unpleasant process of decomposition. His disintegration lacks the cosmic significance apparent in Glatshteyn's earlier work—in the *Shtot* poems, for example. Instead, it is alarmingly mechanical: the apparatus of his body is simply breaking down. The narrator describes his morning ritual of putting himself together, commenting that every day more of the screws necessary to hold him together are missing. Therefore, he must exercise great caution in reassembling himself: *Zol men nisht derzen, nisht derhern,/Vi tandetne-kuntsik ikh bin tsuzamengeshroyft.* ("So that one should not glimpse, not hear,/With what bungling trickery I am screwed together.").

Despite his efforts, however, the narrator finds himself with open crevices of emotional and physical vulnerability. He insists that even with these little agonies he is able to gratify almost all his desires. But the "almost" appears parenthetically, and in Glatshteyn's work, parentheses indicate more, rather than less. Thus, the unachieved satisfactions assume an importance unacknowledged by the narrator. His submissions and protestations culminate in the claim with which the poem concludes: even pain, since it indicates life, must be regarded as a gift in the uncertainty of old age.

The conflict between fading away gracefully and rebelling against the inevitability of growing older is reflected with particular clarity in those of Glatshteyn's poems where he once again probes the delicate interactions of men and women. During and immediately after the Holocaust, he had scrupulously avoided manifesting direct interest in this theme. Now, and through the end of his career, he returned to the special joys and problems of personal relationships. In some ways, he is more torn now than before, for while capable of savoring the pleasures of a fully mature response, he is unwilling to accept the limitations attendant upon his progressing years.

There is a striking difference between poems in which Glatshteyn discusses relationships through a first-person narrator and those in which he employs a more distanced voice. The former radiate peace, contentment, self-awareness; the latter, confusion, ambivalence, regret. Moreover, whereas a number of the first-person poems exude a sense of destiny and deep significance, the others, although they may mention classics of art and psychology, convey none of the same aura of permanence. The poem *Bavunder* ["Admiring"][5] is an exception to this pattern in its use of a third-person narrator to describe a positive association; however, it incorporates a reference to the biblical Jacob which, as a possible allusion to Glatshteyn himself, thereby creates an immediacy similar to that of a first-person narrator. In some ways, the woman in *Bavunder* is viewed as an ornament, a wonderful embellishment for her man. As the narrator asserts: *Er hot zi avekgezetst far alemens bavunder* ("He seated her for everyone's admiring"). From this position, she is able, cleverly and like a young girl, to rule as a queen over a household of desiring men. The issue of public respectability is obviously an important one to the narrator, but it does not eliminate his need for private approval, of an avowal that he is indeed special to his woman. Thus, the narrator declares that, although she is successful with men in general, she is nonetheless totally faithful. Her loyalty assumes legendary proportions: it is like *a shverer shteyn/Af a brunem,/Vos bloyz eyn yankev/Kon im aropkoyklen.* ("a heavy stone/On a well,/Which only one Yankev/Can roll off."). This is both a biblical reference to the enduring and devoted love of Jacob and Rachel, which began at a well as Jacob pushed off the stone that covered it, and a pun on *eyn yaakov*, the name of that well.[6]

While *Bavunder* concentrates on the interpenetration of public and private sides of a relationship, *Gutskeyt* ["Goodness"][7] and *A nes* ["A miracle"][8] each concern only one of these two aspects. In *Gutskeyt*, the woman, like her counterpart in *Bavunder*, is a regal figure in public: *Un vu du zitst/Falt af undz alemen/Der finkl fun dayn kroyn.* ("And wherever you sit/On all of us falls/The sparkle of your crown."). *A nes*, in contrast, focuses completely on private intimacy. The miracle is that the narrator and his woman can still find so much zest and meaning in life. Everything is an object of wonder and substance to them. Here, the narrator admires not the woman's social expertise but, instead, the challenging intelligence of her responses: *S'mindste gornit vert a seykhldiker epes/Durkh dayn fartaytsh, zog, un freg.* ("The least nothing becomes a prudent something/Through the way you interpret, say, and ask."). He goes on to elevate the relationship by stating that the two of them have received the biblical blessing of long days. Hence the title of this work gains additional importance: at first apparently culled from one line in the poem in which modest joy occurs like a miracle, it in fact refers to the entire relationship.

These three poems, appearing in sequence in *Di freyd fun yidishn vort*, form a kind of unit. In *Bavunder*, the age of the couple is ambiguous—maturity implied but not confirmed—but the men and women of *Gutskeyt* and *A nes* are definitely no longer young. In the first line of *Gutskeyt*, the narrator proclaims: *Dayn gutskeyt iz dayn yungshaft*, ("Your goodness is your youth,") indicating that the woman is youthful in personality rather than body. The narrator refers as well to *Der parmet fun ponem* ("The parchment of the face")—either hers or his own—implying not only old age, but also a subtle sense of durable importance. In *A nes*, however, the narrator states explicitly that *Mir vern alt* ("We are becoming old").

The unions specified in *Bavunder, Gutskeyt,* and *A nes* are all longstanding, their basis not only unquestioned, but apparently unworthy of mentioning. However, some of Glatshteyn's most moving comments and interesting images occur in poems where stability is a relatively new component of the relationship, as in *Tsvey* ["Two"].[9] In this work, past difficulties, although resolved by now, are recalled and discussed by the narrator in the context of depicting enduring passion. He speaks of himself and his woman as *Tsvey tsuzamengeflokhtene heylike akrobatn* ("Two braided-together holy acrobats"); through each other, they purge themselves of sadness and are calmed, both together and in the solitude that accompanies even the greatest intimacy. But there are hints that this equanimity has been achieved only after bitter experiences of trial and rebuke. As the narrator comments, the acrobats have made peace with *ale betn fun forvurf* ("all beds of reproach") and now remain as pure as fresh bed linen. They have come to terms with old conflicts: the woman has accepted her appearance and the narrator finds nothing more beautiful than this sign of maturity, admiring her as she looks at him *On shotns fun forvurf* ("Without shadows of reproach").

Not all of Glatshteyn's narrators were so fulfilled, however. The two poems together entitled *Tsvey lider vegn altn* ["Two poems about the old man"],[10] for instance, concern the thwarted need of an older man to prove that he is still a virile lover. These poems,

connected both by the events they recount and by the figure of
Freud, who in each case dominates the action, are also significant
in that they indicate Glatshteyn's return to the brilliant humor so
evident in his pre-Holocaust work and understandably absent from
his output of the 1940's and 1950's. The title's reference to an old
man is ambiguous: on one level an allusion to Freud, since he is
described as *der alter froyd* ("old man Freud"), it also implies the
would-be lover of the work, whose major conflict is his anxiety over
a sexual incident with a young woman.

The first poem concerns an act of love-making, viewed meta-
phorically as a chess game. The principal figures are thus doubly
distanced. Not only are they the anonymous objects of an omniscient
narrator's interest; in addition, they become symbols, the king and
queen of a game, playing out their affair on a chessboard blanket.
The mood of sporting competition is accentuated by the queen's
behavior, which is simultaneously playful and aggressive. Into this
loaded atmosphere walks Freud—at the very moment when the
king is becoming *rirevdik vi a ber*. ("mobile as a bear."). The title
of this poem, *Der driter tsukopns* ["The third one at the head of
the bed"], thus assumes a special meaning, hinting that this sexual
encounter has a psychological component rendering it as appropri-
ate for the analyst's couch as for the bed. Immediately, the king
feels constrained by Freud's presence; he begins to sweat, he be-
comes hesitant. Fearfully, he attempts to discover what the psy-
chiatrist, pen and notebook in hand, is writing about him. But he
knows that every move has already been worked out, for there is
no free choice in Freud's tidy formulations: *Bashtimt yeder hoyb
un fal./Alts iz tabulirt* ("Every rise and fall is decided./Everything
is tabulated"). The king of this chess game, then, is in fact a pawn
of psychological determinism.

The queen, in contrast, remains unflustered by the presence of
Freud. Continuing to be frivolous, she attempts to push Freud off
the bed, thereby indicating on another level the woman's desire to
help the man over his difficulties. But it is all in vain. Suddenly,
Freud makes his own move: an attempted assassination of the king.
And, in a brilliant conclusion to both chess game and poem: *In dray
getsvungene tsugn/Vert der kenig mat*. ("In three forced moves/The
king is check-mated [or: lackluster]."). Here, the two levels of this
poem converge. The check-mating of the king is at the same time
the man's sexual defeat. And in both instances the villain is Freud-

ian, so to speak: metaphorically represented by the analyst himself, in actuality the implicit constraint inspired by the lover's own emotional state causes him to be vanquished sexually, rendered impotent by his musings and insights.

The second poem, *Mayn shmues mitn altn—dernokh* ["My conversation with the old man—afterwards"], is again marked by narrative distance: the chess game figures have disappeared, and now a first-person narrator engages in discussion with Freud about the sexual disaster that has occurred, while disassociating himself from the event, however. The narrator accuses Freud of taking revenge on the hapless lover because the latter had not believed in him, and therefore had to be shown the validity of psychoanalytic theories. Freud defends himself, citing his Viennese gallantry as proof that he would never intrude uninvited. The man had wanted him there, Freud insists, to provide the excuse for his inevitable failure. The problem, Freud states bluntly, is that *Er iz vi ikh—alt.* ("He is, as I am—old."). The would-be lover had not truly wanted to complete his sexual act and had sought, ultimately successfully, to subvert it: *Er hot zikh aleyn nisht fargunen./Biz—nisht nor zayn, nor ir brunen,/Hot er fartruknt mit taynes tsu zikh.* ("He begrudged himself/Until—not only his, but her well,/He dried up with self-reproach."). The reason for the man's guilty response is two-fold, Freud explains. First, he is not ordinarily partial to one-time sexual favors; second, the woman's youth, which had seduced him, had also terrified him, making him unable to accept the possibility that she would find an old man attractive. Interpreting her positive responses as negative, he had heaped abuse upon himself. Now, unable to rid himself of guilt and fear, he puts himself on trial—by going back to his familiar bed. Despite the amusing tone of these poems, then, the pain of the older lover is clearly conveyed.

II   *The Flight from Heritage Continues*

Glatshteyn's reaffirmation of an active interest in male-female relationships did not obscure his other poetic concerns; nor did it signify his return to a purely introspective point of view. While insisting on his right to discuss whatever private issues moved him, he understandably continued to be preoccupied with what for him was both an intimate and a very public problem: the fate of Yiddish and *yiddishkeyt* in Israel and the United States. Ostensibly, the

three poems that comprise *Kibya* ["Kibia"][12] are the narrator's re-
action to an Israeli attack on an Arab village. In fact, however, his
response to that event shifts into a generalized complaint that Israel
is abandoning the Eastern European part of its heritage. The first
of these three poems begins with blunt indignation: *Kas, nekome,
roykh./A kleyne makhne mit retsikhe in di oygn.* ("Anger, revenge,
smoke./A small multitude with violence in its eyes."). Hinting at
the un-Jewish nature of brute force, the narrator goes on to assert
that Israelis have: *Rakhmones in zikh opgeshmadt/Un posl gemakht
dem parmet fun mayn lebn.* ("Apostasized their mercy/And defiled
the parchment of my life."). The use of this latter image, which
suggests the scrolls of the Torah, emphasizes the narrator's view
that the formalized religious tenets of Judaism are only part of a
broader Jewish framework—one that he associates with Eastern
Europe and the avoidance of belligerence. The ironic conclusion
of the poem underscores the narrator's resentment as he tells God—
explicitly and significantly, the God of the *geduldikn besmedresh*
("patient prayer and study house"), of traditional, unaggressive Jew-
ish life—that he finds it difficult to forgive the spurious heroism
represented by Kibia.

The second poem of the *Kibya* series is a paeon to the Jews of
Eastern Europe. This work begins with the narrator's assertion that
he would not trade the Jews of his heritage for any amount of
physical strength. Just as the initial two lines of the first poem had
been sputterings of rage that were exclamations rather than sen-
tences, so, too, do the first lines of the second poem constitute an
elliptical, if rhapsodic, dedication: *Mayn folk, mayn folk fun rakh-
mones,/Yidn fun mayn gants lebn.* ("My people, my people of mer-
cy,/Jews of my entire life."). The narrator links his past directly and
specifically to Poland, the exilic soil upon which he nonetheless
received a solid training in goodness. Moreover, the strength of his
people had been compatible with revered tenets of Jewish life. And
the narrator concludes by expressing the hope that Israelis will one
day allow themselves to accept the teachings of Eastern European
Jewry. He pleads with them: *Bafray zikh nisht fun mayne gerekhte
dalet-amos.* ("Do not free yourselves from my ethical four ells.").[13]
Remaining within the bounds of tradition will yield the Israelis a
paradoxical reward, he intimates, since by eschewing freedom they
will be spared enslavement by the *blutike keytn* ("bloody chains")
of world savagery.

A state of nonviolence is realized through a dream-vision in the final section of *Kibya*. Here, the narrator addresses an enemy and posits a time in which Jewish fighters will be not only strong, but just, even in battle revealing themselves as *Nisht keyn onfalers,/Nor bashitsers, zigers, hoykh derhoybn.* ("Not aggressors,/But protectors, victors, highly elevated."). Far from being pitiless, this new breed of warrior will actually heal the wounds of its victims when the time comes to lay down the *sholem-shteyn* ("peace-stone"), the foundation for the future. As in the past, then, Glatshteyn turns to fantasy in order to achieve a resolution that his present reality cannot provide.

In actuality, Glatshteyn harbored little faith that his Eastern European heritage and orientation would find favor and be appreciated in generations to come. As he contemplated the future, not from the perspective of world annihilation or political eventualities, but rather with an eye to his own prospects of individual and cultural immortality, he was filled with profound pessimism. A poignant demonstration of his pain is the poem *Eynikl-doyres* ["Grandchild-Generations"],[14] in which the narrator speaks to his descendants. Try though he may, he confesses to them, he cannot understand their handwriting: *Kh'blend zikh di oygn/Iber tsukunftike hiroglifn.* ("I am blinding my eyes/Over future hieroglyphics."). On the surface, everything seems clear; it even reminds the narrator of Yiddish or Hebrew. But just as he fancies himself on the verge of comprehension, the writing becomes *Lopetes mit kotsheres*. This image functions ingeniously as an indication of how valuable it is to understand not only the rough outlines of Yiddish but its subtleties as well: the literal meaning "spades and pokers" can be comprehended idiomatically as "scrawling handwriting" only by those who have an intimate knowledge of the Yiddish language.

But the generation of his grandchildren will possess no such thing, the narrator fears: immediately after admitting his failure to figure out their writing, he asks: *Vos iz s'geayl/Fun mir azoy gikh tsu antloyfn?* ("What's the hurry/To run away from me so quickly?"). In their haste to flee from him they have already put more distance between themselves and him, their grandfather, than he had seen fit to place between himself and the eighteenth-century Hasidic master, the Baal Shem Tov. The issue here is not so much one of time span as of perspective: in two generations, these heirs have thrown over two hundred years of flourishing tradition.

The narrator of *Red tsu mir yidish* ["Speak Yiddish to me"][15]
illustrates the consequence of rejecting Yiddish in lines both rich
in humor and subtly moving. By playing on the Hebrew-Aramaic
component of Yiddish, he points out the flexibility and indepen-
dence of the language. The poem begins and concludes with the
same lines, which by the end can only be understood as ironic: *Red
tsu mir yidish, mayn yidish land,/Un ikh vel tsu dir redn ivrit
mimeyle.* ("Speak Yiddish to me, my Jewish land,/And I will speak
Ivrit [modern Hebrew] to you as a matter of course."). The narrator
delineates the conflict between the two languages, and uses as his
vehicle a meeting with the biblical Abraham and Sarah near their
burial caves. Greeting them with a friendly and colloquial *Got helf,
zeyde-bobeshi.* ("Hello, grandfather and granny."), he is answered
in homey, traditional Yiddish by Sarah; Abraham, however, refuses
to speak to him. Sarah attempts to comfort the narrator, explaining
that in Israel, a man must be actively mute in Yiddish. But she
assures him that one day: *ale ivrit-kinder/Veln ufhern yidish
shvaygn.* ("all Ivrit children/Will cease to be silent in Yiddish.").

The use of Hebrew-Aramaic component words in *Red tsu mir
yidish* is a cynically jocular comment, not on the contribution of
Hebrew-Aramaic to Yiddish, but rather on the ways in which Yid-
dish has adapted and embellished the Hebrew that it has incor-
porated and integrated into itself. When Abraham pretends that he
does not understand the narrator's Yiddish, for example, Sarah in-
dicates that her husband is *meyvn kol diber* ("understands every
word"). This is a favorite cryptic comment used among Yiddish-
speaking Jews when a non-Jew in their midst understands Yiddish:
since the non-Jew's knowledge would not generally extend to He-
brew-Aramaic origin terms, the safest form of warning would be
one made up entirely of words from that component. Here, how-
ever, the expression is employed in reverse to indicate that Abra-
ham, despite his pretense, in fact understands Yiddish very well.
Thus, although *meyvn kol diber* is derived from the Hebrew-Ara-
maic component of Yiddish, it assumes its second meaning—and
the one that Sarah intends—only in Yiddish.

Similarly, Sarah refers to herself as *a yidene fun yidish-taytsh*
("a Jewish woman of Yiddish-translation"), playing upon the Yiddish
term *ivretaytsh* ("a stylized archaic Yiddish used, for example, in
the translation of sacred [Hebrew] texts"). Here, however, it is not
the rendering of Hebrew into Yiddish but its opposite that is evoked.
Underlying this term is the memory of the broad accessibility and

lively significance of Yiddish—and not Hebrew—to Eastern European Jews in their well-developed day-to-day tradition of interpreting and discussing religious texts. Finally, Glatshteyn refers to Israel as *khamishoser-land* ("Tu Bishvat [the fifteenth day of Shebat, the Jewish New Year's Day for trees] land"). While this term conjures up visions of vegetation and fruitfulness, it is at the same time an expression of condescension, because *khamishoser*, a Hebrew-Aramaic origin term (meaning "fifteen," hence synonymous with *tu*, its numerical equivalent in a counting system based on Hebrew characters rather than numeral words), exists today in Yiddish despite a different modern Hebrew word for the same holiday. The use of *khamishoser* underscores how Yiddish, even when gleaning aspects of itself from Hebrew-Aramaic, retains its unique and independent identity. When the first two lines of the poem are repeated at its conclusion, the dual meaning of *yidish*, i.e., both Yiddish and Jewish, becomes clear; the narrator implies that a truly Jewish land, unwilling to forsake Yiddish, would instead find the relationship between the two inevitable and natural. Behind all the joviality, then, lies a sharp barb of bitterness and disappointment.

Although he employed different evaluative criteria, Glatshteyn's fear for the future of American Jewish life was no less severe than his concern over Israel. In the United States, he continued to believe, the problem was less one of rejection than of assimilation: although active disdain for Yiddish and Eastern European values played a role in the decline of *yiddishkeyt* in America, it was secondary to passive weakening of religious ties and the desire to forget a recent immigrant history. Glatshteyn reveals his dismay in several poems, for example *Tsu lange teg* ["To long life"][16] and *Vi a pastke* ["Like a trap"],[17] in which he caustically mocked the American Jewish style of worship. Nonetheless, at least a semblance of connection with the past is retained in these works. In contrast, *Dermonungen* ["Reminders"][18] sketches a vignette in which even this link has been severed.

The poem is divided into two parts, the first of which finds the narrator on a train, reminiscing as he travels. During the entire journey he is occupied by thoughts of a previous era, of the Lower East Side in bygone days. He recalls years of immigration, poverty, loneliness, illness, hunger, and hard work in sweat shops. The narrator has all this in mind because he is on his way to visit a beneficiary of that generation, one *yidishn historiker ben shnayder* ("Jewish historian, the son of [a] tailor"). This version of the traditional patronymic is ironic, first of all because the use of occupational titles instead of names points up the status difference that has occurred between father and son in just one generation; secondly, and more important, because it emphasizes the intrusion of purely secular priorities into what had been an integrated cultural framework based on religion.

The second part of the poem contains a description of the historian's environment: he lives *fardorft* ("ruralized") where a Jew is *nisht geshtoygn, nisht gefloygn*, literally "entirely untrue," but here signifying an impossibility. Wryly, the narrator explains that there is no *shul* ("synagogue"), no *talmetoyre* ("American Jewish elementary school"), not even a *sinagoge* ("non-orthodox synagogue"), but that, because of this: *Zenen zayne kinder voyl dertsoygn* ("His children are well brought up"). The historian, accompanied by his bulldog, greets the narrator and treats him to a lavish meal. But the narrator must remind his host—and with this the poem abruptly concludes—that it is the anniversary of his father's death, *Un s'kumt dem orimen/Iyst-sayder shnayder a kadesh.* ("And the poor/East-side tailor deserves a kaddish [a prayer said by a mourner, especially by a son for his dead parent]."). This final pair of lines points up the extent to which the historian, for all his supposed desire to uphold and appreciate the past, has disregarded his own heritage, both religiously and personally. The narrator's specific criticism emerges as he points out the son's thoughtlessness; but a larger criticism is revealed fully through juxtaposition of the poem's two parts. By describing how an immigrant group had suffered, the narrator suggests that the sons of that generation—no matter how superficially successful—are failures in the deeper sense that involves their individual history and that of their parents.

The infiltration of the American milieu into the values and lifestyle of Eastern European immigrants and their progeny is reflected in Glatshteyn's brilliant use of vocabulary, his ability to weave into his work a strikingly large number of words that evoke the English language. Some of these are names; the rest are acceptable Standard Yiddish terms that happen to have close cognates in English. A central motif in the poem *Tsu lange teg,* for example, is the word *oytomobil;* moreover, in the second strophe, three consecutive lines conclude with words that resemble their English counterparts: *simptomen* ("symptoms"), *vizit* ("visit"), *mashin* ("machine"). The placement of these terms serves to accentuate them and leave a lingering impression. The same technique is employed in the poem

Vi a pastke, where *long-ayland* ("Long Island"), *konservativ* ("conservative"), *studio* ("studio"), *adres* ("address") all appear in line-final position.

The situation in *Dermonungen* is different, because two types of English are employed in keeping with the separate time periods that the poem encompasses. The position of the historian son is made clear by the use of *sinagoge* ("non-orthodox synagogue") and *buldog* ("bulldog"), both of which occur in the second part of the poem. Most of the cognates with English, however, are situated in the first part of the poem, and it is here, too, that the majority of names appear: *dolar* ("dollar"), *borders* ("boarders"), *iyst-sayd* ("East Side"), *iyst-river* ("East River"), *elis ayland* ("Ellis Island"). Not only do these terms approximate, or borrow from, English, but they recall the spirit and significance of the era they describe. In this sense too, then, the *Dermonungen* of the poem's title are reminders: of a past time, and of years when immigrant Jews sought to adopt, but had not yet fully integrated, the ways of America and its language.

III   *The Second Annihilation*

The subject of life in the United States had always fascinated Glatshteyn and continued to occupy an important part of his poetic attention even now, as he watched the rapid decline of Yiddish and *yiddishkeyt* in its midst. Following his desire to address a broad range of issues, partly in order to help insure his competence as a poet with a future, he chose American society as a principal focal point for his remarks. *Di freyd fun yidishn vort* and *A yid fun lublin* are marked by Glatshteyn's return to the themes he had discussed at the outset of his career: the problems of life in New York City, the different position of American blacks, and—in his poem *Sharfe reyd fun a 'bitnik'* ["Harsh talk from a 'beatnik'"][19]—the important function of social rebels in the tradition of Luther Boddy and Sheeny Mike. There are new topics as well, for example, the Vietnam War and the style of American politicians.

Yet, after the intensity of his Holocaust writings, these poems tend to seem pale and mild despite the obvious concern that lies behind them. There was only one subject that could legitimately replace the Holocaust as a cosmic question for Glatshteyn: the atomic bomb. In several poems, he probed the implications of this modern threat, discussing its significance for humanity and touching as well on the ambiguous position of God in a new post-Holocaust context.

For the narrator of *Teg fun elnt* ["Days of loneliness"],[20] atomic fallout symbolizes the culmination of all mankind's sins, the sign that it has transgressed once too often. Humanity must try to clean up its mess without the aid of religious solace, for between man and God there exists *A barg fun ongekristikte,/Ongemistikte zind.* ("A mountain from a heap of Christian,/Manured sins."). The narrator explains the reason for this isolation: over centuries, Judeo-Christian religions had relied on the concept of confession and forgiveness, finally allowing themselves to poison their environment with the *tayvlskoyt fun undzere zind* ("devil's-dirt of our sins"). Only then, breathing in the "death-dust," had they realized their self-deception. Rather than a cycle of sin and forgiveness, a different pattern exists in the world: *Der himl iz hart/Un hot nit fargebn di mindste aveyre.* ("Heaven is hard/And has not forgiven the least sin."). In the end, then, humanity must understand that, after its heinous deeds, it is enjoined from any relationship with God and must accept censure from an impersonal heaven.

The problem of human beings overstepping ultimate boundaries, to their own subsequent dismay, is dealt with differently in *Hit zikh* ["Beware"].[21] Here, the narrator connects the atomic age and its horrors with the atrocities of the Holocaust, using the term *khurbn* ("Holocaust") to refer to the bomb: *S'knoylt zikh iber dir der khurbn-roykh,/S'falt af dir zayn shprey/Mit yeder mindstn vintl.* ("The holocaust-smoke is curling over you,/Its drizzle falls on you/With every least breeze."). Here there is no question of divine forgiveness; rather, the *veltmentsh* ("world person") is everything; having seized control of earth, he has usurped the attributes and power of a deity, and will soon control heaven as well. God either no longer exists or has retreated rather than be associated with such a species: man's prayers are to himself. Finally, the narrator warns the *veltmentsh* that his resemblance to God rests chiefly in his ability to destroy: *Eyder mir vern ale opgevisht,/Hit zikh, dershrokener veltmentsh,/Zolst nisht makhn—eybike nakht.* ("Before we are all wiped out,/Beware, frightened world person,/That you do not make—eternal night.").

In an even grimmer perception of the future, the narrator of *Fun dos nay* ["Anew"][22] describes a final rewriting of history, using images from the Book of Genesis. It is a vision of destruction that begins with the biblical *vayehi: vayehi, s'iz geven, ("vayehi,* and there was,"). This verb, used continually in the story of Creation, has another meaning in Yiddish: "misfortune, disaster." Both connotations of the word are operative here—Creation has been struck by catastrophe. In an allusion to the ravaging of Sodom and Gomorrah, cities which God annihilated because they were utterly lacking in righteous men, the narrator comments that the end of the world has occurred because *ale lender zaynen gevorn sdomen* ("all countries have become Sodoms"). In his account, it was not two cities, but all countries that had fallen into iniquity. And the destruction was not at the hand of God *per se*, but rather through *A mabl fun atomen.* ("A flood of atoms."). The noun *mabl* assumes particular significance in this context because it signifies not the rain of fire and brimstone which was God's means of destroying Sodom and Gomorrah (Genesis 19.24), but rather the flood that destroyed all the world except for Noah and those on his ark.

This is an image that contains a nexus of implications. Since the destruction of Sodom and Gomorrah occurred after the Flood in Genesis, the reversal here suggests that in this new interpretation, a different order of the world exists than before: rather than total destruction followed by a covenant between God and the descendants of Noah, now there is no fresh and hopeful beginning. There will be no regeneration; God's covenant with the Jewish people is obsolete. Thus, the title of *Fun dos nay* takes on an unexpected irony: at the beginning of the work, it had appeared that "anew" referred to the cyclical violence of humanity; but, as the poem concludes, it is clear that there will be no new start after all.

In *Teg fun elnt, Hit zikh,* and *Fun dos nay,* while mankind is clearly responsible for its own potential demise, Glatshteyn once again raises the question of the position of God vis-à-vis His creation. In the face of an atomic threat, He has proven Himself to be as distanced and powerless as during the Holocaust. Glatshteyn has still not come to terms with his anger, frustration, and disappointment: he is perpetually like the Jew in *On yidn* who must leave God in order to return and respond to Him.

IV *Declining Artists, Vanishing Language*

As important and resonant to Glatshteyn as many of these social problems obviously were, their general significance had to compete with more personal implications. In particular, the unabated decline of Eastern European Jewry created specific literary difficulties that Glatshteyn and his colleagues were forced to confront. By the 1960's, these artists were getting on in years. The narrator of *Alt* ["Old"][23] admits that: *Mayn tsekh iz alt.* ("My guild is old."). Because of their diminished numbers, he continues, their cirtical standards have necessarily been lowered; now, work that in a more potent and vivacious environment would be considered second or third rate, is greeted with acclaim: *Di melokhe falt fun di hent,/Ober alts muz toygn.* ("The craft falls from our hands,/But everything must qualify.").

The question of value and evaluation in Yiddish literature weighed heavily on Glatshteyn during this period, and his worry about the judgments of contemporary and future readers was justified. The concept of awarding praise as if it were charity is the central idea, as well as the initial image, of the poem *Reyd vi tsdoke-pushkes* ["Speech like alms boxes":][24] *Reyd klapn vi tsdoke-pushkes,/Varfn on a moyre mit zeyer loybn.* ("Speech clanks like alms-boxes,/Horrifies with its praise."). Decimated in their ranks, Yiddish writers can look only to each other for appreciation; hence they are impoverished and needy, reduced to an existence in which *Der blinder groyst dem toybn./Eyner dem andern nemt zalbn.* ("The blind man extols the deaf one./One begins to anoint the other."). The inevitable result of this condition is a cheapening, not of subject matter, which had been a principal concern of an earlier postwar period, but of the artists themselves, of their total output and vision. There is a sense of phoniness, the narrator asserts, about the entire process of assessment, where even those who are seen through and recognized for what they are during their lifetime must be "rehabilitated" when they die, in yet another act of gratuitous charity.

The prognosis for the future is grim, according to the narrator, particularly viewed in light of the past. A previous generation in Eastern Europe had devoted its energies to creating Yiddish literature: now, that literature has lost its richness and its connection with an older spirit. Worse still, even this meager heritage is unlikely to be retained: as the few remaining artists die off, their caretaker searches pathetically for an heir *Vos m'zol im helfn oyshinken kadesh.* ("Who will help him limp out the mourning prayer for the dead.").

The narrator of *Kh'shtey in toyer* ["I stand at the gate"][25] amplifies on the difficulties of laboring to transmit the cultural baggage of Yiddish language and literature. He describes himself standing by a gate hawking Yiddish honeycake with raisins, an obvious metaphor for the attempt to peddle Eastern European Jewish culture. However, he realizes that what he has to offer is inappropriate and obsolete in a world where *Merkhokim vern tseribn supersonish.* ("Distances are crushed supersonically."). There is neither time nor space for the poetic heroes of Bialik and Perets, whose difficulties in resolving the clash between tradition and change had at one time excited a huge reading public and drawn its attention to the two artists who would become pillars of modern Hebrew and Yiddish poetry. Now, however, in this jet-age equivalent to the world of *1919*, Yiddish writers must face the bitter truth that their art is the merchandise of a slower era and has no marketability. The narrator has no choice but to join the *marsh fun untergang* ("march of extinction").

The defensive pride that the narrator exhibits to the outside world in *Kh'shtey in toyer* is evident as well in *Mayn getselt* ["My tent"][26] and *Mayn Mi* ["My toil"],[27] both of which concern the struggle against groveling for recognition. In the first of these, the narrator asks to be bound to the tent of Yiddish, suggesting by his oblique evocation of the biblical desert both his chosenness and his intense separateness. He claims, however, to be unconcerned by his isolation from others; in fact, he prefers not to mix with them, not to be known by them: *Loz mikh vern shtum-loshn far der velt,/Afile in der bester iberzetsung* ("Let me become mute language for the world,/Even in the best translation").

Despite his realization that loyalty to Yiddish is a burden, even an imprisonment, the narrator has no interest in being set free. Although he does not say so directly, his relationship to the language is covenantal. Seeing that he cannot achieve universal acclaim, he is nevertheless satisfied that when he dies, he will leave as his bequest a path for his people to follow; again alluding to the Bible, he declares that he will become a pillar of clouds leading Jews through the desert and a beam of light over the small ark where the Yiddish language is preserved.

By elevating both his own status and that of his language to a level where they assume the highest possible national importance, the narrator of *Mayn getselt* makes translation seem possible but contemptible. In contrast, the narrator of *Mayn mi*, although he too rejects the prospect of translation, knows that the choice is not his to make. He knows that his work is written for a select few, some of whom will never see it anyway. But he would rather pawn his last shirt than go crawling outside that milieu—*tsu der fremd* ("abroad"), as he puts it. An unidentified other voice tells him: *Afile iber hundert un tsvantsik, vint un vey,/Vestu voglen in umfarshtey.* ("Even after one hundred and twenty years, alas,/You will wander in non-comprehension."). The narrator claims to be unperturbed, however, insisting that in the world to come a small tent will be prepared for him: there, amid skimpy furnishings, an old Jew will come to hear his poetry and appreciate it. The narrator's ironic description of his envisioned future reveals resignation but neither resentment nor despair. As in *Red tsu mir yidish,* he enjoys hinting to his cognoscenti that they are in possession of a special treasure beyond the grasp of those outside the province of Yiddish.

But Glatshteyn's concern with the privatization of Yiddish was not limited to his anxiety about a waning audience. In the five poems that comprise *Di freyd fun yidishn vort* ["The joy of the Yiddish word"],[28] after which Glatshteyn's 1961 volume is named, he expresses his profound emotions about writing in Yiddish but also reveals his fear that he himself is losing touch with a beloved part of his life. Although the title of this work implies optimism, the poems themselves yield precisely the opposite impression. Indeed, their narrator reports that the pleasures once furnished him by the language have become elusive—in fact, inaccessible. In the first poem, he outlines a primary cause of this hardship: at this juncture in its history, too much meaning is being forced into Yiddish. The narrator, addressing himself, declares: *dos gezang/Shprotst vi frish groz,/Nor du tretst despotish/Un grinkeyt vert umgebrakht mit a geshrey.* ("song/Sprouts like fresh grass,/But you step despotically/And verdure is killed with a scream."). Thus he himself is responsible for the destruction of his own happiness: sentencing *dem gantsn horizont tsu fartaytsh* ("the entire horizon to interpretation"), he has become *der tsoymer fun azoy fil vilder sheynkeyt,* ("the tamer of so much wild beauty,").

In the second part of *Di freyd fun yidishn vort,* the narrator alludes to the biblical vision of resurrection in the valley of the dry bones (Ezekiel, Chapter 37) in order to imagine the revivification of Yiddish. Singing into the valley of *beynerdike verter* ("boney words"), he commands them: *Nemt os tsu os, in varemen tsiter/Un meynt gornit,/Nor tantst antkegn velt.* ("Join letter to letter, in a warm shiver/And mean nothing,/Simply dance toward the world."). But even as he seeks to recapture Yiddish and the dead milieu of his youth—where definition had been secondary to the sheer delight of existence—he realizes that he will encounter doubters who will ask instead: *Vos iz di taytsh fun dem alts?* ("What is the meaning of all this?"). Thus, even were the miracle of new life possible for Yiddish, the narrator comprehends that the essence of the language would continue to go unappreciated.

Much of the third poem in this series is rendered in the first person, as the narrator begs for an avenue to the enchantment of Yiddish. He avers his wish to be released from all vanity, his willingness to accept a spartan existence, as long as he is granted: *gantse, fule meslesn,/Lozt mikh nisht dos yidishe vort/Af a rege fargesn.* ("Whole, full twenty-four hour periods,/Do not let me forget the Yiddish word/For a moment."). Due to his preoccupation with earning a living and enjoying creature comforts, the narrator has permitted himself to neglect his language; thus as the poem concludes, he pleads: *O zing, derzing zikh tsu naketer knapkeyt.* ("O, sing, sing yourself into naked meagerness."). His imagery is erotic at the same time as it contrasts the material and spiritual aspects of his existence: while the world grows fat on his bed, threatening to usurp his space as well, the Yiddish word—his true lover—awaits him, faithful and mute. In his inflamed dream he sighs to it: *Ikh kum, ikh kum.* ("I am coming, I am coming.").

In this section, then, the narrator's dream overtakes the biblical prophecy of the previous poem. In the fourth work of this series, the dream continues; the narrator fancies himself *oysgeton un oysgeshpant* ("undressed and unharnessed"), as Yiddish glitters from afar like fool's gold. He wants to run towards it, but *di keytn fun dayn kholem/Klingen knekhtik un vegn shver.* ("the chains of your dream/Clank slave-like and weigh heavily."). Even as he realizes that he will soon wake up, however, he knows as well that he has been deeply affected by his dream, which leaves him with a thought he cannot digest.

The last poem of *Di freyd fun yidishn vort* connects the arenas of sleep and wakefulness, prophecy and day-to-day experience, to illustrate the impossibility of the narrator's desired union with his cherished Yiddish. In a semi-somnolent state, he perceives a warm hand and a bright face solving the riddles of the night. Morning and breakfast bring a ively reality and, as he rouses himself, the narrator relinquishes his vision while relating it; having spent a day together in the world of dreams, he and the joy of Yiddish must part: *O, zay gezunt, zay gezunt./Nit farlir mikh, zukh mikh op.* ("O, goodbye, goodbye./Do not lose me, recover me."). Yet, although he recognizes the ephemeral and unreal nature of his dream, the narrator nonetheless finds solace in having felt even this tenuous communication: *A shmeykhl geyt mit mir a gantsn tog in shpan.* ("A smile keeps step with me all day.").

The final message of *Di freyd fun yidishn vort* is thus just the opposite of what might be inferred from the title itself: the joy of the Yiddish word, while undeniably inherent for the narrator in the substance of the language, is no longer readily available to him. For Glatshteyn, this relegation of Yiddish to dreams was particularly poignant. At the beginning of his career, his language and literature had been his sanctuary, the only area of his poetic existence where reality was hopeful and nonthreatening. Initially, it was the social problems of the outside world—as, for instance, those of *Harlem: Zuntik*—whose resolution had been sought in the domain of fantasy. Now he feared that Yiddish itself would be confined to that realm.

V *Reinterpreting the Past*

Glatshteyn's changing relationship to Yiddish was not the only aspect of his personality that he held up for reevaluation in the 1960's. With advancing years, he delved further and further back into his past, scrutinizing specific events and attitudes in an apparent effort to better understand himself and the man he had become. In *Ibershpil* ["Replay"],[29] for example, he explored the question of sexuality, not by observing it as a detached psychological or social phenomenon, as he had done in *Nakht, zay shtil tsu mir* or *Tsu dir,* but rather by recalling a personal incident of childhood sexuality. This poem begins as a nostalgic attempt on the narrator's part to play back a scene from his annihilated past—and here, annihilation has a double meaning: the past, forcibly destroyed by the Holocaust, is also destroyed because its temporal essence cannot be recaptured. During a Sabbath visit to his aunt and uncle, pleasant smells and sensations that impress the child narrator yield quickly to his concentration on tension between himself and his childless aunt. As his uncle retires to nap, his aunt's kisses become *shtiler, shener, on-geleygter* ("quieter, more beautiful, more welcome"). The boy simply experiences, without reflection, the dampening of his face by her tears. The mood is uneasy: as if echoing the changing atmosphere, the house canary, who had at first jumped about with curiosity, now *zingt nisht/Nor git nerveze signaln.* ("does not sing/But rather emits nervous signals."). The scene described by the narrator reaches its climax with his description of how, burning with the thirst of a young wanderer, he rambles in his aunt's arms, kissing her hands and stroking the hair that, contrary to all rules of traditional modesty, is exposed to him rather than covered. The boy revels in his explorations: *Kh'vander mit farmakhte oygn./Kh'zukh berglekh, toln, taykhlekh, kvaln.* ("I wander with closed eyes./I look for hills, valleys, streams, springs.").

But, despite the superficial similarity between this incident and an adulterous encounter enacted almost within the presence of the wronged party, the reality, of course, was otherwise. Looking back, the narrator understands how his aunt's motivations and response had differed from his own; he admits, however, that it had taken sixty years until he finally realized and understood *Der mumes akoredik ponem,* ("My aunt's barren face,"). What for the boy had been a situation of erotic excitement and imagery, an experience of childish sexual adventure ripe with possibility, had been for his aunt an opportunity to express her desire for a child and her sadness that she had been denied this wish. By reevaluating his own past, then, the narrator gains the additional insight that permits him to perceive others from a new vantage point.

Glatshteyn's rethinking of old events did not stop at childhood, but rather carried him all the way back to infancy, where he claimed to discover the roots of his future sexual, intellectual, and religious behavior. His five-part *Oytobiografye fun an intelekt* ["Autobiography of an intellect"][30] charts the course of a modern mind that develops for a time free of conflict and doubt but is finally forced to wrangle with important spiritual questions. When he was still in the cradle, the narrator asserts in the first poem, he had mocked his father's belief in God. Nonetheless, with all his mental precocity, he had remained dependent at this point on the deaf-mute servant who changed his clothes and kept him pacified.

As if to demonstrate his dismissal of his father, who symbolizes faith in God, the narrator ignores him entirely in the second poem of this series. Instead, he concentrates on his relationship with the servant, before whom he had begun to feel ashamed because he still needed to have her clean and diaper him, a weakness that struck him as incongruous with his extraordinary intellectual ability. The narrator's father reappears in the next poem, but functions only as a point of departure for a discussion of the development of his budding genius. Now, the issue of faith is eclipsed, sheer intellect having become knowledge and bodily comfort having shifted into sexuality. In the pursuit of erudition, he had buried himself impatiently in difficult and forbidden books. The servant, who in the past had been the narrator's major link with his uncontrolled physical functions, now provided his outlet for erotic urges: *Mit hits hob ikh di kleyder/Fun der shtumer dinst gerisn.* ("With heat I ripped/The clothes off the mute servant.").

By the time he left the cradle, the narrator had become an intellectual adult. In heavily rhymed, brief lines that lend an air of urgency and desperation to his words, he relates how he had chosen to relegate all phenomena to chance: *Di ayzerne ram/Far alts iz geven/Un gevorn,/ . . . Tsufal, blinder geshen,* ("The iron frame/For everything was/And became,/ . . . Chance, blind happening,"). With all his knowledge and skepticism, however, the narrator is haunted in the end by the importance and wisdom of his father's faith. In an epilogue, he muses over the fact that man has now almost reached the moon and that he himself still worships before the idol of randomness. Nevertheless, he finds his intellect disturbing and wonders whether he has in fact ever left the cradle. The root of his doubts emerges in the final strophe, as the narrator states—for the first time mentioning his Jewishness directly—that perhaps it would be wiser for him to go to a small Hasidic house of prayer and there, together with other Jews, recite the memorial prayer for the dead.

This final section of *Oytobiografye fun an intelekt* is clearly post-Holocaust, and the narrator realizes that logic cannot help him comprehend the horror of this time; nor can his notion of an arbitrary universe. Rather, the only way to achieve some acceptance of this catastrophe, he suggests, is through faith and a belief in hidden purpose. Moreover, he asks himself whether the appropriate response to life in a post-Holocaust world should be not the glorification of technology and intellect, but rather traditional acts of prayer and mourning.

VI *Coming to Terms with the Past*

Glatshteyn's difficulties with accepting an inherited Jewish faith were clearly related to the fact that he, the skeptic, had been permitted to live through the Holocaust while so many believers had perished, despite—or because of—their trust. This grim realization led him, in *Tsum tatn af yontev* ["To my father on *Yontev* (Jewish holiday, festival)"],[31] to face explicitly what he had before only implied: his guilt at having survived. In this work, Glatshteyn once again manages to bring together a number of salient poetic characteristics: his replaying of the past, his use of fantasy as a means of positing the solution to an irreconcilable problem, and the conflicting feelings about his role as a Jew.

The dual meaning of *Tsum tatn af yontev* is suggested by its title: it is both the narrator's abstract tribute to his father and a dream of actually going to him. In this vision, the narrator recalls, it was evidently Passover, but the son was unprepared for celebration; he was *farkhometst*, contaminated by the leavening forbidden during this holiday. Moreover, he had arrived dressed in weekday clothes and *Mitn shtoyb fun reder/Un ayngetrotenem hunt-koyt.* ("With the dust of wheels/And pressed-down dog dirt."). However, his father, to whom the narrator addresses his comments, welcomed him immediately with the words *gut yontev*, the greeting used on Jewish holidays, and offered him a glass of sacramental wine. Then, not waiting for his son to wash himself, either as a means of cleansing himself or as a ritual act, he led him at once to the table.

The narrator remarks that his father seated him at the table just as he was: *On oysreyd, on fardrosn*, ("Without rebuke, without resentment,"). He means, of course, not only his travel-weary appearance but also his avoidance of traditional observance, a far deeper type of uncleanliness. The father, in contrast, was not only pure but literally shining with blinding light. He was dead. The narrator realized this even in his dream, both by observing that his father's heart had been shot through, and in his sense that he could communicate with his father simply through his powers of understanding.

Suddenly, he and his father, together with the ceremonial table, were carried off to a forest whose trees and flowers smelled like Jewish meals. The narrator states that his father had been dead a long time; of himself, he laments, however: *Halevay af mayn vundshuld,/Vos hot nokh gebrit un gebrent/Un frishe yesurim getsundn.* ("If only the same were true of my wound-guilt,/Which still boiled and burned/And ignited fresh agonies."). It soon becomes clear why the narrator feels guilty: the forest to which he and his father had been brought, summarily and without their consent, was the Maidanek death forest next to Lublin. Now, however, as the smells of his native dishes reached him even more clearly, the narrator constructed a fantasy scenario of his past. This time he would die along with his father in the Maidanek Forest: *Der tish hot undz beydn/Gefirt tsum maydanek-grub/In yidishn veldl.* ("The table led both of us/To the Maidanek grave/In the Jewish grove.").

The poem ends with a twist: the narrator had heard footsteps and experienced a sensation of horror, but his father knew that these were not the steps of a stalking enemy. Rather, they belonged to the Jewish God who, much like an escapee or partisan, was hiding out in the forest: *Er hot nokh alts moyre aroystsukumen/Af der mentshlekher fray.* ("He is still afraid to emerge/Into human liberty."). Defeated, guilty—or both—He, like the narrator himself, felt more comfortable among the dead.

Tsum tatn af yontev reveals the narrator's complicated concept of what his Jewish identity entails. He is not traditionally observant; his father is. Yet, both of them suffer the same fate in the poet's vision; and they are carried to their deaths by tradition itself, in the form of a holiday table. Thus, although the narrator's outlook is nonobservant, his ties to heritage drive him, in his dream, to suffer with his people rather than face his waking reality.

Glatshteyn's guilt over having survived the Holocaust, and his realization that he had abandoned the observant ways of his parents, lent a particular urgency to his efforts at making peace with the past. For, having at the beginning of his career rebelled against his elders with all the enthusiasm of youth, he had lost the chance to be reconciled with them when they and their entire world had perished. Such was Glatshteyn's need to recapture the world from which he once had run that at times he came to look for the kind of faith that Jews had for generations upheld, lived and died for. However, this desire was not without conflict. The poem *Fargleyb mikh* ["Make me have faith"][32] for example, is a prayer in which the narrator asks God for the simple relationship with Him enjoyed by a child: *Fargleyb mikh mit der kindisher taytsh/Fun hartsike tfiles.* ("Make me have faith with the childish meaning/Of hearty prayers."). Sensing God's distance from him, he begs: *Farknip tsurik mayn lebn mit dir,/Shrump ayn dayn groyzamen umendlekh* ("Reconnect my life with You,/Shrink Your horrible infinite").

Whereas his impulse toward faith was problematic and sporadic, Glatshteyn continued to integrate and discuss the more consistent and abiding change that had taken place over the years: his development into a highly involved and responsible Jewish poet, radically different from the *Inzikhist* Jewish poet he had originally professed himself to be. In a certain sense, this identification ameliorated his conflict over faith. The poem *Oysderveylt* ["Chosen"],[33] for instance, contains statements about a sense of Jewishness that on one level does away with the power of God and with man's need for Him. The poem is like a song of praise to God, extolling His virtues and His uniqueness. However, the object of the narrator's effusion is not God, but the Jew: *Vi sheyn iz der yid,/Shener fun boym,/Shener fun im iz nisht keyner./Kh'heyb uf di oygn tsum yid.* ("How beautiful is the Jew,/More beautiful than the tree,/No one is more beautiful than he./I raise my eyes to the Jew.").

Oysderveylt concludes with an ironic twist that again eliminates God, not only as a unique force, but as the supreme power that had forged a covenant with Israel and created His Jewish people. Now, although the Jews are still the chosen ones, it is not God who chooses. Instead, the narrator singles out his own people and forms a new bond within the framework and vocabulary of the original covenant: *In binyen fun felker/Hob ikh zey ale ibergetseylt,/Dikh fun ale umes/Afsnay oysderveylt.* ("In the edifice of peoples/I have counted them all,/You of all nations/[I have] chosen anew.").

It is not the faith of the Jew that attracts him, however, but rather the values inherent in Judaism, the way of life that grows naturally out of following a system of commandments. This is uppermost in the narrator's mind when, instead of studying and praying Jewish religion, he studies and prays the Jew. In this way he can remain *Opgekert fun a velt/Vos iz gevorn rishesdiker, treyfer.* ("Turned away from a world/That has become meaner, more impure."). Indeed, the Jew becomes an *alt-fartifter seyfer* ("old pored-over religious book") for him, thereby replacing actual books that, even though they may inspire and influence traditional Jews, do not fulfill his own needs.

The narrator of *Oysderveylt* indicates that he has always upheld traditional Jewish values, at least in his mind, even though it has required a process of clarification to realize their final importance to him. For the narrator of *Di kroyn* ["The crown"],[34] however, the path is far more tortuous. In this climactic work, Glatshteyn attempts to chart the course of a return to Jewish heritage, using a mixture of Jewish and Christian imagery. The central symbol of this poem is a silver crown worn by the narrator, the presence of which he needs to explain. Moving backwards in time, he relates how once, on a sea voyage, he had thrown his *tfiln* ("phylacteries")—the crowning glory of Israel and the symbol of his membership in the Jewish covenant—into the water. Years later, like cast-off bread, a silver crown returns to him instead.

Coaxing his memory even further back, the narrator describes his departure from home, his embarkation on a forty-year wander, like the children of Israel: *Durkh dem eymedikn midber fun undzer yorhundert*. ("Through the horrible desert of our century."). Each year in the desert had constituted a thorn for his crown. As he wandered, avoiding ritual observance, he had nonetheless searched for God. But his parents, whom the narrator describes as *gotgeshtaltike* ("formed in the image of God"), and whom he encounters on several occasions during the years, reprove him for his bareheadedness, the blatant disavowal of his heritage. Now the narrator realizes that it had been a futile gesture to cast his bread on the water, to discard his *tfiln*, with the leather straps that represented his bond to his people and his faith: *In a sakh teg arum vest es gefinen*. ("Many days later you will find it."). And, at the conclusion of *Di kroyn*, the narrator acknowledges that his parents have finally been rewarded; he has returned to the fold, his head crowned *Mit grayzgroyer yidishkeyt*. ("With grey-haired yiddishkeyt.").[35]

The silver crown, then, is *yiddishkeyt*. The narrator may have thrown away his *tfiln*, part of which are placed on the forehead, but he cannot escape what they symbolize. After a poetic journey through the desert of civilization, after a rebellious period where he had rejected the commandment to cover his head with *tfiln*, after all this, the narrator returns to an acceptance of *yiddishkeyt*—not in the same way as his parents had taught him, but in a fashion that does not deny them.

Glatshteyn's drive to embrace *yiddishkeyt* was not only a way of perpetuating the past, but also a means of asserting the continuity between his present and that past, of showing that his early advocacy of change had not in fact been so drastic. The stimulus for *A yid fun lublin* ["A Jew from Lublin"][36]—the title poem of Glatshteyn's 1966 volume—is a winter walk on the streets of New York, during which memories of his youth as a poet in the city flow into the narrator's mind. The juxtaposition of current perceptions and images of a previous era forms the underlying structure of this work. Throughout, a subtle shift in grammatical tense serves to indicate the presence of the two temporal areas affecting the narrator. Initially, his comments reflect the integration of these two periods: *S'iz gornit gegangen farloyrn./S'iz epes aroysgekumen derfun.* ("Nothing has been lost./Something has emerged from it."). The second strophe of the poem is a description of his immediate responses as he walks along. His feet sing out one poem after another, and he asserts that he is: *a bateylikter yid,/Mitn yidishn got/In a frayer shtot.* ("an engagé Jew,/With the Jewish God/In a free city."). In the narrator's contemporary self-definition, then, he is an artist with a commitment, carrying with him the symbol of his people's faith and tradition as he moves through a secular world.

The third strophe of *A yid fun lublin* is a flashback to the narrator's younger years. In certain essentials, he recalls, his life was already then what it would remain: involved, Jewish, poetic, free. But, rather than walking with the Jewish God, the narrator relates that, as a poor young man, he had paced the city: *Mit mayne yidishe gezangen,* ("With my Yiddish songs,"). His Jewishness had emanated from within him then, and it had proved sufficient to sustain him. At that time, he had viewed the entire outside world in terms of himself: *In alts vos mayne oygn hobn gezen,/Bin ikh geven,* ("In everything that my eyes saw,/I existed,"). The narrator confides—shifting back to the present tense—that now, even as the past grows continually more distant, it returns to him with ever increasing force, reviving old hungers and making him long for that stage of his life when, confident and actively involved in his surroundings, he had known that his future extended before him.

At the conclusion of *A yid fun lublin,* the narrator not only achieves some measure of synthesis between present and past, but exposes a deeper layer of his identity. Still walking in the now subdued city, and still feeling the hunger of his youth, he allows himself to realize additional Jewish ties: those of *gedenkte psukim* ("remembered verses of sacred books"), those of *yidishn farshtand* ("Jewish understanding"). In the end, then, the narrator comes to see that despite his longstanding devotion to artistic independence and secular Jewish culture, his life and work have been, and always will be, rooted in a framework of tradition.

VII   *Two Aging Chinese Poets*

Glatshteyn's attempts to understand his past and its effect on him, his feelings about himself as artist, lover, Jew, his visions of the future—all these concerns merge in several groups of poems in which he uses as mouthpieces not one but two Chinese poets: Li Tai Po and Po Tshu Iy. Although both exotic voices are employed as a deterrent to excessive exposure, Glatshteyn varies the type and degree of masking with the persona. Li Tai Po is the more confessional and personal, revealing his diary entries and concentrating, there and elsewhere, on his innermost thoughts and feelings. In contrast, Po Tshu Iy is guarded; he communicates through letters and is given to hinting rather than commenting outright. In addition, his constellation of topics more closely approximates the totality of Glatshteyn's own than do Li's. Two aspects of the way personae functioned for Glatshteyn are hereby illustrated. First, they enabled him to connect issues that he ordinarily discussed separately, thereby allowing him to summarize himself. Second—by contrast—they permitted him to accentuate differing aspects of himself.

At the outset of *Der khinezer poet po tshu-iy shraybt a briv tsu zayn fraynd yuan tshen* ["The Chinese poet Po Tshu Iy writes a letter to his friend Yuan Tshen"],[37] Po sets himself up as a measured, sober man, as opposed to Yuan, who is a glutton and a guzzler. Beginning his letter with formal and courteous greetings for his friend, he soon begins to discuss himself, defining his writing as intended for his people. Po goes on to defend himself for spending three years in seclusion, mourning the death of his mother and attempting to assuage his guilt over the fact that he had neglected her during her last, blind years in order to pursue his own reputation. But, he asserts, he had not failed to minister to his people, both as ruler and as judge; and since they could respond to the traditional teachings of religion and he could not, it was his mother who had guided him and, in turn, enabled him to lead them. But he admits that he has not sung in some time, preferring instead to think of Honan, the city of his people which he is confident will stand firm for as long as his people exist, outliving harsh rulers, bitter seasons and cold days.

Po laments the suffering of his people and juxtaposes it with his own comfortable and fulfilled past. In particular, he has been successful with women; explaining his progress from a youthfulness that he does not consider worth recapturing to an unworried old age, he relates: *Kh'bin ayngeshlofn mit likhtikn dank/Tsu di koykhes mayne,/Tsu mayne boyglekhe glider.* ("I went to sleep with bright thanks/To my strength,/To my supple limbs."). Nonetheless, he worries about the future and, in thinly veiled comments, reveals his extreme pain at the prospect of aging, a thought that has caused him to cry where even his mother's death had left him dry-eyed. He feels trampled by youth, yet compelled to chase it, to fuse *yunge basherte freydn,/Mit tsugeshporte.* ("young predestined joys,/With saved-up ones."). Thus he is left to watch over the young woman who lies stretched out next to him. While he remains awake, she sleeps, exhausted from the strain of love-making.

Commenting that he does not like to reveal himself in his writing, and that he deems it unsuitable for a leader to open his diary to the public, Po concludes by announcing that he is at work on a new ballad: a song of eternal regret. This will be a work *fun eybikshaft,/Vos iz freydike eynzamkeyt,/Ayngeshveyst in mayn blut.* ("of eternalness,/That is joyful loneliness,/Sweated into my blood.").

Despite the cloaking technique of employing Po as a narrator, the Chinese poet's letter clearly refers to events in Jewish history. The questions Glatshteyn raises are neither new nor surprising, but the way in which they are combined and connected is unusual. For example, while his dilemma over private experience versus public responsibility was well explored by him elsewhere, here three levels of conflict obtain rather than two: commitment to his people, who represent a particular religious tradition and way of life; his need to assess old values, having left them behind only to return to them in the realization that they are significant to his people; and, finally, the desire for self-fulfillment, both in his career and in relationships with others.

Furthermore, Glatshteyn freely admitted that his agony over the Holocaust had never left him. But here, he reveals the complex of contrasting emotions that was in part responsible for his guilt feelings. Po feels uncomfortable as the voice of his people, when its collective misery has been so much greater than his individual unhappiness. Moreover, he feels ambivalent about the city of Honan, a symbol for Eastern European Jewish life. He admires its ability to exist in the face of destruction and its continued struggle to stave off death. But his combined feelings of sympathy for his people and distress over their fate were not sufficient to override his quest for private thoughts and personal pleasure.

Perhaps the most interesting indication of Glatshteyn's mood in the 1960's is that, for Po, the deepest sadness and worry arises from his realization that he is growing old. After all his broader, more abstract involvements, it is this inevitable fact that causes him the most anguish, that can move him to tears. His only real comfort amid the pain and regret continues to be his art, his abiding love of language. At one point, Po says: *Kh'hob lib fule verter,/Vos vegn vi zey meynen./Kh'hob lib brenendike verter*, ("I love full words,/That weigh as they mean./I love burning words,"). Thus, a partial solution to the certain misery of old age and aloneness lies in his ability to compose a new ballad, in which he can express both his remorse over the past and his realization that, despite attempts at relationships in later years, he will finally emerge alone. Through the letter of Po, then, Glatshteyn once again gives voice to his aesthetic loyalties, discussing explicitly the implicit, though major, motivating force behind his initial choice of Li Tai Po as an artistic mouthpiece.

The words of Li Tai Po, while manifestly more confessional than those of Po Tshu Iy, focus as well on problems in relationships, especially those between an older man and a young woman. Although the burden of public responsibility and other issues confronting the artist are not ignored by Li, they are clearly less important to him than the purely individual trials and guilts attendant upon his interactions with women. But Li differs from Po not only because of his choice of subjects and his willingness to expose his secret thoughts. For, where Po is sedate and disciplined, Li is wild: his central difficulty seems to lie in his compulsion to carouse and behave rashly, despite his knowledge that he cannot cope with the consequences of his actions. However, the poems *Fun li-tay-po's gedenk-bikhl* ["From Li Tai Po's memory-book"][38] and *Mit li-tay-po* ["With Li Tai Po"][39] probe Li's inner strife from diverse perspectives. The five poems that comprise the first series are separate reflections; the second series consists of three poems that relate to one another and form a progression. In both series, however, Li is cared for by a woman whom he regards as a mixed blessing, because her goodness accentuates his guilt.

In *Fun li-tay-po's gedenk-bikhl*, the presence of this long-suffering woman is not immediately apparent; rather, as the series begins, Li is discussing his efforts at romantic liaisons. The first lover is a younger woman, addressed by Li as *kind* ("child"). He suspects that to her the prospect of an affair is at worst a game and at best some sort of mission: *Dem hekhstn khesed zukhstu/Tsu ton un gebn,/Oystsuleshn an alt lebn.* ("You are searching for the highest grace/To do and give,/To extinguish an old life."). The imagery of this poem centers around the color grey, mirroring Li's age and fatigue: he asks her whether her desire is to *Vern vayb tsum grayz-groy/Ibern gantsn layb.* ("Become the wife of grey hair/Over an entire body."). His heart, fluttering toward her as the only treasure of manhood that he still retains, is *grayz-groy* ("grey-haired") as well. Moreover, if she does come to him, the woman herself will be rewarded with a silver crown, her adoption of his essence thereby imbued with her own glitter.

The obstacle of age in this poem yields to a different barrier in the next section of Li's memoirs. Here, although he makes a valiant attempt to ignore his sense of public duty, it nonetheless manages to intrude upon and disrupt his private desires. Wishing to accommodate his would-be paramour's impatient demand that he temporarily abandon his national yoke, he literally locks it outside her home. But he is uneasy, and feels how *Mayn alt natsyonal harts hot gemont.* ("My old national heart demanded its due."). Realizing his dilemma, the woman endeavors more concertedly to seduce him. But as his excluded burden becomes vociferous, Li responds with increasing nervousness. Finally, he sees the bitter truth reflected in an angry mirror, which hurls back at him the image of *A naketn khinezer.* ("A naked Chinese."). Thus, Li cannot escape his sense of national commitment, which infiltrates his life even against his will and causes him to become a mere reflection of his own conflicts.

However, Li is less troubled by his thwarted wish to evade communal obligation than by his very real failures with respect to a single woman. In a frank admission of guilt, he confesses that, after having been with another woman, he will have to endure a day of chagrin because he has treated his wife shabbily. For, while with his lover he experiences the fulfillment of *borvise, shtiferishe fis* ("bare, mischievous legs"), his wife is devotion personified, waiting at home *grayz-geduldik* ("with grey-haired patience"). Li declares that he can overcome her clever head, her refined hands, but he is no match for her forgiving eyes.

In some sense, Li is angry at his wife for enhancing his own sense of wrongdoing by her virtuous conduct. The concept of a faithful woman as onerous is continued in *Mit li-tay-po* ["With Li Tai Po"]: this set of three poems begins with a depiction of Li's powerless anger and shame over his need to be cared for by his wife. Upon realizing that he is aging, however, he comes to recognize and appreciate her loyalty. All three works are conveyed through third-person narration; Li is referred to directly in the title and in the first poem but only indirectly alluded to elsewhere. This removal of Li from center stage is in fact a double distancing. As always, the Chinese poet's words are a means of camouflaging the voice of the Yiddish poet; now, however, Li's own thoughts are hidden.

The narrator explains in the first poem that Li regularly returns home drunk, to be undressed, put to bed and "re-assembled" the next morning—all by his wife with a *shtiln moyl* ("quiet mouth"). He is completely transparent to her, yet each day she repeats her ritual: *A gantsn tog trogt zi im vi a kroyn,/Biz er kumt vider bay-nakht an ayngerister* ("All day long she carries him like a crown,/Until he returns at night, blackened with soot"). Li's response to their situation is one of fear combined with the desire to flee, to remain alone.

But in the second poem, Li perceives that he is growing old; he discovers a new appreciation of nature, which in the past had eluded him. And, through an even more fundamental insight, Li understands the interrelation, indeed the juxtaposition, of life and death: *Kukn af a lebedik vigl,/Hern dem vig fun toyt!* ("To look at a living cradle,/To hear the rocking of death!"). Building on this new tendency toward reconciliation, he is able, in the third poem, to admit that, even while chasing the excitement of new lovers, he had in reality been searching all the time for his own wife. Now that he sees himself as old and isolated, she no longer seems uncomfortably good and oppressively close; instead, she appears wonderfully understanding and companionable. Li is ashamed of his obtuseness and asks: *Bistu geven mit mir dem gantsn veg,/Di gantse tsayt?* ("Were you with me the whole way,/The whole time?"). Finally, the woman's dogged dedication to her man is revealed as a sign of strength and wisdom rather than weakness, for she had been guided by only one basic question: *Ven vestu zikh bazinen/Un mikh nit zukhn dort,/Vu du konst mikh nit gefinen?* ("When will you consider/And not look for me,/Where you cannot find me?").

If Glatshteyn's personae function as a means of granting him the freedom to confess thoughts and emotions kept hidden elsewhere, then the placement of Li Tai Po himself in a distanced position may be presumed to indicate a special need. Indeed, the mood developed in *Mit li-tai-po*—one of resolution and a measure of peace if not contentment—is absent from the other "Chinese" poems. It seems that, even with the aid of disguise, Glatshteyn could not allow himself to be reconciled, his work of exploration and reevaluation completed. For, while able to pose certain ultimate questions concerning his life, he was evidently not yet ready to answer them definitively.

Songs of Reconciliation

*G*EZANGEN *fun rekhts tsu links*—Songs from Left to Right—
(New York, 1971)[1]—was Glatshteyn's final volume of poetry,
appearing just prior to his unforeseen death at the age of seventy-
five. Despite the suddenness of his demise, though, it is clear from
internal evidence that his book is a summing up, the completion
of a circle. The poetry itself is calmer, Glatshteyn's tone milder.
Above all, this is a work of reconciliation. Glatshteyn emerges as
a man who has attained equilibrium if not peace, whose life is
simpler, less discordant than before. On occasion, this sense of
resolution is expressed in a tone that borders on the celebratory.
The short poem *Ven* ["When"] (p. 44), for example, contains the
narrator's declaration that, if he could, he would concentrate on
singing the praises of his wife, *Vos zet oys azoy frish,/Baym ufshteyn
vi ven zi leygt zikh shlofn.* ("Who looks as fresh,/Upon arising as
when she goes to bed."); and on becoming "national-sentimental,"
always dedicating his poetry *Tsum pintele yid.* ("To the essence of
the Jew."). The narrator realizes, however, that in an era of universal
bitterness and danger, he cannot indulge in such happy pursuits,
for to do so, he believes, would be irresponsible. Yet, while his
innermost yearnings remain unfulfilled, the narrator does not pro-
ject the frustration and anger evident in earlier Glatshteyn poems:
instead, he has accepted the essential and unchangeable dilemma
of his role.

I The Lover at Peace

This does not mean that Glatshteyn renounced his desires com-
pletely. Indeed, *Di zilberne lorelay* ["The silver Lorelei"] (pp. 47-
48), one of the most resonantly beautiful poems in *Gezangen fun
rekhts tsu links,* comes as close to being a paean to his wife as the
164

nonconfessional Glatshteyn, who uses a third-person narrator in this work, would allow himself. As its title suggests, the poem plays on the legend—immortalized by Heinrich Heine in his poem "Die Lorelei"—of a fairy who lived on the Lorelei cliff overlooking the Rhine, luring sailors to a watery grave with her beautiful singing. The potentially frightening analogy is transformed in the first three lines of the poem: *Di zilberne lorelay iz a gute kekhin,/Zi fangt im mit ir ponem dem frumen,/Mit ir gutskeyt vos hot nisht keyn grunt.* ("The silver Lorelei is a good cook,/She catches him with her pious face,/With her goodness that has no bottom."). Here, it is not evil that ensnares the man, and not the dangerous Rhine that is unfathomable. This is a Jewish Lorelei, who feeds her aging man homey meals and guards his health. She is no longer young: hers is the silver, not the golden, hair of the legendary Lorelei. This woman's gold lies in her hands, the narrator asserts, to which the paintings on the walls of her peaceful home testify.[2]

As the poem progresses, the narrator incorporates the man into the Lorelei legend, again, however, reversing the tale. For this is hardly a helpless victim; he has gladly chosen his present life. Commenting that the silver Lorelei's nets—which she had earlier used while swimming from one conquest to another—now lie abandoned, he adds that the man possesses his own nets, but that these too have become unnecessary equipment. And the narrator concludes by stating that this contented couple, rather than pursuing new loves, will relive old experiences in the comfort of familiar confidentiality: *Zey veln beyde ruik un farginerish zikh teyln/Mit amolike nakhesn un alts oysdertseyln./Nokh a yor, nokh a yor.* ("They will both quietly and unbegrudgingly share/Past pleasures and tell everything./Another year, another year.").

The union depicted in *Di zilberne lorelay* is in keeping with the tone of peace and resolution that suffuses *Gezangen fun rekhts tsu links.* Both parties have come to terms with their maturity and its implications. While actively aware of his sexuality, the narrator of *Di zilberne lorelay* exhibits none of the wistful regret displayed in previous poems. In *Gezangen fun rekhts tsu links,* even the opportunity for a sexual relationship with a younger woman, which had ultimately confounded Glatshteyn's earlier narrators, is greeted with humor and the ripe understanding of an older man. The encounter in *A froyd-epizod* ["A Freud episode"] (p. 119), for example, is radically different from the one discussed in *Tsvey lider vegn altn.*

In those poems, the aging lover was trapped in a psychological morass; here, the man is able to maintain some distance in the face of a younger woman's subtly revealed neurotic desires. The first lines are a clever exposition of her difficulty that at the same time discreetly avoid the explicit mention of sexual intercourse: *Zi hot im ongegrifn bay ir foter-kompleks,/Plutsem, un fest gehaltn,* ("She assaulted him by her father-complex,/Suddenly, and held on tightly,"). Although he has been "attacked," the man does not cry out for help; instead, he looks at the woman with *farshemte groye hor* ("ashamed grey hair") and *farveynte oygn* ("tearful eyes"), asking himself whether what is occurring can be true, whether it is actually sex. But by the final strophe of the poem, as the narrator mentions the man's delight at being seduced, the woman's erotic intentions are clear. In another meaningfully ambiguous sexual reference, the narrator relates the man's query: *Ober kon es lang hobn a mamoshes?* ("But can it have substance for long?"). Here the "it" refers both to the nature of the relationship and to the old man's capacity for seduction, his potency. The answer is implicit in the question, for the man is *a rezignirter* ("resigned") as he asks it. And, to be sure, having challenged himself, he immediately swoons, bringing both the sexual incident and the poem itself to an abrupt halt.

II *Jewishness Redefined*

Glatshteyn's increased acceptance of his life and limitations allowed him at times to express a sense of comfort and well-being in personal relationships—despite the disclaimer, voiced in *Ven*, that he would not concentrate on them. So, too, was he able to turn with a certain equanimity to the second issue that had claimed his attention in *Ven:* his identity and position as a Jew. Indeed, in *Du shenkst mir* ["You grant me"] (pp. 43–44), even his response to God, which had always been intense and problematic, is now cheerful and relaxed. This work is an off-beat prayer of thanks to God for His return of the narrator's soul.[3] The narrator recounts that his initial concern in the morning is not the traditional *rozhinkes mit mandlen* ("raisins and almonds") of commerce, but rather leisurely worship. However, his words of praise are rendered not through the canonized morning service but rather as an accompaniment to eating breakfast. He puts himself together much as the narrator of *Inderfri* had—gradually readying himself for the day—but here, there is no sense of parts being out of order, of pieces missing. Instead, there is simply the pleasure of gathering strength, giving thanks, and enjoying a new morning. As the narrator drinks hot tea, he feels his limbs being cleaned out; with his orange-grapefruit juice he experiences the full power of day pouring into him; his legs are steadied by cereal with milk. This is the narrator's own *shakhres,* or morning prayer, his opportunity to bless everything to which he is destined—including, by implication, his old age. And he trusts that, although the day will contain its harsh burdens, throughout it the voice of God will accompany him.

Here, as in earlier poems concerning his heritage, Glatshteyn emphasizes his acceptance of essence but not necessarily of form. Although he sometimes appealed to formal religion for the sake of argument in his work—as in *Undzer got* ["Our God"] (pp. 77–78), where he claims belief in Jewish resurrection, simultaneously dismissing Christianity as idolatrous—his stance toward ritual was essentially secular. His commitment to *yiddishkeyt* as a national, historical, philosophical, geneological, and even psychological entity—all of which have common borders with theological Jewishness—was total. And as he came increasingly to make peace with the complexities of his identity, Glatshteyn was forced to confront the fact that this reconciliation, like his romantic one, could be reached only by relinquishing certain long cherished beliefs and dreams about the world and his place in it.

For in *Gezangen fun rekhts tsu links,* Glatshteyn expressed an outlook that was in total opposition to his very earliest pronouncements in the *In zikh* manifesto and in his first volumes of poetry: the notion that to be Jewish is to be perpetually separate from the wider world. Despite the possibility for connection with others, Jews ultimately stand alone—partly because they have been forced by circumstances to accept insularity as legitimate and appropriate. The concept of Jewish isolation is expressed with particular succinctness in the poem *Az der kultur-yid* ["When the culture-Jew"] (p. 39), a work whose pithy message is accentuated by the breathy shortness of its lines. The narrator wonders what the "culture-Jew" expects when wandering alone in the desert. The answer is straightforward: *S'zoln im antkegnkumen/Pikaso, oder sartr.* ("That he should be catered to by [literally: approached by]/Picasso, or Sartre.").[4] But as this two-line strophe ends and the next one begins, it becomes clear that the Jew's expectations will not be realized:

instead of the luminaries of European culture, his only secure companion in the wilderness is *a tanakhisher posek* ("an Old Testament verse").

The image of the isolated wanderer in the desert is used intriguingly here. On one level, it evokes the forty-year wandering of the Jewish people prior to their entry into the land of Israel. In this context, the culture-Jew's solitude signifies loss of contact with his own people: he has chosen to separate himself from them, preferring to follow a nontraditional path. But precisely by being a culture-Jew, he inhabits another desert, segregated from the larger society that he seeks to join. In this desert, he is not alone of his own volition, but rather because others reject him. Like the narrator of *Di kroyn*, whose discarded *yiddishkeyt* had swum back to him, the culture-Jew must acknowledge that his only companion is the haunting presence of what he has unsuccessfully tried to escape: his historical, parochial heritage.

The narrator of *Maranen*["Marranos"] (p. 117)[5] sharply summarizes the plight of the Jew in an alien culture: *Tsvishn goyim zenen ale yidn maranen.* ("Among non-Jews, all Jews are Marranos."). As an endangered minority, he contends, Jews must always compromise themselves to some extent; how much they choose to do so is another matter. At worst, they may become *bifresye khazerfresers* ("public pork-gluttons"), zealously attempting to conform to the dominant milieu by spurning the laws of their people. But although it is possible to stop short of such betrayal, there are few alternatives for the diaspora Jew. Playing on the old Enlightenment ideal, the narrator declares that, at the very least, the Jew must be: *Yid in hoyz, mentshl in gas.* ("Jew in the house, little man in the street."). Yet the diminutive *mentshl* implies that even this degree of compliance with the dictates of a secular environment is a degrading capitulation. Inevitably, then, life among non-Jews is fraught with complications and riddled with pain and discomfort. As the narrator of *Tfutses* ["The Jewish Diaspora"] (p. 40) explains: in the *keynems-land* ("no-man's land") of the diaspora, *Mir veysn dokh—mir zaynen arumgeringlte yidn/Bay azoyfil sine-grenetsn.* ("We know, of course—we are Jews encircled/By so many hatred-borders.").

III   *The Diaspora Spurned: Israel Embraced*

The general sense of malaise inspired by an atmosphere perceived as inherently hostile to Jews caused Glatshteyn to feel uncomfortable about life in America, which had by 1971 been his home for over half a century. But his uneasiness was more metaphoric than actual. Glatshteyn had always criticized aspects of American life; however, whereas in the 1920's he had felt intimidated and impotent, he was merely irritated by the foment of the late 1960's. Disgusted with leaders of both sides in the Vietnam war for allowing the deaths of innocent people while they—he asserted—indulged in megalomaniacal celebrations, he was annoyed as well at what he deemed the irresponsibility of youthful antiwar protesters who had never known true hardship. And, in a clever *reductio ad absurdum* (*Mayn rasistishe biografye* ["My racist biography"]), (pp. 121–24), the poet of *Luter bodi* and *Harlem: zuntik* vented his resentment at the Black Panthers.

After the Holocaust, Glatshteyn's map consisted of only two locations other than the Eastern Europe of his memory. As a corollary to his dissatisfaction with the United States, he attempted, at the end of his life, to finally resolve his conflicts about Israel, particularly with regard to that nation's use of violence and its disdain for things Eastern European. *Ziger* ["Conqueror"] (pp. 35–36), for instance, is a poem about the Six Day War that contains strong praise for the Israeli military, whose prowess, the narrator insists, goes hand in hand with nonbelligerence. He encapsulates this view in the poem's first line, where he addresses a soldier as *Troyeriker ziger*, ["Sad Conqueror,"]. Indeed, in the narrator's interpretation, the Six Day War illustrates the antipathy of the Israelis to combat: reluctant to fight, they had conquered swiftly simply to extricate themselves from the fray. For these soldiers are not *kikhol hagoyim* ("like all the non-Jews"), but rather *kikhol hayidn* ("like all the Jews")—they do not enjoy violence.

The narrator continues his comments in this vein, minimizing the political import of the 1967 Arab-Israeli conflict and, rather, converting it into a predominantly religious or national battle in which Jews and their Jewish God had been forced *Nisim tsu vayzn.* ("To perform miracles."). In reality, however, this wonder rests not in the Jews themselves but in misperception on the part of their enemies: believing that they would be confronting a nation of cowards, they had been shocked and frightened to discover *shtol un ayzn* ("steel and iron") instead. By construing this negative view of Jews as something imposed by Israel's adversaries, the narrator thus obviates the need to explore what other Glatshteyn narrators had felt compelled to discuss: the presence of this same stereotype in the Israeli notion of Eastern European Jewish life. Indeed, the narrator wishes to consolidate these two versions of Jewish culture and oppose them to the rest of the world. He declares that his soldier is *nisht keyn ish milkhome,/Nor a man fun fridn.* ("not a man of war,/But a man of peace."). With this formulation, the narrator subtly implies that the gentleness he so admires is rooted in Eastern European *yiddishkeyt;* for whereas *ish milkhome*—"man of war" stems from the Hebrew-Aramaic component of Yiddish, *man fun fridn*—"man of peace" does not. This synthesis culminates in the narrator's assertion that, for Jews, religion and history still take precedence over any latter-day attraction to violence: *Hot men badarft zayn a novi,/Az loyfst vos gikher zikh oysveynen/Bay der koyslhamaarovi?* ("Did one have to be a prophet,/[to predict] That you would run as quickly as possible to cry your eyes out/At the Wailing Wall?").

The dual nature of Israel as ancient homeland and thriving new state finally led Glatshteyn to experiment with the idea that it was the appropriate home for all Jews, a concept which he developed in *Funvanen iz a yid?* ["Where does a Jew come from?"] (pp. 29–30) and *Letster opshtel* ["Last stop"] (pp. 33–34). The first of these poems concerns the arrival of the narrator at the Israeli border and his interaction with the clerk who is to issue him his visa. The latter, weary after a day of work, greets the narrator with a yawn and perfunctorily asks to know his previous home. He is unprepared for the response: *"Yeder yids funvanen/Iz fundanen,"* ("Every Jew's whence/Is hence,"). At first the clerk does not comprehend. Once he does, however, he is delighted, summoning a *minyen* ("minyan [prayer quorum]") of clerks to observe the narrator, who meanwhile has broken into song. Now everyone understands and appreciates the importance of the narrator's Jewish visa: it is heritage—his own and that of all Jews. Their communal joy rises to ectasy, peaking in a dance that the narrator and the clerks perform *vi lyubavitsher khsidim* ("like Lubavitsh hasidim").

On a purely narrative level, the point of this poem is uncomplicated: the home of all Jews, no matter what their apparent origin, is ultimately the Jewish land. However, *Funvanen iz a yid?* gains sophistication from its imagery, which suggests both the myriad of influences that converge in Israel and the possibility of their harmonious integration. The picture of a *minyen pkidim* ("minyan of clerks"), for example—a religious grouping of secularly occupied individuals—indicates the natural connection in Israel of what may be experienced in the Diaspora as two ways of life, an interpenetration that climaxes with the spectacle of these bureaucrats dancing like Hasidim. Although they are citizens of a modern nation, Glatshteyn thus implies, Israelis have not broken the thread that ties them to Eastern Europe—and, by extension, to other areas where Jewish life has flourished.

The thought that Israel is the natural home of all Jews because it incorporates the entirety of Jewish heritage becomes part of a larger vision in *Letster opshtel*. The title of this work suggests the end of a journey, and its first two lines indicate that, in fact, the trip has been an ultimate one: *Keyn vayter fundanen iz nishto,/Keyn brik tsum tsurik oykh nisht.* ("No further hence exists,/And no bridge to back either."). Both *fundanen* ("hence; from here") and *tsurik* ("back") are employed as nouns here; yet, as the narrator continues, it is clear that places and experiences other than those of this last stop, even if endowed with substance, are becoming peripheral. Israel is the supreme nucleus, the embodiment of Jewish history and beliefs, the spot from which Jews will never again be driven away.

Time itself assumes a new form here, as past and present coalesce. In the central image of this poem, the narrator recommends going outside to the living earth, where *Vest vern dayn eygener arkheolog,/Vest ufzukhn di trit dayne di ayngeknotene.* ("You'll become your own archeologist,/You'll find your embedded footsteps."). In this land, then, it is possible for Jews to find their true selves, the original configurations of their existence. As with an archeological object, they will have to clean away layers of *mitgeshlepte greytkeytn* ("dragged-along willingnesses") and *fartreyfte goyishkeytn* ("impure non-Jewishnesses") before uncovering this source of being; but the reward—self-recognition—makes the effort worthwhile. In the end, the final stop of *Letster opshtel* is revealed as the last stage of a complex journey back to Jewish origins: back to the historical Jewish land, back to an appreciation of Jewish history and the development of a timeless Jewish heritage, back to a set of pure Jewish values. At the same time, this last stop, where past and present come together, is the point from which a future of purity will emanate. Thus, in *Letster opshtel*, Glatshteyn makes his peace with

Israel, accepting it as the one place in all of space and time where a full and uncompromised Jewish existence can be maintained in all its richness.

IV   *The Rebel Reneges*

Even more pronounced than Glatshteyn's efforts to reflect a harmonious Jewish identity is his pursuit of reconciliation with his literary forebears. *Gezangen fun rekhts tsu links* opens with an essay entitled *Tsuriktrakhtungen* ["Thinking back"] (pp. 11–18), a reevaluative look at the history of Yiddish poetry in America. In this unusual work, Glatshteyn deliberately minimizes the differences between *In zikh* and its precursor, *Di yunge*, and downplays the extent of his own group's radical nature. In retrospect, the appearance of *Tsuriktrakhtungen* is a special event in Glatshteyn's career: just as he had announced himself to the literary world in his prose introduction to the *In zikh* anthology, so he takes his leave—fifty years later—in the same fashion.

Glatshteyn begins this essay by explaining the impetus for his comments: an opportunity he had had to witness the enthusiasm of a young writer. Making explicit what is merely intimated in some of his poems, he recalls the almost sexual excitement that his first steps as a poet had aroused in him, going on to lament that, in later years, it is regrettable but natural for a kind of artistic arteriosclerosis to set in, forcing even the most daring to be less extravagant with creative energy.

The prospect of chronicling his career is in a way unattractive to him, Glatshteyn admits, because it is a sign that his future has become vague; nonetheless, he allows himself to discuss some moments from his initiation into the world of Yiddish poetry. Two main topics absorb him: the character of his own originality, and the relationship that he and the other members of *In zikh* had sustained with *Di yunge* as well as with that group's literary predecessors. His first poems, he maintains, although absolutely new in form and in expression of content, were by no means an indication of disrespect for the elders of Yiddish belles lettres; on the contrary, he had felt himself deeply tied to a great literary tradition, one that incorporated both *Di yunge* and earlier writers. In this, he contends, he was profoundly different from the members of *Di yunge*, who not only objected to the work of their older colleagues but also disliked them personally. Taking his point still further, Glatshteyn claims that, while he was indeed trying to assert himself against his literary fathers, a simultaneous sense of piety had caused him to soften his criticism of them so that they would not feel maligned. He even begins to question the reality of his insurgency, speculating that perhaps he had only appeared to rebel because he was responding to the rhythms of American and English poetry, which until that time had not influenced Yiddish literature.

These musings lead Glatshteyn to declare that in actuality *Di yunge* were greater literary revolutionaries than the *Inzikhistn*, because they had truly rejected their past whereas *In zikh* had not chosen to do so. Any impression that the younger group was more extreme is by dint of the fact that they, as opposed to *Di yunge*, had written about their own poetry (something *Di yunge* had not done), and thereby created an illusion of substantial innovation.

Even as he and his colleagues engaged in literary battles, Glatshteyn concludes, they had recognized that they were attempting to appropriate a literature of significance; thus, his own superficial demeanor of haughty defiance had been tempered by his realization that he was honored to be a member of the same literature as his adversaries. And, harking back to the original impulse of the essay, he regrets the present straits of his literary generation: having grown older, they should by now be fathers, accepting the respectful rebellion of a new group of poets. But that continuity has been denied them.

V   *A Last Word on Yiddish*

Tsuriktrakhtungen, though a benign and peacemaking look at the past, leaves no doubt about the grim fate of Yiddish literature. Glatshteyn's prognosis for the future of the Yiddish language itself was equally bleak. In *Gebentsht zol zayn* ["Blessed should be"] (p. 109), the narrator claims to be pleased that no one speaks or reads Yiddish any longer. His reasoning is curious: language as a tool has become debased. Honestly intended words are extinct and all that remains is *Reyd venerish durkhgefresn* ("Speech venereally eaten through"). Thus, the narrator accepts as a blessing the position of Yiddish, or *bobe yidish* ("grandmother Yiddish"), as he calls it. Neither spoken nor read, but rather preserved in a *genizah*,[6] the language is protected from the impurity of lips that would defile it.

And the narrator concludes with the somber statement that he and others of his generation—refugees from their own descendants—*Trogn a gedekhenish vi a bashertn yokh.* ("Carry a remembrance like a predestined burden."). Thus, the nightmare vision of *Di freyd fun yidishn vort* has come to pass: Glatshteyn's cherished Yiddish exists no longer, except in the distant and elusive realms of dream and recollection.

VI   *The Personae: Slipping Masks*

Emblematic of Glatshteyn's need to achieve closure in *Gezangen fun rekhts tsu links* is the reappearance in this volume of both Reb Nakhmen of Bratslav and Li Tai Po, his two favorite personae. By and large, these figures continued to fulfill their previous function for Glatshteyn: through them, he was able to discuss the issues that concerned him elsewhere in his work, but either more openly or with a different slant. In this last volume, however, there were some changes. The two poems in which the Bratslaver's voice is heard, for instance, contain nothing to identify their narrator, save his characteristic manner of speech, and the fact that his words are addressed to Nosn, his scribe. Moreover, in one of the two works, *Zay nisht keyn shoyte* ["Do not be a fool"] (pp. 69–71), Nosn's name does not appear until the end. Thus, distancing devices are much less obvious here than in the earlier Bratslav poems, suggesting a Glatshteyn so reconciled that he no longer desired, or needed, to mask his comments as fully as before.

Still, in *Zay nisht keyn shoyte* Glatshteyn expresses sentiments concerning man's relationship to God that do not emerge in the other poems of *Gezangen fun rekhts tsu links.* For all his attempts to come to terms with a Jewish God, none of Glatshteyn's poems so displays the totality of belief that emerges in the lines of *Zay nisht keyn shoyte,* and certainly none of them manages to combine naivete and a kind of brilliant logic as this work does. Nakhmen begins by warning Nosn not to make a fool of himself by believing in God, since God is too powerful to need such gestures from His creatures. Furthermore, belief implies its opposite, and this Nakhmen dismisses as idolatry. Nakhmen goes on to contrast Judaism with Christianity; the latter religion, he asserts, with its concepts of Trinity and virgin birth, requires faith because its tenets are indeed impossible to accept at face value.

Nakhmen concedes that human beings must respond to God's deeds with trust, because these are beyond the realm of mortal comprehension. But this is not the same as subjecting His being to the test of belief. The latter is heresy, Nakhmen admonishes Nosn, since he would never think to question the existence of a human being, a cat, or even a worm in such a manner. Moreover, he concludes, apparently unaware of his circular reasoning, the question of belief is irrelevant in the end, since the world and everything in it belongs to God and is permeated by His radiance. Thus, Nakhmen uses the guise of sophistication to make an apparently complicated argument out of what is essentially a simple statement of faith. His language, by contrast, is at its plainest when his thoughts are most complex. He forms nouns from adverbs to concretize abstractions; the impact of this technique is particularly strong because four such terms are crowded into three lines: *Iber der aldoikeyt un nishtoikeyt,/Er vos iz dort iber ale dortikeytn/Un umetumikeyt,/Darf az du zolst in im gleybn?* ("Over the allthereness and notthereness,/He who is there over all therenesses/And everywhereness,/Needs you to believe in him?").

Unlike *Zay nisht keyn shoyte*, it is clear from the very first line of *Zolst zikh nisht vundern* ["You shouldn't wonder"] (pp. 72–73), with its reference to Nosn, that this is a Bratslav poem. *Zolst zikh nisht vundern* lacks both the linguistic play of *Zay nisht keyn shoyte* and its unique point of view. What the two poems do have in common is their simplicity and their expression of transcendent faith. In *Zolst zikh nisht vundern*, Nakhmen is disturbed about humanity's unending misconduct, which is especially inexplicable because Nakhmen cannot imagine mankind functioning autonomously (in this his view diverges from that of other Glatshteyn narrators).

Once again Nakhmen's solution involves reification—here, of the soul. In Nakhmen's view, human beings cannot be better than they are because there are no more fresh and pure souls with which to fill them. Using the metaphor of tailoring, he decides that those who labor in the heavenly soul workshop, refurbishing souls for their next home—and he refrains from mentioning God in this regard—no longer have good material from which to work: *Alts iz tserisn, tseflikt, mies farflekt.* ("Everything is torn, ragged, loathesomely spotty."). In olden times, used-up souls would come back in good condition, requiring only a smoothing out before being ready to inhabit a young body, but for several generations, the soul tailors have had to resort to mending. Therefore, Nakhmen explains, given the raw material that people innocently and helplessly receive, better behavior cannot be expected of them. Nakhmen thus refuses to blame the human condition on either heavenly or earthly forces.

Nakhmen's complete faith, which remains intact because essentially contradictory principles are never examined, ties together *Zay nisht keyn shoyte* and *Zolst zikh nisht vundern*. It also separates them from the rest of Glatshteyn's work, where a paradoxically secular peace with God is attained on the basis of values accepted and heritage remembered. Precisely because he could not bring himself to exhibit unquestioning belief in a Jewish deity, Glatshteyn used the guise of Reb Nakhmen to explore and test out the possibility of such a faith.

Just as the Bratslav poems represent, on one level, a break with Glatshteyn's earlier pattern of distancing, so, too, does the first of three poems collectively entitled *Fun li-tay-pos notits-bikhl* ["From Li Tai Po's notebook"] (pp. 91—97). Glatshteyn had created the persona of Li Tai Po in part to establish a culture entirely removed from the world of Jews. Yet the first of these poems, *Der bsomim-hendler* ["The spice merchant"], concerns a Jewish Chinese man, Vang-Tshien, through whom the difficulties of the Jew in Diaspora— a major issue for Glatshteyn in *Gezangen fun rekhts tsu links*—are held up for observation.

Although Vang-Tshien has a Chinese name, he is nonetheless described in terms of standard Jewish stereotypes: he is a merchant, his beard is full and blacker than others. Despite the fact that his grandfather before him had been a spice merchant on the same street, Vang-Tshien is a foreigner with foreign blessings on his lips; he is cautious, measured and reflective in his speech. His wife, too, behaves in uncustomary fashion, laughing more loudly and bowing less low than her Chinese counterparts. Above all, Li Tai Po is afraid of Vang-Tshien because the latter has admitted to him that, as a Jew, he is guilty of killing a god. Although the narrator is not himself a believer, he is intimidated by this knowledge—even as he sits with the Jewish couple, drinking their wine. Li Tai Po concludes his description of Vang-Tshien with an expression of fear inspired by the latter's assertion that one day all of Cathay will be ruled by a foreign beard like his own; hence the narrator falls prey to the classic suspicion of nonJews that Jews plan to take over the world. The mollifying efforts of Vang-Tshien's wife apparently do nothing to assuage this anxiety.

In *Ven ikh bin alt geven* ["When I was old"], Glatshteyn returns to a pet topic: the relationship between an old man and a young woman. The poem is unusual, however, in that its narrator is the woman, who addresses the old Li Tai Po. It is a work of great tenderness; there is no sense of female irresponsibility and potential readiness to hurt a declining man, traits that mark the women in other poems where Glatshteyn confronts the same issue. The title of this poem highlights its central question, that of chronological disparity. Devoid of context, it suggests old age, while in fact, corresponding to the first part of the poem's first line: *Ven ikh bin alt geven tsvelf yor,* ("When I was twelve years old,").

The incident recalled by the narrator involves her experience of initiation into young womanhood, an event for which she credits Li Tai Po. One evening, while walking in the garden with members of her family and being ignored by them, the young woman found herself approached by Li Tai Po, who took her hand and spoke, maturing her in the process. The woman is grateful to Li Tai Po for knowing: *Vifl froy s'voynt/In a tsvelf-yorik meydele,* ("How much woman lives/In a twelve-year-old little girl,") as well as for his subsequent restraint on that fateful evening.

In repayment for his generosity of spirit, sexual intelligence and sensitivity, the woman, now fully adult, has returned to Li Tai Po, who has become an old man. Despite his substantial loss of power, she wishes to consummate the union that he had so benignly avoided when, as she puts it—stressing in a new way the age difference between them, as well as the passage of time—*kh'bin yung geven tsvelf yor.* ("I was twelve years young."). This is not an act of pity, but rather one of compassion and gratitude. Now it is her hand that will move him, bringing back all that he has lost, and transforming him just as she had been transformed so many years before.

This poem, although poignant, presents a final view of Li Tai Po, not as the old hedonist, nor the doddering fool who must depend on his wife to help him out of his drunken states, but rather as a clever and gentle man who deserves to be rewarded for his kindness. Any doubts or conflicts he may feel are hidden by his silence. But, unlike the encounter depicted in *A froyd epizod,* or in other poems where the motivation of the woman was questionable or questioned, this relationship is based on affection and respect rather than on spurious desires.

Beyond the internal closure achieved in *Ven ikh bin alt geven,* a broader resolution is evident as well. For, one area in which Glatshteyn's narrators in *Gezangen fun rekhts tsu links* exhibit resignation, rather than peace and satisfaction, is that of interactions between old men and younger women. In every instance, except for *Ven ikh bin alt geven,* the man is finally a buffoon or a helpless, impotent object of seduction. By allowing the woman's perspective to emerge, Glatshteyn suggests that here too—although it may be difficult to recognize and accept—there is every reason for an aging male to enjoy feelings of well-being and calm.

Not so the Li Tai Po poem *A zun* ["A Son"], which concerns the unnatural situation of a father who outlives his son. Although this description is on one level a straightforward discussion of personal tragedy, it is also an allusion to national disaster, in which the living thread of death and remembrance is torn, leaving the father with a burden of guilt for being an illegal heir, and resulting in a peculiar merging of life and death because he has not managed to support his son, *Vi s'shteyt geshribn,* ("As it is written,") until the moment of his own death. This tragedy is so immense and obvious, that strangers come to mourn as if for a member of their own family.

A zun reflects a bitter truth from which Glatshteyn could not escape and simultaneously reveals an underlying motivation of *Gezangen fun rekhts tsu links.* As he lamented in *Tsuriktrakhtungen,* there would be no younger generation of writers to approach him in the spirit of rebellion; as a Yiddish poet, he was without heirs, without even readers to memorialize him. Glatshteyn grasped that in a sense he would have to be his own son, that he would have to achieve reconciliation and continuity by himself. Thus he concluded his final volume with *1919, In roykh,* and *Tirtl-toybn,* the poems with which he had inaugurated his career as a Yiddish poet. Perhaps he was hoping to find permanence, not in his father's shadow now, but in his own.

CHAPTER 8

Conclusion

Y ANKEV Glatshteyn was above all else a poet of crisis: turmoil
was the dramatic pivot of his career. Although in the 1930's, he
seemed to be approaching a kind of equilibrium, the cataclysmic
events of the Holocaust destroyed any chance for him to fully ac-
complish it. With the exception of his discussions about personal
relationships, the final reconciliations of *Gezangen fun rekhts tsu
links* seem forced on occasion, as if emanating from a need for
resolution rather than its actual achievement. At the end of his life,
he was racing against time to come to terms with a world that was
moving step by step with him towards death.

Glatshteyn lived to see his worst youthful fantasies borne out and
the treasures of his existence annihilated. His sensitive and loving
employment of Yiddish, and his keen sense of the past—both of
which had enriched his work as early as *Tirtl-toybn*—were now, he
feared, instruments in the service of that which had already slipped
forever into the realm of memory. Underlying Glatshteyn's worries
and his need to make his own peace with all aspects of his past and
present, however, was the desperate feeling that there would be
no future for his artistic contributions, that, as the narrator of *Undzer
dor* had lamented so many years previously, the wick of his gen-
eration was flickering dimly and would be extinguished with his
death.

Against this grim prediction of literary oblivion, there remains
only the greatness of Glatshteyn's work. It should suffice.

179

Notes and References

Chapter One

1. Most of the general information for this chapter comes from the following sources: *Leksikon fun der nayer yidisher literatur* (New York, 1958), II, col. 256–61. Yankev Pat, "Yankev glatshteyn." In *Shmuesn mit yidishe shrayber* (New York, 1954), pp. 79–95. Avrom Tabatshnik, "A Conversation with Jacob Glatstein." Trans. Joseph C. Landis. *Yiddish* 1 (Summer 1973): 40–53. Ruth Whitman, "The Man and His Work." In *The Selected Poems of Jacob Glatstein.* Trans. Ruth Whitman (New York, 1972), pp. 11–23. Quotations and specific references from these works will be cited in the body of the text.

2. Glatshteyn, camouflaged as Klara Blum, evidently wanted to carry his joke as far as possible. The following strophe from one of these pseudonymous poems, *A gezang* ["A song"], shows him employing a style quite unlike his own adventurous one; moreover, it is a clear attack on the literary "establishment" of his time:

> *Oy, s'iz umetik azoy*
> *In kafe tsu zitsn,*
> *Hern alte khokhmes,*
> *Oysgedroshene vitsn.*
> *Un der roykh mit tempkeyt*
> *Filt undz on di moykhes.*
> *Tsvishn groyse mentshn*
> *Geyen oys di koykhes.*
> *Oy, s'iz umetik azoy.*

> (Oy, it's so sad
> To sit in the café,
> To hear old witticisms,
> Hackneyed jokes.
> And the smoke fills up our
>   brains
> With dullness.

Among great men, one's
strength expires.
Oy, it's so sad.)

3. Y. Glatshteyn, *Dray studentn zenen mir geven* ["We Were Three Students"], in *In der velt mit yidish* (New York, 1972), pp. 286–88.

4. Arn Glants-Leyeles, *Tsu aykh dikhter yidishe* ["To You Yiddish Poets"], in *A yid afn yam* (New York, 1947), p. 201.

Chapter Two

1. A. Afranel, Al. Gurye, Yankev Glatshteyn, Bernard Luis, Ruvn Ludvig, A. Leyeles, N. Minkov, Yankev Stodolski, contributors, *In zikh* (New York, 1920).

2. This group included in its ranks the poets Mani Leyb, Moyshe Leyb Halpern, Avrom Moyshe Dilon; and the prose writers Yoysef Opatoshu and Dovid Ignatov. For a good brief introduction in English to the Yiddish literary milieu in America, see Irving Howe, "The Yiddish Word," in *World of Our Fathers* (1976; paperback rpt. New York, 1977), pp. 417–59.

3. Y. Rapoport, *Yankev glatshteyns dikhterisher veg: fun zilbekstsentrishkeyt tsu groys-natsionaler dikhtung,* ["Yankev Glatshteyn's poetic path: from syllablecenteredness to great national poetry,"] in *Oysgerisene Bleter* (Melbourne, 1957), pp. 97–137; Shmuel Lapin, "Jacob Glatstein: Poetry and Peoplehood," *American Jewish Yearbook,* 73 (1972), 611–17.

4. B. Alkvit, *Yankev glatshteyn* ["Yankev Glatshteyn"], *Getseltn,* 2 (Oct.–Dec. 1946), 205–18; Arn Glants-Leyeles, *Yankev glatshteyns veg* ["Yankev Glatshteyn's path"] (1946; rpt. in *Velt un vort: literarishe un andere eseyen,* New York, 1958), pp. 136–44.

5. These poems appeared in *Poezye,* June 1919, pp. 5–6.

6. The study of sacrifices in Leviticus, during which the term *tirtl-toybn* would arise, was traditionally the first biblical lesson for a boy in *kheyder.*

Chapter Three

1. *Yankev glatshteyn,* pp. 66–68.
2. *Fraye ferzn,* p. 10.
3. *Fraye ferzn,* pp. 7–8.
4. *Yankev glatshteyn,* p. 39.
5. *Fraye ferzn,* p. 46.
6. "Miss Negro Slayer by Half an Hour," *New York Times,* 7 Jan. 1922, p. 1, col. 3.
7. *Yankev glatshteyn,* pp. 29–30.
8. *Yankev glatshteyn,* pp. 46–47.
9. *Fraye ferzn,* p. 27.

10. *Fraye ferzn*, pp. 22–23.

11. *Fraye ferzn*, pp. 14–16.

12. Glatshteyn's use of blacks in this way is quite different from their stereotypical image in the 1920's. Frederick J. Hoffman—*The Twenties: American Writing in the Postwar Decade*, 2nd. ed., rev. (1962; paperback rpt. New York, 1965), p. 308—describes the predominant artistic view of blacks in this period: "Since the Negro lived differently, seemed to have reserves of wisdom not available to the white consciousness, his life, art, and society were given special examination and praise. His was a free, uninhibited, unmechanized soul, and his 'dark laughter' provided an interesting commentary on the fretful, petty obsessions of the white man."

13. *Yankev glatshteyn*, p. 7.

14. *Fraye ferzn*, p. 21.

15. *Yankev glatshteyn*, pp. 41–42.

16. These examples are all from *Yankev glatshteyn*—the first two appear in the poem *O ambasadore* ["Oh ambassador"], pp. 16–17; the third occurs in *Du* ["You"], pp. 46–47.

17. *Fraye ferzn*, pp. 80–81.

18. Respectively, *Kredos*, pp. 52–63; *Yidishtaytshn*, pp. 51–52, and 56–58.

19. *Kredos*, pp. 34–37. According to Moses Rischin, in *The Promised City: New York's Jews 1870–1914* (1962; rpt. New York, 1970), p. 89, Sheeny Mike was the nickname of Michael Kurtz, reputedly the "'champion burglar of America'." In a note on her translation of *Shini mayk* in *The Selected Poems of Jacob Glatstein* (New York, 1972), p. 181, Ruth Whitman indicates that Glatshteyn's Sheeny Mike is an "imaginary composite of several real gangsters who grew up on the lower East Side in New York in the nineteen-twenties."

20. See, for instance, *Di froy fregt* ["The wife asks"], *Kredos*, p. 21.

21. *Kredos*, pp. 31–33.

22. *Kredos*, pp. 27–29.

23. Even Lamed Shapiro, who otherwise took a jaundiced view of Glatshteyn's love poetry, found this work to be a healthy exception. Reviewing *Kredos* in *Vokh*, 11 Oct. 1929, p. 18, Shapiro panned all Glatshteyn's works on the subject—save *Fun undzer yokh*—as combined proof that the poet was "puritan on the one hand, a cynic on the other—both attitudes merge to render sexual love loathsome."

24. *Yidishtaytshn*, pp. 10–11.

25. *Yidishtaytshn*, pp. 14–15.

26. See, for example, his scathing *Tayere itsiks* ["Dear Itsiks"] (*Kredos*, p. 81).

27. *Yidishtaytshn*, pp. 67–69 and 70–72 respectively.

28. See, for instance, the poems *Watch Your Step* (p. 31) and *In goldenem land* ["In the golden land"] (pp. 32–33), both of which appear in Halpern's

first volume of poetry: *In nyu york—In New York—*, 3rd ed. (1919; rpt. New York, 1954).

29. *Khokhmes hayudaike* refers to the *Wissenschaft des Judentums*, the so-called enlightened, scientific—as opposed to strictly traditional—study of Jewish subjects. This method, which began to flourish in the late eighteenth century, is based on criteria of general European scholarship.

30. Respectively: *In nyu york*, p. 78; *Di goldene pave—The Golden Peacock*—(New York, 1924), pp. 16–18.

31. *In nyu york*, p. 109.

32. *In nyu york*, pp. 44–46.

33. *In nyu york*, p. 152.

34. Glatshteyn discussed his bond with Halpern in a 1955 taped interview with the critic Avrom Tabatshnik, published as "A Conversation with Jacob Glatstein," trans. Joseph C. Landis, *Yiddish*, 1, (Summer 1973), 47: "I think Moshe Leyb's was a great achievement. He too broadened poetic terminology, poetic language. He demonstrated that you could use ordinary words in poetry. But it must be pointed out that Moshe Leyb was not always successful in creating a hostel for these words. His hostel was not so successful. I think that I often took the commonplace, idiomatic, succulent, folk expressions and even the heavy prosaic words, and I tried to harness them in the traces of poetry."

35. See Glatshteyn's sharp critique of Sh. Y. Abramovitsh's novel *Fishke der krumer* ["Fishke the lame"] in *In tokh genumen—Sum and Substance*, (New York, 1947), pp. 453–69.

36. See Glatshteyn's poem *Nayvort* ["Newword"] (*Kredos*, pp. 39–40). A less direct but equally strong reference to Joyce's influence is seen in Glatshteyn's *Ven dzhoys volt geshribn yidish: a par-ode* ["If Joyce had written Yiddish: a par-ode(y),"] *In zikh* 3, (July, 1928), 68–70; in this work Glatshteyn imitates Joyce's style.

37. *Yidishtaytshn*, pp. 108–11, 99–102, and 97–98, respectively.

38. Ladino is popularly used to designate the language of Sephardic Jews. However, it is more appropriately reserved for the language they used in translating sacred texts. Their vernacular is better designated as Dzhudezmo.

39. Arn Glants-Leyeles, *Yankev glatshteyns naye vendung* ["Yankev Glatshteyn's new turn"], *Vokh*, 13 Dec. 1929, p. 9.

40. *Yidishtaytshn*, pp. 79–81.

41. *Yidishtaytshn*, pp. 85–93.

Chapter Four

1. Although he originally published *A gute nakht, velt* in January 1938, Glatshteyn canonized this poem with the date April 1938—the month it appeared in *In zikh*, 8 (1938), 66–67.

2. The translation of these lines is by Ruth Whitman. See *The Selected Poems of Jacob Glatstein*, p. 59. The following is a more literal translation: "My leaves of sacred books, my twenty-four [books of the Tanakh],/My *gemore*, to arduous/Talmudic subjects, to bright *ivretaytsh* [stylized archaic Yiddish used e.g. in the translation of sacred texts],/To Jewish law, to deep meaning, to obligation, to that which is just."

3. See, for example, H. Leyvik, *Vegn geyn tsurik in geto* ["About returning to the ghetto"], *Tog*, 15 March 1938, rpt. in H. Leyvik, *Eseyen un redes* (New York, 1963), pp. 127–30. Leyvik argued that Glatshteyn appeared to be making light of an important issue by advocating a return to Eastern Europe without acting on it; and he challenged Glatshteyn to seek the ghetto if he seriously meant the words of his poem. Yeshaye Ostri-Don also took issue with Glatshteyn. During a lengthy discussion of *A gute nakht, velt* in his monograph *Bloye horizontn* (Mexico, 1945), Ostri-Don comments: "We stand not only alienated, but in fact resentful, not before the image, but against the desire to return" (p. 130).

4. Glatshteyn seems to have been influenced by the charges made against him. Years later, even as he asserted that *A gute nakht, velt* was meant as "a wounded Jewish scream of disappointment in the great Western world, which had ostensibly emancipated us and left us alone to confront total calamity when Hitler's fateful decree swept over us," he nonetheless found it necessary to defend himself. As he put it: "When Hitler came, to return to the ghetto by choice was not in our power. The ghetto was not a ghetto, but a death trap." *Fragn un entfers* ["Questions and answers"], *Yidisher kemfer*, 9 Nov. 1956, p. 13.

5. *Gedenklider* (New York, 1943).

6. For a discussion of this form, see A. Zaretski, *Praktishe yidishe gramatik* (Moscow, Farlag shul un bukh 1926), p. 82.

7. Joshua Trachtenberg, in *Jewish Magic and Superstition: A Study in Folk Religion* (1939; rpt. New York, Atheneum 1975), p. 85, defines a golem as "a homunculus created by the magical invocation of names."

8. Lawrence L. Langer deals with this problem in his book *The Holocaust and the Literary Imagination* (1975; rpt. New Haven and London, Yale University Press 1977). Speculating that "life may be an immortality in reverse, a 'demortality' " (p. 62), he goes on to say: "death has replaced life as the measure of our existence, and the vision of human potentiality nurtured by centuries of Christian and humanistic optimism has been so completely effaced by the events of the Holocaust that the future stretches gloomily down an endless vista into futility" (p. 76).

9. The interrelationship of life and death stressed in this poem is just the opposite of what Terrence Des Pres discusses in his book *The Survivor* (1976; rpt. New York, Pocket Books 1977), p. 114. Probing the mentality necessary in order to survive the Holocaust, Des Pres notes: "The essential

paradox of extremity is that life persists in a world ruled by death. Life-in-death characterizes every aspect of the survivor's experience. . . ."

10. During an interview with Yankev Pat—published as part of *Shmuesn mit yidishe shrayber* (New York, 1954), pp. 79–95—Glatshteyn mentioned that his father had died in Maidanek at the age of seventy-six (p. 83). In the same interview, Glatshteyn commented on his father's attitude to Yiddish literature: "He as much as consecrated his son to Yiddish literature. He brought Perets, Sholem–Aleykhem, Reyzen into the home for me. He was delighted when I read out loud from Yiddish literature. It seems to me that he wanted a Yiddish writer for a son" (p. 82).

11. For an overview in English of Reb Nakhmen of Bratslav's life and personality, see the introduction to Arnold J. Band, *Nahman of Bratslav: The Tales* (New York, Paulist Press 1978), pp. 9–48; and Arthur Green, "Rabbi Nahman of Bratslav: A Critical Biography," Diss. Brandeis, 1975. Hereafter referred to as *Green*.

12. This formulation is not original to Nakhmen, but is based on a traditional Kabbalistic interpretation.

13. *Pos "rob"* ["Poe's 'Raven',"] in *In Tokh genumen* (New York, 1947), p. 300.

14. *Shtralndike yidn* (New York, 1946).

15. See Exodus Rabbah 28:6.

16. Langer *(The Holocaust and the Literary Imagination,* p. 164) makes an interesting point about the special use of children in the literature of the Holocaust: "In most literature of atrocity, the specific forces behind the suffering of the victims are as anonymous as they themselves are destined to become; and the choice of children as victims compounds the anonymity (because of the even more limited comprehension of the children) and intensifies the atmosphere of intimidation."

17. Glatshteyn evidently had second thoughts about considering *A yidishe kroyn* as a Holocaust-related work. In *Fun mayn gantser mi—Of All My Labor—*, Glatshteyn's volume of selected poems (New York, 1956), p. 206, the final strophe of *A yidishe kroyn*—where the father's death is announced—has been omitted. Moreover, the poem does not appear in Glatshteyn's *Kh'tu dermonen—I Remember* (New York, 1967), a volume devoted specifically to his Holocaust poetry.

18. An exception is Glatshteyn's inclusion, in his final volume, *Gezangen fun rekhts tsu links,* of a retrospective essay and a playlet from the year 1921.

19. In his 1955 interview with Avrom Tabatshnik in *Yiddish*, 1, (Summer 1973), 41, Glatshteyn commented: "No matter how hard he may wish to ensilence his impressions within himself, the poet today cannot refrain from speech." The most difficult task of the Yiddish poet in a post-Holocaust environment, he continued, was to reach the point where "the 'chaff' of

his poem, the so-called prosaic element of his poem, is on a par with its musical element" (p. 42). Elsewhere, Glatshteyn warns against neglecting form because of the enormity of content inherent in the subject of the Holocaust—*Far a novene*—*form un inhalt* ["For a change—form and content"], in *In tokh genumen* (1947), p. 381. Thus, it appears that in *Lublin, mayn heylike shtot*, Glatshteyn chose to avoid the risk of unfulfilled poetic aims.

20. *Green*, pp. 312–13, contains a lucid explanation of the dialectical process of religious growth as it occurred for Nakhmen, based on his "descents" and "ascents."

Chapter Five

1. All further references to this work will appear in the body of the text.

2. For some critics, this new volume was greeted with a certain disappointment. Y. Rapoport, for instance, expresses his reservations in *Yankev glatshteyns nay liderbukh* ["Yankev Glatshteyn's new book of poems"], *Gk*, No. 19 (1954), pp. 210–13. In a hierarchy of Glatshteyn's works, Rapoport contended, *Dem tatns shotn* would certainly rank higher than *Yidishtaytshn*, but its language was below the standard of *Gedenklider* and *Shtralndike yidn*. Shmuel Niger objects to *Dem tatns shotn* on different grounds in a 1953 critique that also appears in a later collection of essays: *Dem tatns shotn*, in Vol. II of *Yidishe shrayber fun tsvantsikstn yorhundert* (New York, 1973), pp. 9–16. Niger complains that the unselective composition of Glatshteyn's book forces the reader to wade through considerable inferior poetry in order to arrive at truly first-rate material.

3. Although it was difficult for him, Glatshteyn evidently wished to appear optimistic at this point in his career. During his interview with Yankev Pat (*Shmuesn*, p. 90), he asserted: "The world, humanity, must come to a 'happy end'. . . . If not for optimism, if not for the striving for good, we would already have had the third atomic war. . . . The liberation movements, the screams of thousands of books, the cries of poems, the waves of thoughts have accomplished a great deal. . . . I mean all of us, myself included—are part of world optimism."

4. Assimilation seemed more dangerous to Glatshteyn when it was ignorant than when it occurred as part of a conscious program. And, as he commented to Yankev Pat (*Shmuesn*, p. 94), it was this ignorance that he sought to expose and attack in the poem *Yidish*.

5. Glatshteyn was reluctant to forgive breaches of literary loyalty for the sake of nonliterary aims. Thus, even his reaction in *Dem tatns shotn* to the 1952 Stalinist liquidation of Yiddish writers (*Vi flaterlekh* ["Like moths"], p. 191) contains a barb of anger at the conformist attitudes of the slain artists.

6. Glatshteyn's anxious attempt to make peace with the past represents the effort to overcome what Lawrence L. Langer terms "the absurd position of man as Survivor." *(The Holocaust and the Literary Imagination,* p. 270). Langer goes on to describe the contradictions inherent in the survivor's experience: "the act of recollection, instead of forging links with the past, only widens the exasperatingly impassable gulf between the dead and the living, creating a void which makes new beginnings for the future equally impossible, until some way of reconciling the fate of those dead with the present can silence the influence they continue to exert on the living."

7. Sambation is the legendary river of rocks beyond whose impassable boundaries, according to Jewish lore, the Ten Lost Tribes of Israel live.

8. In his volume of selected poems, *Fun mayn gantser mi—Of All My Labor* (New York, 1956), Glatshteyn has rearranged *Shneyike shnitn,* although it remains a work in four sections. The first poem of the original has been omitted and the third poem divided in two. Thus, the narrator's greeting of the cow is no longer part of the same poem as his musings about eternity.

9. In a very early essay—*In zikh* 1, 2 (1920), p. 82—Glatshteyn reviewed Arthur Waley's translations of Chinese poetry and short stories into English, granting the work high praise and stating further: "However much possible, *In zikh* will acquaint its readers with the Chinese poetic oeuvre. In future issues we will also have critiques of them." Moreover, his volume *Fraye ferzn* contains a poem entitled *Khinezish teater* ["Chinese theater"] (pp. 58-62). Years later, Glatshteyn stated in his taped interview with Avrom Tabatshnik *(Yiddish* 1, [Summer 1973], pp. 51-52) that he had been: "a frequent visitor to the Chinese theater on the Bowery. . . . I read Li Tai Po, and I liked him very much. Wherever I saw a poem of his in whatever translation, I read it. My interest in Chinese verse comes also from my feelings about the lyric. When I saw the Chinese plays, I sensed the undemonstrated emotion of the Chinese. . . . Precisely . . . this very lack of a fuss about one's own feelings is what always interested me in Chinese poetry.

10. Significantly, neither of these poems is included in *Fun mayn gantser mi.* Since only four of the original ten appear—and the introduction is omitted as well—this deletion is not meaningful *per se.* But the title has also been changed to leave out any reference to youth: the cycle is called simply *Umgeklorte gezangen* ["Unclarified songs"].

Chapter Six

1. *Di freyd fun yidishn vort* (New York, 1961). Hereafter cited as *Freyd.*
2. *A yid fun lublin* (New York, 1966). Hereafter cited as *Lublin.*
3. *Lublin,* p. 63.
4. *Lublin,* pp. 84-85.

5. *Freyd,* p. 196.

6. In this image, Glatshteyn plays with two allusions to his own name, both of which he employed in other poems as well. One, his identification with his biblical namesake, Jacob, was particularly clear in the poem *Ge-zangen* (*Gedenklider,* p. 76), where the narrator called himself *Yankev-Yisroel* ("Jacob-Israel"), referring to the patriarch's two names. The other, more subtle, connection is to Glatshteyn's surname, which means "Smoothstone." In the poem *Bayshpiln* ["Examples"] (*Kredos,* pp. 44–46), Glatshteyn focused explicitly on the definition of *Glatshteyn* during a discussion of his writing: having cited his own name in this work, he later comments: *Shlayfshteyn, shlayfshteyn, shlayf dem shteyn* ("Polishstone, polishstone, polish the stone").

7. *Freyd,* p. 197.

8. *Freyd,* p. 198.

9. *Lublin,* p. 121.

10. *Lublin,* pp. 122–24.

11. Additionally, these poems are indicative of Glatshteyn's long interest in Freudian theory and methods. His awareness, if not concern, was evident already in the earliest days of the *Inzikhistn,* implicitly in their call for a free-associative poetic technique, and explicitly—if loosely—in the following comment from the *In zikh* manifesto (p. 10): "If such a poem [the type they intend to write] will then be . . . material for Freudian theory, if traces of something morbid [and] sickly are found in the poet, that does not bother us." Years later, Glatshteyn was to tell Yankev Pat during their interview together (*Shmuesn mit yidishe shrayber,* p. 86): "Our generation . . . published Sigmund Freud, who expressed the soul-struggle of our generation." See also Glatshteyn's poem *A froyd-epizod* ["A Freud-episode"], in his *Gezangen fun rekhts tsu links,* p. 119.

12. *Freyd,* pp. 102–03.

13. Four ells is a rabbinic metaphor signifying the measurement of a person's own domain.

14. *Freyd,* pp. 151–52.

15. *Freyd,* pp. 105–06.

16. *Freyd,* p. 165.

17. *Freyd,* p. 173.

18. *Freyd,* pp. 153–54.

19. *Lublin,* p. 33.

20. *Freyd,* p. 122.

21. *Lublin,* p. 55.

22. *Freyd,* p. 124.

23. *Freyd,* p. 14.

24. *Lublin,* pp. 25–26.

25. *Freyd,* p. 141.

26. *Freyd,* p. 142.

27. *Freyd*, p. 170.

28. *Freyd*, pp. 203–06.

29. *Lublin*, pp. 79–80.

30. *Lublin*, pp. 39–42.

31. *Lublin*, pp. 66–68.

32. *Freyd*, p. 167.

33. *Lublin*, p. 15.

34. *Freyd*, pp. 157–58.

35. Glatshteyn's is a new understanding of Ecclesiastes 11.1: "Cast your bread upon the waters, for you will find it after many days." Rather than applying the traditional interpretation that the giver of charity will eventually receive the fruits of that generosity, Glatshteyn uses the biblical verse to indicate that heritage cannot be cast away ultimately.

36. *Lublin*, pp. 72-73.

37. *Lublin*, pp. 101–06.

38. *Lublin*, pp. 114-18.

39. *Lublin*, pp. 119–20.

Chapter Seven

1. All further references to this work will appear in the body of the text.

2. Glatshteyn's second wife was the artist Fanny Mazel.

3. The last prayer said before retiring, the bedside *krishme*, entrusts the soul to God during sleep, and the first prayer of the morning, *modeani*, gives thanks for its return.

4. At the end of his life, Glatshteyn was evidently much interested in Picasso. During a 1971 conversation, he commented that his poem *A briv fun adolfo dem eltern tsu zayn khaver adolfo dem yingern* ["A letter from Adolfo the Elder to his friend Adolfo the Younger"] (*Gezangen fun rekhts tsu links*, pp. 51–54) alludes to Pablo Picasso and Pablo Casals. In this work, an aging cellist berates an aging painter for refusing to acknowledge his limitations.

5. The term Marrano refers to a secret practitioner of Judaism in Spain or Portugal, whose ancestors, to escape persecution, converted to Christianity at the end of the Middle Ages.

6. The term *genizah* refers to the storeroom of a synagogue where torn leaves of damaged books are kept until they can be buried.

Selected Bibliography

PRIMARY SOURCES

1. Yiddish Editions

In zikh: a zamlung introspektive lider. Contributors, Glatshteyn et al. New York: Mayzl farlag,1920.

Yankev glatshteyn. New York: Farlag kultur, 1921.

Fraye ferzn. New York: Grohar & Stodolski, 1926.

Kredos. New York: Farlag yidish lebn, 1929.

Yidishtaytshn. Warsaw: Farlag Kh. Bzhoza, 1937.

Ven yash iz geforn. New York: Farlag inzikh, 1938.

Ven yash iz gekumen. New York: Farlag M. Sh. Shklarski, 1940.

Emil un karl. New York: Farlag M. Shklarski, 1940.

Gedenklider. New York: Farlag yidisher kemfer, 1943.

Yosl loksh fun khelm. New York: Makhmadim, 1944.

Finf un zibetsik yor yidishe prese in amerike. Ed., with Shmuel Niger and Hillel Rogoff. New York: Perets shrayber farayn, 1945.

Shtralndike yidn. New York: Farlag matones, 1946.

In tokh genumen. New York: Farlag matones, 1947.

Dem tatns shotn. New York: Farlag matones, 1953.

In tokh genumen. New York: Farlag fun yidish natsionaln arbeter farband, 1956.

Fun mayn gantser mi. New York, Issued with the help of the World Jewish Congress 1956.

In tokh genumen. 2 vols. Buenos Aires: Kiem farlag, 1960.

Di freyd fun yidishn vort. New York: Der kval, 1961.

Mit mayne fartogbikher. Tel Aviv: Farlag Y. L. Perets, 1963.

A yid fun lublin. New York: CYCO, 1966.

Af greyte temes. Tel Aviv: Farlag Y. L. Perets, 1967.

Kh'tu dermonen. New York: Farlag bergen belzen, 1967.

Anthology of Holocaust Literature. Ed., with Israel Knox and Samuel Margoshes. Philadelphia: Jewish Publication Society of America, 1969.

Gezangen fun rekhts tsu links. New York: CYCO, 1971.

In der velt mit yidish. New York: World Jewish Congress, 1972.

191

Prost un poshet. New York: Knight Printing Press, 1978.

2. English Editions

Homecoming at Twilight. Trans. N. Guterman. Foreward by Maurice Samuel. New York: Thomas Yoseloff, 1962. [Translation of *Ven yash iz gekumen*.]

Homeward Bound. Trans. A. Zahaven. New York: Thomas Yoseloff, 1969. Translation of *Ven yash iz geforn*.

Poems. Trans. and Ed. Etta Blum. Tel Aviv: I. L. Peretz Publishing House, 1970.

The Selected Poems of Jacob Glatstein. Trans. Ruth Whitman. New York: October House, 1972. Contains an excellent introduction.

3. Hebrew Editions

Mikol amali: shirim ufoemot. Trans. Shlomo Shenhod. Jerusalem: Bialik Institute, 1964. Selected translations from *Fun mayn gantser mi;* contains an important foreward by Dov Sadan.

Uvehagiya yash. Trans. Shlomo Shenhod. Tel Aviv: Dvir, 1957. Translation of *Ven yash is gekumen*.

SECONDARY SOURCES

1. Articles in Yiddish

ALKVIT, B. "Yankev glatshteyn." *Getseltn*, 2 (Oct.–Dec. 1946), 205–18. Asserts essential continuity in Glatshteyn's work.

BIKL, SHLOYME. "Yankev glatshteyn: gezamlte lider." In *Shrayber fun mayn dor*. Pp. 108–15. New York: Farlag matones, 1958. Insightful article about *Fun mayn gantser mi;* written in 1957.

ERLICH, RACHEL. "Vegn yankev glatshteyns poetisher shprakh." In *For Max Weinreich on His Seventieth Birthday: Studies in Jewish Languages, Literature, and Society*. Pp. 382–69. The Hague: Mouton & Co., 1964. Engaging analysis of the language of *Di freyd fun yidishn vort*.

GLANTS-LEYELES, ARN. "Yankev glatshteyns naye vendung." *Vokh*, 13 Dec. 1929, pp. 8–9. About Glatshteyn's poetic experimentations in the late 1920's.

———. "Yankev glatshteyn tsu zekhtsik yor." *Di goldene keyt*, No. 25 (1956), pp. 150–63. Interesting essay commemorating Glatshteyn's sixtieth birthday, positing his career as an upward spiral.

———. "Yankev glatshteyns veg." In *Velt un vort: literarishe un andere eseyen*. Pp. 136–44. New York: CYCO, 1958. About *Shtralndike yidn;* written in 1946.

GRINBERG, ELIEZER. "Yankev glatshteyns derekh in der yidisher poezye." *Tsukunft*, 62 (March, 1957), 108–11. An interesting article whose starting point is *Fun mayn gantser mi*.

————. *Yankev glatshteyns freyd fun yidishn vort.* New York: CYCO, 1964. Monograph about *Di freyd fun yidishn vort.*

GROBARD, B. "Fun onheyb biz onheyb: vegn yankev glatshteyn." *Zaml-bikher,* 7 (1948), 410–23. Concerns Glatshteyn's first six poetry volumes; stresses notion of metamorphosis.

LEYVIK, H. "Vegn geyn tsurik in geto." In *Eseyen un redes.* Pp. 127–30. New York: Congress for Jewish Culture, 1963. About the poem "A gute nakht, velt"; written in 1938.

NIGER, SHMUEL. "Rozhinkes mit mandlen" and "Dem tatns shotn." In *Yidishe shrayber fun tsvantsikstn yorhundert.* II, pp. 17–25, 9–16. New York: Congress for Jewish Culture, 1973. About *Shtralndike yidn* and *Dem tatns shotn,* respectively. The first of these—a begrudgingly admiring critique—was first written in 1946; the second, in 1953.

OSTRI-DON, YESHAYE. "Inem gang fun yankev glatshteyn's *gedenk-lider.*" In *Bloye horizontn.* Mexico: Drukeray di shtime, 1945. Pp. 85–179. Monograph about *Gedenklider.*

PAT, YANKEV. "Yankev glatshteyn." In *Shmuesn mit yidishe shrayber.* Pp. 79–95. New York: Martin Press, Inc., 1954. An informative and entertaining interview with Glatshteyn.

RAPOPORT, Y. "Yankev glatshteyns dikhterisher veg: fun zilbekstentrish-keyt tsu groys-natsionaler dikhtung." In *Oysgerisene bleter.* Pp. 97–137. Melbourne: Melbourne Committee to Celebrate the Author's Sixtieth Birthday, 1957. Argues that Glatshteyn's work became more valuable as he began to write about national issues.

————. "Yankev glatshteyns nay liderbukh." *Di goldene keyt,* No. 19 (1954), pp. 210–13. About *Dem tatns shotn.*

SHAPIRO, LAMED. Review of *Kredos.* *Vokh,* (11 Oct. 1929), p. 18.

2. Articles in English

FAERSTEIN, CHANA. "Jacob Glatstein: The Literary Uses of Yiddish." *Judaism,* 14 (1965), 414–31. Excellent article exploring change in Glatshteyn through text analysis.

HOWE, IRVING. "Journey of a Poet." *Commentary,* 53 (Jan. 1972), 75–77. Concise look at Glatshteyn's contribution to Yiddish poetry in America.

LAPIN, SHMUEL. "Jacob Glatstein: Poetry and Peoplehood." *American Jewish Yearbook,* 73 (1972), 611–17. Views Glatshteyn's later poems as vastly superior to the earlier ones.

TABATSHNIK, AVROM. "A Conversation with Jacob Glatstein." Trans. Joseph C. Landis. *Yiddish,* 1 (Summer 1973), 40–53. Revealing interview, taped in 1955.

For a fuller bibliography of works by and about Yankev Glatshteyn, see Zaynvl Diamant's bio-bibliography in *Leksikon fun der nayer yidisher literatur.* New York: Congress for Jewish Culture and CYCO, 1958. II, col. 256–61; also, "Works in English by and about Jacob Glatstein:

A Selected Bibliography," by Janet Hadda. *Yiddish*, 1 (Summer 1973), 63–70. Numerous short articles—with particular critical emphasis on *Mikol amali: shirim ufoemot* and *Uvehagiya yash*—have also appeared in Hebrew newspapers and literary journals.

Index

Abramovitsh, Sh.Y. (Mendele Moykher Sforim), 54–55
Afn vaser, 58–59
Alkvit, B., 22
Alt, 146
Alte beyner, 132–33
Az der kultur-yid, 167–68

Baal Shem Tov, 106, 139
Bavunder, 134, 135
Bialik, Khayim Nakhmen, 147
  El Hatsipor, 80–82
Bratslav, Reb Nakhmen of, 106, 186n11
  use of as a persona, 73, 78–80, 95, 110, 124, 128. *See also Davhen minkhe, Der bratslaver git aroys a tshuve, Der bratslaver in a nakht fun yeride, Der bratslaver tsu zayn soyfer, Der bratslaver zingt nigunim, Faran aza gekekhts vi hunger, Her un shtoyn, Zay nisht keyn shoyte, Zolst zikh nisht vundern*
bratslaver git aroys a tshuve, Der, 126
bratslaver in a nakht fun yeride, Der, 95–98
bratslaver tsu zayn soyfer, Der, 73–80
bratslaver zingt nigunim, Der, 123–24
briv tsu zikh, A, 112, 113–14

Davnen minkhe, 124–25
Dermonungen, 141–42
Di yunge, 19
  separation from by *In zikh,* 20–21, 39, 40, 172, 173
Do lign, 102–103, 105
Dovid edelshtat, 111

Du, 33–34
Du shenkst mir, 166–67

Eastern European Jewry, relation to Glatshteyn's poetry, 62, 95, 106, 110, 114, 115–16, 122, 132, 137–39, 141, 145–46, 160, 169, 170
Edelshtat, Dovid, 19, 111, 112
Eygns, 31
Eynikl-doyres, 139

Faran aza gekekhts vi hunger, 125–26
Fargleyb mikh, 154–55
farziglter briv, A, 39–40
Finfundraysik, 34
firer, Der, 42
Fort a yid, 115–16
Freud, Sigmund, 136–37, 189n11
froyd-epizod, A, 165–66, 177
Fun a briv, 94–95, 113
Fun dos nay, 144–45
Fun li-tay-pos gedenk-bikhl, 160–62
Fun li-tay-pos notits-bikhl, 176–78
Fun undzer yokh, 47–48, 55, 104–105, 130
Funvanen iz a yid?, 170, 171

Gebentsht zol zayn, 173–74
geferlekhe froy, Di, 13
getselt, A, 104–105, 130
gezang, A, 181–82n2
Gezangen (Dem tatns shotn), 115
Gezangen (Gedenklider), 71–73, 114
Glants-Leyeles, Arn, 13, 17, 19, 22, 58
Glatshteyn, Yankev
  biography, 11–18

Blum, Klara, pseudonym, 14
personae, use of, 158–60, 174, 176

POETRY VOLUMES:
  Fraye ferzn (1926), 28
  freyd fun yidishn vort, Di (1961),
    132, 135, 143, 148–50
  Gedenklider (1943), 17, 63, 64, 65,
    67, 82, 96, 101, 104
  Gezangen fun rekhts tsu links (1971),
    18, 23, 164, 165, 167, 172, 174,
    176, 178, 179
  Kredos (1929), 41, 61
  Shtralndike yidn (1946), 17, 63, 82,
    90, 91, 93, 95, 101, 103, 104
  tatns shotn, Dem (1953), 17, 102,
    103, 104, 105, 107, 110, 114, 123,
    128, 132
  Yankev glatshteyn (1921), 28, 39
  yid fun lublin, A (1966), 132, 143
  Yidishtaytshn (1937), 41, 59, 61, 63;
    See also Bratslav, Reb Nakhmen
    of and Li Tai Po

Glatshteyn, Yitskhok (Itsik), 12, 70–71,
  122
Goldfaden, Avrom, 52
Got iz a troyeriker maharal, 67–68
gute nakht, velt, A, 42, 62–63, 64, 79,
  99, 185n3, 185n4
guter yid taynet zikh oys, Der, 103–104
Gutskeyt, 134, 135

Harlem: zuntik, 36–38, 150, 169
Halpern, Moyshe Leyb, 51–52, 53–54,
  55, 111, 112
  Benk aheym, 53
  Gingili, 54
  Mayn umru fun a volf, 54
  Memento mori, 53
  Zlotshev mayn heym, 53
Her un shtoyn, 126–28
Hit zikh, 144, 145
Holocaust
  changed perspectives resulting from,
    99–101, 119, 150
  effects on Glatshteyn's poetry, 17–18,
    22–23, 28, 41–42, 55–56, 58, 63–64,
    67, 70, 71, 79, 82–83, 86, 91–92, 93,

94, 95, 98–99, 101, 102–103, 104,
  105, 107, 112, 113–14, 116, 124,
  126, 129, 133, 136, 145, 154–55,
  159–60, 179
  Post-Holocaust themes, 143–44, 152–
    53, 169
HOMO, 32–33, 36, 49

Ibershpil, 150–51
In der fintster, 40
In roykh, 15, 23, 24–25, 178
In zikh,
  Glatshteyn's break from, 27, 28, 155
  manifesto, 19–22, 39, 59, 167
  separation from Di yunge, 20–21, 172,
    173
Inderfri, 133, 166
Israel, 102, 107, 114–17, 124, 137–39,
  141, 169–72
Iyev in nyu york, 30

Joyce, James, 57

Kh'davn a yidish blat in sobvey, 93–94
Khelm. See Yosl loksh fun khelm
khinezer poet po-tshu-iy shraybt a briv
  tsu zayn fraynd yuan tshen, Der, 158–
  60
kholem, A, 65, 80–82
Kh'shtey in toyer, 146–47
Kh'tu dermonen, 88–91, 92, 93
Kh'vel zikh ayngloybern, 117–18, 119
Kibya, 138–39
kroyn, Di, 156, 168

Lapin, Shmuel, 22
Letartsat, 68–69
Letster opshtel, 170, 171–72
Leyeles, Arn. See Glants-Leyeles, Arn
Li Tai Po, use of as persona, 78, 128,
  129, 131, 132, 158, 163. See also Fun
  li-tay-pos gendenk-bikhl, Mit li-tay-
  po, Tsen umgeklorte gezangen fun
  yungshaft
Loew, Rabbi Judah, of Prague (Maharal),
  67; See also Got iz a troyeriker ma-
  haral
Lublin, mayn heylike shtot, 90, 91–93
Luter bodi, 31–32, 36, 42, 169

Maranen, 168
Mayn bruder binyomin, 86–88
Mayn getselt, 147
Mayn mi, 147, 148
Mayn rasistishe biografye, 169
Mayn tate-mame shprakh, 105–107
Milyonen toytn, 69–70
Minkov, Nokhem Borekh, 13, 14, 19
Mit li-tay-po, 160–61, 162–63
Monolog in driter perzon, 109–10
Moyshe leybs kol, 51–54, 109

Nakht, zay shtil tsu mir, 48–50, 150
Nakhtlider, 98–101, 103
nes, A, 134, 135
1919, 15, 23, 24, 26, 27, 28, 30, 64, 68, 147, 178
Nisht di meysim loybn got, 83–84, 86

On yidn, 83, 84–86, 87
Onhoyb, 103
Ovntbroyt, 34–36, 45, 47, 49
Oysderveylt, 155–56
Oytobiografye fun an intelekt, 151–53

Park evenyu, 30–31, 32
Poe, Edgar Allen, "The Raven", 80–81

Rapoport, Y., 22
Red tsu mir yidish, 140–41, 148
Reyd vi tsdoke-pushkes, 146
Rozenfeld, Moris, 19

Sako un vanzetis montik, 42
Sharfe reyd fun a 'bitnik', 143
Shaykevitsh, N.M.(Shomer). *See Shomer*
Shini mayk, 42–45
Shlos fun yo, 41
Shneyike shnitn, 121–22
Sholem-Aleykhem, 54–55
Shomer, 51, 54–56, 109
Shtot, 28–29, 30, 37, 49, 133
Shvartse khoges, 42
S'redt der alter yid, 116–17
S'yidishe vort, 64–65

Teg fun elnt, 144, 145
Tfutses, 168
Tirtl-toybn, 15, 23, 25–26, 27, 40, 58, 119, 120, 178, 179

Tsayt, 118–19, 120
Tsen umgeklorte gezangen fun yung-shaft, 128–31, 188n10
Tsu a fraynt, 57
Tsu dir, 50–51, 150
Tsu lange teg, 141, 142
Tsum kopmayster, 57
Tsum tatn, 70–71, 79, 88
Tsum tatn af yontev, 153–54
Tsuriktrakhtungen, 172–73, 178
Tsvey, 135
Tsvey lider vegn altn, 135–37, 165–66
Tsvishhn minkhe un mayrev, 107–108

Undzer dor, 39, 179
Undzer got, 167
Undzer tsikhtik loshn, 65–67, 70
United States, the, 52, 55, 93–94, 102, 107, 108–10, 117, 137, 141, 143, 168–69
Unter fremdn dakh, 45–47, 48, 49

Ven, 164, 166
Vi a pastke, 141
vort, A, 119–21

yid fun lublin, A, 157–58
Yiddish language
   attitudes toward, 40–41, 65, 102, 105–109, 114, 139, 147–50, 173–74
   compared to English, 110, 142–43
   compared to German, 65–67, 70
   compared to Hebrew, 107–108, 140–41
   experiments with, 40, 56–58, 127–28
Yiddish literature, attitudes toward, 17–18,94, 102, 146–47
Yidish, 107, 108–109, 110
yidishe kroyn, A, 88,186n17
Yidishkeyt, 112–13
Yisker, 87–88
Yortsayt lid: M.L. Halpern, 111–12
Yosl loksh fun khelm, 59–61

Zay nisht keyn shoyte, 175, 176
Ziger, 169–70
zilberne lorelay, Di, 164–65
Zing ladino, 57–58, 107
Zolst zikh nisht vundern, 175–76

DATE DUE